CW01022784

WHAT IS A PLAYHOUSE?

This book offers an accessible introduction to England's sixteenth- and early seventeenth-century playing industry and a fresh account of the architecture, multiple uses, communities, crowds, and proprietors of playhouses.

It builds on recent scholarship and new documentary and archaeological discoveries to answer the questions: what did playhouses do, what did they look like, and how did they function? The book will accordingly introduce readers to a rich and exciting spectrum of "play" and playhouses, not only in London but also around England. The detailed but wide-ranging case studies examined here go beyond staged drama to explore early modern sport, gambling, music, drinking, and animal baiting; they recover the crucial influence of female playhouse owners and managers; and they recognise rich provincial performance cultures as well as the burgeoning of London's theatre industry.

This book will have wide appeal with readers across Shakespeare, early modern performance studies, theatre history, and social history.

Callan Davies researches the cultural, literary, and theatrical history of early modern England. He has taught at universities across the UK and at Shakespeare's Globe, and he is part of the project teams *Before Shakespeare and Middling Culture*. His work includes studies of Elizabethan playhouses, rhetoric, practice-as-research and a monograph with Routledge, *Strangeness in Jacobean Drama*.

"We thought we knew the answer to Davies' title question, but it turns out that playhouses were much more various, multiple, and collaborative venues than traditionally allowed. Based on new archival work and a refreshing critical intelligence, Davies' exciting and readable book is a theatre-history gamechanger."

Emma Smith, *Hertford College, Oxford*

"In *What is a Playhouse? England at Play, 1520–1620*, Callan Davies brilliantly explores and expands our understanding of what an early modern playhouse was in London and beyond, resulting in a book which is a much-needed addition to the field of theatre study."

Heather Knight MCIfA, FSA, *archaeologist who led the excavations of Curtain, Theatre and Boar's Head playhouses*

"What was a playhouse and how was it used in the sixteenth and seventeenth centuries? Davies' detailed study capitalises on recent archaeological discoveries and offers new archival research to revisit and reassess what we think we know about early modern playing venues, a concept which was more elastic and varied than traditional narratives have conditioned us to believe. Rigorous yet engaging, *What is a Playhouse?* is a welcome corrective to Globe-centric conceptions of playing spaces, accentuating a plurality and diversity of venues that 'housed' play in all its forms."

David McInnis, *University of Melbourne*

"Callan Davies' new book, *What is a Playhouse? England at Play, 1520–1620*, offers a fresh and stimulating perspective for anyone interested in the history of theatre and popular entertainment. His decentring of older London-centred narratives of a male-dominated theatre world opens up a more generous view of the multipurpose functions of playhouses and a well-researched view of the wide range of indoor and outdoor spaces used and supported by diverse participants -- men, women, children and animals -- in the Shakespearean era and earlier. An important reassessment of the pervasive influence and meaning of play in early modern England."

Sally-Beth MacLean, *Professor; Director of Research / General Editor, Records of Early English Drama (REED)*

WHAT IS A PLAYHOUSE?

England at Play, 1520–1620

Callan Davies

Routledge
Taylor & Francis Group

LONDON AND NEW YORK

Cover image: Designed and created by Tyler Davies, copyright

First published 2023
by Routledge
4 Park Square, Milton Park, Abingdon, Oxon OX14 4RN

and by Routledge
605 Third Avenue, New York, NY 10158

Routledge is an imprint of the Taylor & Francis Group, an informa business

© 2023 Callan Davies

The right of Callan Davies to be identified as author of this work has been asserted
in accordance with sections 77 and 78 of the Copyright, Designs and Patents Act 1988.

British Library Cataloguing-in-Publication Data
A catalogue record for this book is available from the British Library

Library of Congress Cataloging-in-Publication Data
Names: Davies, Callan, 1990– author.
Title: What is a playhouse? : England at play, 1520–1620 / Callan Davies.
Description: First Edition. | New York : Routledge, 2023. |
Includes bibliographical references and index. |
Identifiers: LCCN 2022008495 (print) | LCCN 2022008496 (ebook) |
ISBN 9781032138879 (Hardback) | ISBN 9781032138077 (Paperback) |
ISBN 9781003231127 (eBook)
Subjects: LCSH: Play–Great Britain–History. | Recreation–Great Britain. |
Architecture and recreation–Great Britain. |
Children's playhouses–Great Britain–History.
Classification: LCC GV1200 .D38 2023 (print) |
LCC GV1200 (ebook) | DDC 790.0941–dc23/eng/20220427
LC record available at https://lccn.loc.gov/2022008495
LC ebook record available at https://lccn.loc.gov/2022008496

ISBN: 978-1-032-13887-9 (hbk)
ISBN: 978-1-032-13807-7 (pbk)
ISBN: 978-1-003-23112-7 (ebk)

DOI: 10.4324/9781003231127

Typeset in Bembo
by Newgen Publishing UK

In memory of my Dad, Mick

CONTENTS

NOTE ON TEXTS AND SPELLING

Sixteenth- and seventeenth-century English spelling has been modernised throughout: in my own manuscript transcription, in quotations from contemporary printed sources, and (with permission) in citations from the Records of Early English Drama. Readers can follow references to REED materials for the series' original transcription.

ILLUSTRATIONS

INTRODUCTION

The "Playhouse" Canon

In 1635, Cuthbert Burbage wrote a petition to the Lord Chamberlain in which he described his father, James, as "the first builder of Playhouses."[1] Indeed, James Burbage had helped to build, in 1576, an unusual structure in the former monastic land of Shoreditch's Holywell Priory—a round building designed to host (among other things) dramatic performances. Cuthbert mythologised this act of construction into a fantastical family history. His petition can perhaps be seen as achieving a kind of success with posterity, an influence not on the Lord Chamberlain but on all time. After all, James Burbage's supposed theatrical invention launched a persistent narrative of the English playhouse based largely on the idea of the freestanding (often round or "amphitheatrical") structure and rooted in the agency of the (often singular) male entrepreneur. Such an understanding matches the notion of the solitary genius writer that later came to apply to the Burbages' friend and colleague, Shakespeare. There is a parallel between Shakespeare as poster-boy for English literature and the Theatre and then the Globe as his architectural counterparts.

However, we are now accustomed to the idea that Shakespeare was not a solitary genius but was shaped by the collaborative creative practices of early modern drama.[2] The same is true of the playhouses in which that drama was performed. Despite Cuthbert's reified image of his father as *the* builder, vast quantities of archived legal material show quite clearly that the Theatre was a joint venture between James Burbage and his brother-in-law John Brayne, as well as Brayne's wife Margaret, who was so instrumental that she took on, she later explained, some of the physical construction of the building. This group of playhouse proprietors, enterprising though they were, were not "first builders." They were creating a type of venue they would already have encountered on a regular basis: James Burbage travelled around London and across the country as part of the Leicester's Men, performing in a variety of play venues; John Brayne, for his part, had quite literally already built

DOI: 10.4324/9781003231127-1

a playhouse—the Red Lion, in Mile End, in 1567. Other playhouses may not all have looked like the tall, almost-round, outdoor Theatre, but they certainly existed.

Cuthbert's wilful narrowing of the idea of the "playhouse" to refer to his father's venture has come to eclipse the many types of spaces that actually functioned as playhouses. There were a variety of such structures long before Burbage and the Braynes laid foundations for the Theatre—and indeed long after its "conversion" into the Globe on Bankside. Yet, at least to a degree, theatre history of early modern England has until fairly recently been happy to accept Cuthbert's appropriation and to follow a trajectory of playhouse development that began in 1576 with amphitheatrical-style spaces like the Theatre—a prescient case of nominative determinism that positions it as *the theatre*, the original, the archetypal.

This book refutes the idea of an archetypal playhouse and instead sets out a spectrum of archetypes for commercial play venues. Playhouses can be thought of in the way Helen Cooper describes *genre*, "as a lineage or a family" rather than a "series of incarnations or clones of a single Platonic idea":

> A family changes over time as its individual members change, but equally, those individuals can be recognized through their 'family resemblance': a resemblance such as might lie in a certain shape of nose, or mouth, or colour of hair, or laughing in a particular way at a particular kind of joke, or manner of twitching one's eyebrows, even though no one of those is essential for the resemblance to register, and even though individual features (hair colour, eyebrow habits) may contradict the model.[3]

In exactly the way genre functions flexibly for different texts that share some key commonalities, so the architectural appearance and the uses of playhouses differ across time periods, regions, and iterations in early modern England. Yet they are united as constructed or converted sites for commercial *play* of various kinds.

A family or genre model of playhouses allows us to look beyond the way the term has been narrowly defined and fossilised in theatre-historical writing. Although the word itself enters the print market with regularity only in the 1570s, it can be applied to earlier structures, too. For instance, scholars are sometimes happy to recognise the Red Lion of 1567 or John Rastell's Finsbury stage of the 1520s as "playhouses," despite archival records of these venues not using that term.[4] As such, this book is interested in both direct historical uses of the term and in the idea of playhouse-ness: that is, the term's usefulness as a conceptual label for "building[s] in which plays are performed," in the *Oxford English Dictionary*'s capacious definition,[5] sometimes called at the time by other names or synonyms. Only by exploring both can we properly ask what playhouses *were* for someone in the sixteenth or early seventeenth centuries, while countering the now-outdated idea that they appeared out of nowhere in the mid-1570s and represented only a narrow range of buildings.

Indeed, early modern individuals used various names for what we might now call playhouses. Theatrical terms were in flux throughout the years covered by this book, and a new ludic vocabulary reflected both immediate changes and innovations as well as longer historical developments. For instance, a flurry of play-house building in London in the mid-1570s occasioned a raft of antitheatrical invective. But writers were quite literally lost for words to attack the structures. John Stockwood confessed in his sermon on the 24 August 1578,

> I know not how I might … more discommend the gorgeous Playing place erected in the fields, than to term it, as they please to have it called, a Theatre … a show place of all beastly and filthy matters.[6]

Although the Theatre has been positioned as an ur-playhouse from as early as 1635, its earliest audiences and opponents grasped for a range of names: playing place, "houses of purpose built," or its own classically inflected soubriquet, Theatre, dan-cing around the word in the title of this book. The very term *playhouse* was in flux, at once collapsible into synonyms like those used by Stockwood but equally an excessive cobbling together of those synonyms: house, playing place, theatre. Andy Kesson has reconceptualised the London theatre scene of 1580s in an important edited special issue for *Shakespeare Survey*; he observes how "words that appear self-evidently theatrical now" were being developed in these decades and had at the time a wide, polysemous reach.[7] The numerous examples discussed across these pages indicate the long history of the term "playhouse" but also substantiate its flexible application to a range of spaces, dramatic and non-dramatic, in London and far beyond it—some "of purpose built," others temporary, others fashioned from ancient rooms or natural environments.

The spaces addressed in this study therefore include venues we might now regard as very distinct from a twenty-first century idea of a "playhouse," but to which early modern individuals applied the word or its synonyms. Take, for example, a former quarry in Shrewsbury discussed in Chapter 1, which Thomas Churchyard designated, in 1585, a "Theater" and that was lined with wooden seating and used for plays, sports, and other spectator events from the 1560s for over 50 years. "Theatre" has a classical ring to it (pun intended), which indicates the quarry's affinity with Roman, round-ish, outdoor sites of spectatorship, but it is equally syn-onymous with "playing place," or "playhouse," as Stockwood indicates—especially after the Shoreditch venture found widespread fame or notoriety (depending on one's position). The word playhouse itself combines two terms already capacious in early modern English: "play," which covers a multitude of recreational practices, as discussed in Chapter 2, and "house," a term that means far more than "freestanding structure" and could broadly refer to "a space, indoor or outdoor, and not simply an individual building."[8] We can thereby see how a single room in an inn as well as, say, a school building in Witton might be described as a "playhouse," in spite of their apparent architectural dissimilarity.

This book also takes in a tour of spaces called by a variety of other names in a period in which vocabulary for play venues was in flux—spaces that conceptually fit the "family" of the playhouse. As such, I think about the playhouse-ness of a sports complex in Cheshire, which, while it may not have "regularly staged plays," in Kesson's playhouse definition,[9] nonetheless hosted a variety of *play* forms, from music to animal fighting. It also occupied a community position directly comparable to more straightforwardly theatre-like spaces in London and Bristol (as Chapter 4 explains). These structures, just as much as amphitheatres like the Theatre or the Globe, functioned as playhouses.

I therefore unpack throughout this book the "family resemblances" of the early modern playhouse, rather than fixing a precise dictionary definition for the term. As will be clear from the introduction so far, my understanding of the concept is generous: accommodating of provincial spaces, of various models of and motivations for proprietorship, and attuned to the specific community contexts in which they sat. The paradigm of the early modern playhouse offered here is therefore as follows. "Playhouse" was an elastic term, which covered numerous architectural forms and types of venue. They were specifically designed or adapted for commercial play, with some degree of regularity. Playhouses were almost always multifunctional, hosting a range of activity that fell, in early modern English, under the remit of "play." The title of "playhouse" can be and was extended to theatrically adjacent venues, such as those that hosted some combination of sports, music, drinking, and/or "shows" of various kinds. Playhouses drew large crowds, transforming both urban and rural traffic and underscoring anxieties about the close physical proximity of mass gatherings; but they were also permeable spaces, allowing spectators to come and go during entertainment offerings. Playhouses existed outside of London, in diverse forms, and if we are properly to understand these institutions then we must look to both London and provincial experiences of such spaces. Playhouses overlapped with other types of cultural and social institutions, which came together to form early modern notions of "play," including occupational groups, local political structures, and community bodies and identities. In other words, playhouses were embedded in their surrounding communities.

I do not attempt in this book a chronology of playhouses, though I do want to trouble assumptions about order and precedence; I am also uninterested in a "guide" or run-down to the different playhouses in different regions. The Globe, for instance, only features in passing—in part to look beyond its iconicity and in part to pay detailed attention instead to spaces that have not benefited from the Globe's scholarly overrepresentation. This study is rather predicated on a series of less-discussed case studies—some sustained and focused, as in Chapters 3, 4, and 5; some brief and illustrative of the variety of playhouses on offer and of the types of play they offered. As such, this book is not an exhaustive list of English playhouses, much less an account of their evolutionary development, but an analysis of playhouse-ness in a period where play was both controversial and commercially successful at unprecedented levels. Many spaces will be missing and many stories absent—some of them famous and very many of them as yet not told at all. I hope the questions raised here and the playhouse family set out in these pages might help kindle further interest in telling them.

"Firsts" and Dates

Why, then, have so many spaces exhibiting the family traits set out above for so long been omitted from a "theatre history" of England? Why are some early modern structures awarded the label "playhouse" and others not? A whistle-stop overview of the once-dominant theatre-historical narrative of the past 100 years or so— until recent research, discussed below, started to change the story—points to some answers to these questions. Often, the "first" in the history of the English playhouse falls in the year 1576, with the building of Burbage's (and Brayne's and Brayne's) Theatre. Charles William Wallace's important early study of the venue is titled *The First London Theatre*, and Herbert Berry calls his edited collection on the subject *The First Public Playhouse*.[10] Recent accounts, thanks to Janet Loengard's discovery in 1983 of a legal suit concerning stage construction in Mile End, sometimes push this "first" back to the Red Lion, built by John Brayne in 1567, later of the Theatre fame.[11] Following in his wake, there is said to have been a boom of playhouses in subsequent years in London, with the 1570s seeing the opening of Newington Butts, the Curtain, children's commercial venues of the Blackfriars and St Paul's (where plays were performed by companies of children of the ages of 7 or 8 and upward for paying audiences), and early regular mentions of a number of London inn playhouses (Bell, Bull, Bel Savage, Cross Keys). When the Rose was built (in the quieter playhouse-building decade of the 1580s), it added to an already busy scene. The landscape got only busier at the end of the next decade, which saw the building of the Swan (1595) and the conversion of the Boar's Head (1598) and was capped by the transferral of the boards of the Theatre down to Bankside in 1598–9 to be assembled anew in the form of the Globe.

The 1590s therefore represent a teleological crescendo that goes hand in hand with this decade's outsize presence in our cultural imagination today. In these years, two of the most talked-about spaces for us now, the Rose and Globe, sat together on Bankside. Both have equal physical as well as metaphorical legacies, sitting as they do in recovered or reconstructed form in Southwark today. They are therefore emblematic of what E.K. Chambers, in his transformative and extensive work of theatre history, rubber-stamps as "The Elizabethan Stage"[12]: archetypal playhouses. Indeed, the iconicity (cultural and visual) of the 1590s looms large.[13] One of the few visions of the inside of a playing venue generated by any early modern contemporary is Johannes De Witt's sketch of the Swan—a mid-1590s playing venue just along the riverside from the Rose and Globe. This image formed a central visual cue during the reconstruction of Shakespeare's Globe in the 1990s, the amphitheatre that now sits prominently on the twenty-first-century Thames. This 1590s-centric narrative and the commercial impetus today surrounding the Shakespeare industry helps sustain the idea that the Elizabethan playhouse's ultimate evolution looks something like the Globe. It also skews playhouse-ness into a London phenomenon, despite vast evidence that the structures deemed "playhouses" in the capital had plenty of equivalents in other areas of the country.

This above account unfairly glosses over many of the nuances with which scholarship—even that invested, implicitly or explicitly, in the teleology of playhouse development—treats these spaces and their contexts, but it does correspond with a broad received narrative of how the early modern playhouse evolved, one that, in many cases, continues to be perpetuated. Recent scholarship has convincingly all but demolished this model. Nonetheless, a great deal of recent discussion still leans on some of these inaccurate impressions. The British Library's overview of Shakespeare's theatrical infrastructure asserts that "the first public playhouses were built in London in the late 16th century" and divides them into two types—open-air amphitheatres ("usually polygonal") and indoor halls—beginning their selective survey of spaces with the Theatre.[14] Stephen Greenblatt's and Holger Schott Syme's introductory essays for *The Norton Shakespeare* are excellent nuanced overviews of early modern England's playing industry, which emphasise longstanding English playing traditions and the significance of the city inns. Yet Greenblatt asserts that the "first permanent, freestanding public theaters in England date only from Shakespeare's own lifetime," referring briefly to the Red Lion and chiefly to what he questionably describes as "James Burbage's playhouse, The Theatre."[15] In another state-of-the-field volume, *The Oxford Handbook of Early Modern Theatre*, Gabriel Egan also offers a nuanced account of playing venues, warning against teleological "evolutionary terms" of theatre history before conceding they are "not entirely to be resisted."[16] He positions the Theatre not necessarily as *the* first playhouse but instead as "the first of a kind of venue—the open-air amphitheatres." The double emphasis on firstness and amphitheatricality help posit the Theatre as a landmark innovation, even though we do not fully know the architectural features of many earlier playing spaces (including the Red Lion in 1567 or John Rastell's stage in Finsbury in the 1520s). When compared with *known* contemporary or earlier theatre buildings, the only distinct quality that appears to make the Theatre novel as an "open-air amphitheatre" is its roundness. Scholarly over-emphasis on amphitheatrical playhouse structures has created a false distinction from rectangular, smaller, indoor, and/or supposedly more elite spaces, or some mixture of these labels. Yet the recent discovery that the Curtain was rectangular (and surprisingly large), the possibility that Newington Butts was a (likely rectangular) indoor tenement conversion, growing recognition of early indoor children's playhouses, and the increasing recovery of the significance of inn playing spaces all disrupt clear divisions between amphitheatrical and "converted" indoor playing space. Indeed, at the same time, and in the same volume as Egan, Ralph Alan Cohen claims for the (Second) Blackfriars a different first: "the first purpose-built (or refitted) indoor theatre in the English-speaking world."[17] What precisely makes the Blackfriars different from the multitude of other indoor playing spaces before 1608, or indeed the First Blackfriars of 1576—which sat in a different room in the building—is not clear. Even with regard to the earlier space, Sebastian Westcote's (indoor) St Paul's playhouse predates both the Blackfriars and the Theatre by at least a year.[18] As such, we must be wary of investing too much in either the terms "first" or "amphitheatre" as defining points for a narrative of this period's theatre history.

Skewed evolutionary narratives of the English playhouse persist despite important advances in our understanding of sixteenth- and seventeenth-century English theatre history. This book emerges, in part, from the *Before Shakespeare* project, which has recognised the plurality of spaces operating before the 1590s and has established new ways to think about the early modern playing industry.[19] David Kathman's pioneering work on London inns has shown them to be exciting dramatic venues since as early as the 1540s.[20] The research of Mary Erler and Meg Twycross has emphatically shown how commercial playing venues were in operation by the early decades of the century, while Janette Dillon's history of the commercial stage identifies roots in a playhouse built in the printer-playwright John Rastell's garden in Finsbury in the 1520s.[21] Reassessments of the London scene of the 1570s and 1580s have also shown the plurality of approaches, individuals, and motivations at work, with inspiration from William Ingram's impeccably researched *The Business of Playing*.[22] Laurie Johnson has offered the first sustained treatment of the playing venue Newington Butts, concluding that it was known by the name "Playhouse."[23] Kesson has questioned the opening dates of playhouses themselves, observing that we often do not know exactly when a playhouse did open, making timelines for the 1570s particularly thorny.[24] The centrality of the Theatre as a "first" looks ever more untenable when seen both from the focused view of the mid-1570s and with a longer lens, stretching back to the beginning of the century. These observations help us recognise the diversity of London's playhouses and encourage us to focus on their family resemblances as much as their differences. Indeed, Kesson asks that scholarship not overplay admittedly "important differences" between outdoor, indoor, or inn playing spaces, and by turn between children and adult performance venues, and that it rather thinks about the "sheer number of new playing spaces in London in this period. These playhouses are important in their multiplicity, pointing us towards a shift in the way drama was created, sited, funded, and consumed."[25] Archaeological excavations have also shaken assumptions about the period, particularly concerning the Curtain—a playhouse long assumed to be a smaller, less attractive, less successful facsimile of its neighbouring Theatre. The digs led by Heather Knight in 2016 and 2018 and post-excavation analysis has revealed the playhouse to have a much larger stage than assumed and not to have been "round" like its Shoreditch cousin but rectangular. These discoveries have not only prompted reconsideration of theatrical "archetypes" but raise the question of whether there existed a dominant architectural model at all, even (or especially) in this busy period of playhouse construction.[26]

Canonicity

The more generous understandings and wider temporal net cast by these reassessments allow us to challenge the "canon" of sixteenth- and seventeenth-century English playhouses. "Though we tend to think of literary canonization as an effect of the history of authorship," Kesson explains, "theatre history has also been affected by a process of canonization."[27] As I have suggested by reading early family narratives about the Theatre, the playhouse canon is connected to the English literary canon, in particular via Shakespeare, whose works are seen to fit most squarely into a particular type of (amphitheatrical) space and, in turn, supply the governing image of the period's theatrical architecture. Perhaps the most recent "canon" of playhouses might be found in the substantial catalogue of theatrical documents, *English Professional Theatre, 1530–1660* (edited by Glynne Wickham, Herbert Berry, and William Ingram), which lists them as follows: the Red Lion (1567), the Four Inns (often grouped together: the Bel Savage, Bell, Bull, and Cross Keys); St Paul's (c. 1575); the First Blackfriars (1576); Newington Butts (c. 1576); the Theatre (1576); the Curtain (c. 1577); the Rose (1587); the Swan (1595); the Boar's Head (1550s; converted 1598); the Globe (1599); Second Blackfriars (1609); the Fortune (1600); Whitefriars (1607); the Red Bull (c. 1605/6); the Hope (1613); the second Globe (1614); the Phoenix (or Cockpit) (1616); the second Fortune (1621); Salisbury Court (1629).[28]

Even among this sizable selection (itself remarkable in its quantity), theatre-historical discussion sometimes applies a hierarchy of playhouse-ness. Spaces that look or function slightly differently to the Theatre or the Globe, such as the small indoor Blackfriars or St Paul's playhouses that hosted children's performances in the 1570s and 1580s, are still sometimes marginalised as secondary or "so called" playhouses.[29] In part, this is because these spaces are multiple, rather than singular, in their purpose. For instance, documents might describe them as "rehearsal" spaces, or, as with the inns, it is clear that they had other or equal primary functions. Yet a brief look at perhaps the earliest canonical playhouse, the Theatre, quickly disabuses us of any sense of the difference between amphitheatrical "purpose-built" playhouses and multi-use rooms. The Theatre was built for "play"—that is why it is undeniably a playhouse—yet "play" in sixteenth-century English was used to describe dramatic performance, fencing, bear-baiting, or bowling. True to its purpose, then, the Theatre was home to numerous fencing "prizes" throughout its lifetime,[30] and for all we know such matches may have been more attractive for some spectators than watching the Leicester's Men, the Queen's Men, or the Chamberlain's Men. The same can be said of the inns, often minimised in importance given their status as venues for food and drink where plays also happen. Yet this is indeed no different to the Rose, which was also attached to a victualling house, or to the oysters, nuts, or drink sold in the Theatre (which, recent excavations show, was built adjacent to a medieval building that may well have served visitors snacks), Globe, or Curtain (which was built just down from a property described in the lease as a "victualling house"). As such, we learn of the typical local name for a theatrical "house of multiple occupancy" in 1600s Bristol—an "inn" with multiple chambers and rooms (let to various people) and home to plays "commonly called the playhouse."[31]

As well as broad singularity of purpose, another term used to distinguish "canonical" playhouses from occasional spaces is the label "permanent." Herbert Berry introduces the canon of *English Professional Theatre, 1530–1660* by suggesting such spaces qualify as "permanent structures [...] built for the professional acting of plays."[32] This definition, if we cast aside the singularity of "professional acting of plays" and think more flexibly of "play," is perhaps more useful. It helps distinguish, for instance, between a playhouse and a Guildhall space used for travelling performers, although, as we shall see in Chapters 1 and 4, the lines are often blurred. I accordingly adopt here the importance for playhouse-ness of both intentional design and regular commercial operation. Yet permanency itself is a fraught term, and one not necessarily in tune with early modern architectural understanding. How long must a playhouse stand to be permanent? Many spaces are seen to be fluid from the start, endlessly "convertible" and part of what S.P. Cerasano terms the "the transitory playhouse"—an inherently impermanent architectural space.[33] Indeed, the impermanence of architecture is what both makes and unmakes playhouses. When Richard Farrant was planning the Blackfriars playhouse in 1576, he explains his intention to "pull down one partition and so make of two rooms one."[34] The Curtain playhouse, too, was constructed in an alley-like space, or a plot resembling a "backside," behind an existing house on Curtain Road—spatial overlaps explored in Chapter 1. Playhouses need not survive for decades, or even years, to be awarded the label: the theatrical structure built at the Red Lion complex ran for at least one summer, possibly longer, possibly not (recent excavations suggest a complex changed and developed over decades); the Bristol Wine Street playhouse ran for at least 20. According to Berry, the Swan had a stop-start playing history: it was host to players for three years after its erection in 1595 until 1598, and it was not until 1610 that playing resumed there, for only four years; after this, it had another year of playing in 1620–1 before, in Berry's words, "it ended altogether."[35] Yet *play* did not cease at the Swan in 1621. Like the Rose playhouse, also regarded as "over" by this time, the Swan hosted "prize-fighters," or fencers—a different form of play but one perfectly fitted to a playhouse.[36] After all, the dimensions of the Curtain stage are the exact length of a modern Olympic fencing piste.[37]

The last "category" relevant to this book that is often associated with this list of canonical playhouses pertains to their location. They are at once "in" London and "out" of it. All of these spaces are London playhouses, but, according to Berry, "except four built in inns," they all sit outside City of London territory, "to escape at least partly the jurisdiction of the mayor and aldermen, who were usually hostile to them."[38] London-centricity aside, such a framework sets up an adversarial nature with civic authority at odds with the spaces of this book. Venues discussed in Chapter 1, such as Trinity Hall, squarely in city jurisdiction in St Botolph's Aldersgate, functioned quite happily as a commercial playing space through the 1550s and 1560s. As Berry himself admits, four of the most active playhouses of Elizabethan London—the Bel Savage, Bell, Bull, and Cross Keys—were at the heart of City of London control. The Cross Keys was attractive enough to draw James Burbage from his own playhouse in 1579 and had sufficient staying power to be hosting the Strange's Men in 1593.[39] There was of course tension with authorities like the London corporation, particularly after legislation of 1574 sought to levy a tax on any proprietor hosting a play of some form.[40] Yet such tension continued to apply to suburban spaces, themselves subject to periodic diktats demanding their immediate pulling down. Ingram even suggests that legislation like the City of

London's in 1574 was "designed actually to enable, rather than suppress, the responsible presentation of stage plays in the City."[41] Blanket assumptions that playhouses were "fringe" spaces at odds with authorities—compounded by the popularity of Steven Mullaney's study in dramatic subversiveness, *The Place of the Stage*[42]—not only ignore the numerous spaces that do not fit this model but unhelpfully obscure all playhouses' community connections. The playhouse in Wine Street, Bristol, for instance, was at the heart of a social hub for members of both parish and civic bodies. Elsewhere, the town of Congleton spent huge sums on its animal sport complex as part of a municipal investment in play. Chapter 4 accordingly explores these spaces' relationship with their political and social surroundings.

Commercial and Professional

This book, then, acknowledges the need to define the boundaries of playhouseness but resists the narrowness of the playhouse canon. In so doing, it follows the revisionist scholarly treatment of London spaces outlined above, recognising that multiple factors determine playhouse-ness beyond singular purpose (of "professional" dramatic playing), permanency, and detachment from local authority. The same logic can be extended to a grammar school church-house in East Coker or a quarry pit in Shrewsbury that themselves otherwise share an overwhelming number of the family traits of the early modern playhouse. Indeed, in their focus on London, even recent revisionist treatments of playhouses intimate essential links between the playhouse and the "professional" performance of stage plays, predominantly by patronised troupes. The examples explored in this book point to equal numbers of playhouses that housed different formats for play and performance or that entertained resident or visiting performers (of all kinds) about whom we may well sometimes know very little. The concept of the playhouse at the centre of this book therefore looks beyond the stage itself and thinks about structures of all kinds that "housed" play, game, performance, or sport—both for economic capital (to earn money) as well as for political capital (to earn influence), and cultural capital or even a kind of play-based cultural conviction (that theatricality and performance are desirable in and of themselves—motivations explored in Chapters 4 and 5). This book decentres drama to think about the multitude of "play" and its meanings (surveyed in Chapter 2) and looks instead to playhouses as locations that hosted regular commercial play of all kinds.

The word "commercial" seems better suited to describe the playhouse than "professional"—a term commonly used to circumscribe, or canonise, particular kinds of venues.[43] "Commercial" is more encompassing of the wealth of evidence about playing venues *not* primarily or indeed at all engaged with dramatic acting. Instead, it allows us to explore the ways play was imbricated in all areas of life. Because of proscriptions in England on who could act in a patronised performing troupe, the notion of the "professional" is also very close to the outdated image of the "all-male stage." While excluded from male companies, women were palpably not excluded from the performance industry more generally, including in the management of commercial venues.[44] By looking beyond supposedly "professional" men who ran and performed in playhouses we can continue to recognise commercial actors of all kinds. Kathman has already shown how three of the four inns in London were run by women: Margaret Craythorne (Bel Savage; 1568–91); Alice Layston (Cross Keys; 1571–90); and Joan Harrison (Bull; 1584–89).[45] Three Margarets discussed in Chapter 5 illustrate the point: when Margery Swayne was called upon repeatedly to re-straw the cockpit in Congleton with her expertise as a straw-drawer, or when Margaret Woolfe was described by a visitor as the "face" of the Wine Street box office, or when Margaret Brayne saved money on labour by laying the bricks of the Theatre herself, these women show themselves to be leaders and innovators in the commercial world of the early modern playhouse. Brayne is in fact a central figure in the London theatre scene of the late sixteenth century. She asserted her authority as a proprietor through a series of lengthy legal battles, whose paperwork has happily furnished theatre historians with a sizeable proportion of what we know about London playhouse building and management. These issues, and their significance outside of the capital, are picked up, in particular, in Chapter 5's examination of the business of the playhouse.

London and the Provinces

As I have observed in the above survey of scholarship on early modern English playhouses, almost all studies remain focused on London itself, obscuring regional examples and comparisons, as well as wider national contexts for the development of play. Siobhan Keenan's *Travelling Players in Shakespeare's England* has importantly opened windows onto regional spaces of play, with short accounts of playing spaces outside of London, and though it rests on some of the assumptions about playhouse-ness questioned here, it remains the most focused account of non-London playing spaces to date.[46] Towering over all catalogues of theatre and performance history of this period is the *Records of Early English Drama* project, which collects all archival records of performance and mimetic activity in a given region (typically organised by county, although recent and ongoing collections have broken down the seismic task of London into differently organised outputs). This project has presented an astonishing array of materials relating to provincial performance, from touring professional companies and independent solo performers to displays and tricks of the royal camel. The regional riches contained in *REED* include numerous sites of play, or playing places, but the idea of their *playhouse-ness* has not always been factored into broader scholarship. Keenan, for instance, recognises only three Elizabethan and Jacobean "provincial theatres" (Prescot, Bristol, and York in 1609), with two further tentative candidates, suggesting the scarcity is "not surprising" given smaller populations, lack of wealth, and absence of regular audiences.[47] None of these factors, however, seems either to inhibit or to apply to the popular places of play discussed across this study.

One hope of this book is that it might help shrug off anxieties about applying the label of "playhouse" to venues outside of the capital and thereby instil provincial performance cultures with some of the theoretical and conceptual energy typically reserved for London playhouses. A special issue of *Shakespeare Bulletin* has explored the dramatic energies of England's early modern north west, including paying substantial attention to the playhouse at Prescot—a space so described in a number of documents ranging from the late sixteenth to the early seventeenth centuries. The Prescot Playhouse is at the heart of a regeneration project, Shakespeare North Playhouse, which uses designs for a seventeenth-century indoor court theatre as inspiration for the reconstruction of a performance venue that will bring Shakespearean capital of all kinds to an underprivileged and under-resourced part of the country.[48] The idea of the regional playhouse explored in this book also entertains other design features not necessarily aligned with the formalised, established sense of a "theatre" represented in royal courtly designs or, indeed, by the rebuilt Shakespeare's Globe. These models may well apply to playhouses in places such as Prescot or Bristol—or they may not—but they need not determine our recognition or image of the playhouse outside of London. Prescot, for instance, was home to its own active cockpit, which seemingly tied together the town's interest in dramatic and sporting "play." While the inspiration for Prescot's playhouse remains at least somewhat obscured by historical distance, the success of multiplay cockpit complexes elsewhere in Lancashire and Cheshire, as in Congleton's civic sports infrastructure, equally points to models not rooted in London or court performance. This book accordingly eschews first-ness and London-centricity, to think flexibly across time and the regions of England, in order to recognise the connections between related but temporally or geographically distant spaces—to get closer towards a family history of the playhouse in a period in which England's playing industry grew exponentially.

Contexts and Developments

Why, then, does the century or so following 1520 see the burgeoning of a playing industry across England? The question rather exceeds the ambitions of this book, which seeks not to explain the origins of the playhouse or its transformations, but instead to characterise what playhouses were and how they were used—a study of playhouse-ness. Yet some head-on engagement with the question is necessary to contextualise the chapters that follow, all of which themselves obliquely pick up the *why* of the playhouse in their own ways. Numerous social, cultural, and economic factors contributed to the commercial changes in the playhouse industry, and they require a book or three in themselves. Here, I focus on some of the chief contexts that bear directly on the discussion in the chapters that follow.

Elizabethan theatre did not evolve like a Pokémon but merged in important ways with earlier commercial modes of performance. There has long been debates in late medieval theatre studies about the exact nature of its stages: Richard Southern posited a performance tradition, based on a sketch from a play called the *Castle of Perseverance*, rooted in in-the-round performance. Pamela King and Glynne Wickham have both challenged the idea of the entirely round performance venue for such medieval dramas.[49] Wickham has undertaken a considered discussion of where the "prototype of the Elizabethan public theatres" might lay,[50] recognising the plurality of spaces that overlapped with dramatic performance through the pre-Elizabethan period and acknowledging both similarities and differences with baiting arenas and outdoor circuses. However, his work is now somewhat dated by the emergence of new understandings of the Tudor playing landscape from the revisionist studies noted above and from archaeological discoveries.[51]

Lawrence Clopper has helpfully nuanced approaches to medieval-early-modern staging, rejecting any "evolutionary model" and recognising that "we have applied modern senses of theatrical terms to medieval texts and documents."[52] He traces developments of words like theatre, play, and game to suggest, broadly, that terms like "play" (or *ludus*) might be employed as "a generic term for 'drama' because it is demonstrable that in the medieval languages and early modern English both are used to designate a whole range of sports, games, and recreations."[53] As such, he observes that early uses of terms like *theatrum* need not even designate a physical structure but instead function as rhetorical markers for performance types or events that reached beyond ecclesiastically sanctioned liturgical drama. According to Clopper, clerical antitheatricalism served as a catalyst for new forms of early drama, with the late medieval church's attempted suppression of festive games, gambling, and ales prompting lay groups (especially in cities) to promote and develop fresh types of dramatic presentation.

Vernacular and lay performance activity in late medieval England therefore shaped later models for commercial performance. Developments in drama were also accelerated by social changes. Clopper recognises, for instance, how the growth of strong borough or guild governments spurred forms of enacted drama, thanks to "sufficient population and a lay power base."[54] Such changes combined with rapidly increasing urban populations, especially across the sixteenth and seventeenth centuries, to create new audiences for developing forms of play. Both All Hallows on London Wall and St Katherine's Cree were awarded licences from London to permit an entire summer's worth of play (i.e., a season-long licence) in 1527 and 1528, respectively.[55] Aligning them with the long tradition of church ales (festive celebrations that generated parish income), this licence enabled the parishes to raise funds for church repair. It granted All Hallows' parishioners permission to "make a Stage Play there to begin at Easter next & so to continue unto michaelmas [then] next following."[56] While the profits were designed for the benefit of the church, the plays were run and the infrastructure formed by lay people, as an outward-facing commercial enterprise. At around the same time, John Rastell arranged for a playhouse to be built in his garden in Finsbury, just north of the city of London. Rastell's playhouse was constructed and part of its theatrical activity overseen by the mercer Henry Walton, whom I identify here as a type of playhouse proprietor. Walton also built stages for the parish of All Hallows the year following their official licence, as well as for St Botolph's without Aldersgate in 1529. His role as a playhouse developer and manager is explored in Chapters 1 and 5. Here, however, we can briefly observe how commercial playing venues in the 1520s linked lay dramatic activity on purpose-built parish stages with Rastell's secular venture. This was an industry large enough to sustain repeated work in playhouse-building for Walton. The 1520s thereby furnish us with perhaps the earliest collective evidence for structures functioning as or similar to commercial playhouses and so provide the most convenient starting point for this book, without laying down a straightforwardly evolutionary account based on "firstness."

The Reformation brought with it new possibilities for commercial stage building. The ready availability of land following sales of monastic property in the 1530s and 1540s meant that both individuals and corporations (in some respects like early modern local councils) had access to sites that could be developed for various commercial opportunities—and play sat high amongst them. As such, the quarry in the former Austin Friary in Shrewsbury, the commercial complex at London's Blackfriars, or a priory in Shoreditch presented the chance for affordable space and land for ambitious building or conversion projects. These former ecclesiastical sites were often well-situated for enterprises interested in drawing a crowd, in close proximity to the town or city. As such, not only did the Reformation itself alter the landscape, physically and metaphorically,[57] but the adaptation of recently privatised land for commercial play created new journeys, routes, and traffic that reshaped both urban and rural environments (a subject discussed in Chapter 3).

The mid-sixteenth century also saw an unprecedented expansion in credit lending. While early modern England throughout the years covered in this book underwent harvest failures and repeated episodes of economic dearth, alongside plague and other devastating diseases, it also saw a steady reshaping of the social and economic order. Along with the expansion of literacy and access to education, individuals across the social scale depended on what Craig Muldrew calls a "web of tangled interpersonal obligation" in which "wealth was gained through reputation, not accumulation, individualism, or inward piety."[58] Muldrew's detailed study of early modern credit has demonstrated the social and ethical meanings of borrowing and lending in the period. He identifies a renewed population growth in the 1520s combining with expanding economic activity and a rise in consumption over subsequent decades. With limited cash in circulation, this emerging economic boom was fuelled by individuals buying and selling on credit. Muldrew's research emphasises the moral and community underpinnings of this economic structure and its maintenance through legal processes—debt litigation tellingly reached a staggering high in around 1580—but the "economy of credit" also represented new opportunities in the service and leisure industries, topics raised in Chapter 5. As such, early modern playhouse building was a product of wider economic changes occurring at a particular pace between the 1550s and the 1620s: an exponential increase in alehouses per capita, growth in purchases of non-essential consumer goods, a rise in imported goods and foodstuffs, and nationwide architectural redesigns and renovations (often termed the Great Rebuilding).[59] Indeed, 1620 is a rounded date span for the title of this book. It avoids the encyclopaedic notion of a full sweep up to 1642 and the Civil Wars and Interregnum, but it also offers a manageable date that promises sustained focus on a 100-year period. Robert Tittler groups his study of early modern town hall building and expansion into a period that ends in 1620—a useful yardstick, because in Chapters 1 and 4 I suggest that town halls can help us understand playhouses. After 1620, for Tittler, the type of civic engagement and architectural innovation invested in such halls falls off.[60] Similarly, economic, labour, and fashion historians recognise 1620 as a useful date for appreciating changes in consumption and production that are not tied to regnal years but are instead reflective of daily practice and experience.

Economic and architectural shifts correspond with a wider process of *urbanisation*, which facilitated and shaped the playhouse industry explored in this book. Although a rapidly increasing fraction of the population lived in cities in this period, England remained a predominantly rural and agricultural country. Phil Withington has shown, however, that "early modern England was a more urban society than has generally been acknowledged" and "became more so over time."[61] Cities connected the country ever more centrally, forming the robust skeletal system of its travel routes and exchange networks. Yet urbanisation does not only refer to cities' staggering population expansions and their increased infrastructural importance. It also connotes changes in behaviour and practices across the country. For instance, civic processes became models for national policies; Withington explains how the early modern state applied urban systems of commercial regulation across the whole country (with direct parallels for the recreational and service industries). Moreover, urban institutions developed "codes of conduct and discourse […] expressly civil in nature," rooted in and adapted from medieval urban ideals: corporatism, citizenship, freedom, and commonweal.[62] The increased popularity of such ideals is evidenced by the growth of towns becoming "incorporated"—that is, receiving formal legal recognition of their trading privileges and politico-administrative autonomy. Across this period, then, urban institutionalism proliferated, with consequences for the service and entertainment industries. I build in this book on Tittler's work on the town hall, looking both at and beyond urban locations to show how the playhouse occupied an important, if overlooked, place in what Withington sees as early modern England's "institutional intensification and innovation."[63]

Those institutions bring with them archival elisions. Part of their function and development was to narrow who had access to creating, producing, and preserving documents. Ayanna Thompson has observed how such "archives, and what they preserve, value, erase, write over, and leave scant traces of, are racecraft" (the social process that construct race and racism, or "the underlying imaginative horizon, belief system, or individual and collective mental landscape that seeks to divide humans along unequal lines").[64] As such, histories of early modern institutions or quasi-institutions like the playhouse are faced with an evidence pool skewed towards middling-to-elite and exclusionary visions of the past. This book seeks to think beyond the boundaries of the playhouse wall. It follows Robert Henke's cultural history of theatre by recognising the "quintessentially *social* cultural production and consumption of the 'art' of theatre."[65] At the same time, Clare McManus reminds us that "theatre" is often less helpful a term than "performance":

> in order to understand the role of women in English theatre we have to re-imagine our concept of that theatre: for 'theatre' we now read 'performance,' a broader and more diverse practice which encompasses a range of forms such as dance, music, song, pageantry (both civic and royal), oratory, secular and religious performance, university and school performances, closet drama and jesting.[66]

Many of these elements can be found within the playhouse itself, and here I take forward McManus's enabling sense of "performance" in my understanding of "play," which frequently includes both women's performance as well as ownership, management, and procurement in venues across the country.

This Book

The revisionist "playhouse" paradigm presented in this introduction, applied to a "family" of structures and sites of multipurpose recreational activity, is key to understanding the commercial development of early modern entertainment and dramatic performance. The remainder of this book falls into five chapters and a coda. Chapter 1 undermines the idea of the "archetypal" playhouse to argue for a range of different architectural models. It questions critical and popular assumptions about what Elizabethan theatres looked like (perhaps most emblematic of which is today's Shakespeare's Globe)—assumptions that persist in current theatre-historical writing, including prioritising "amphitheatrical" spaces that are historically atypical rather than representative. Instead, I explore the varying spaces that early modern men and women thought of as playhouses, including company halls like Trinity Hall or the Merchant Taylors' Hall in London, an inn in Bristol, a school building in Witton, or a disused quarry in Shrewsbury. I explore historical models for the development of commercial playing venues, as well as pageant houses in Coventry and Chester and ephemeral elite models such as the Field of the Cloth of Gold. I also look at the way "canonical" London playhouses have close affinities with other spaces of play, such as the bowling alley or the baiting arena. Contemporaries sometimes saw no distinction between these locations, which themselves also presented "plays."

In exploring the multiplicity of playhouse forms, the chapter rejects teleological narratives about playhouse development. It suggests parallels between commercial churchyard stages in the 1520s and children's performance locations in the later part of the century and counters the enduring narrative that playhouses suddenly appeared in the mid-1570s to argue against the notion of "first"-ness. Rather, playing venues developed alongside wider developments in commercial entertainment across the country both before and after the Reformation. Important archival sources like the London corporation records (studied in their entirety) or provincial consistory and quarter sessions records show how playhouses are particularly associated with the rapid growth of buildings for sports, dancing, drinking, and other forms of recreational spectatorship. These contexts help make sense, for instance, of new discoveries about the alley-like space of the Curtain. This chapter therefore sets out a much fuller and more accurate sense of the kind of buildings early modern individuals identified as playhouses.

Chapter 2 builds on recognition of the architectural diversity of playhouses by exploring in detail the different activities that took place within them. It looks beyond dramatic performance to appreciate that even the most canonical of playhouses hosted sporting activities alongside drama. These were fundamentally multipurpose spaces, and contemporaries made visits to them to watch, for instance, a fencing match as much as to see a Shakespeare play. This chapter therefore revisits the meaning of *play* and its implications for and beyond dramatic performance. Indeed, its economic and social connotations across early modern England tie performance to other entertainment forms. As such, this chapter offers an overdue consideration of why a bear-baiting arena on Bankside hosted an audience-immersive "play" in 1584, or why a memoirist writing of the 1610s described it as an extended site of dramatic activity. Similarly, Congleton in Cheshire built and maintained rings designed for animal sport through the 1570s to the 1620s, but these rings were also host to a range of mimetic and musical activity. Once we recognise the multipurpose nature of venues like the Rose or the Theatre, we can then appreciate how locations across England, typically absent from canonical theatrical history, were in fact home to playhouse-like structures that paralleled canonical London venues. We can also recognise the diversity of play forms that took place within such structures. This account of the multipurpose playhouse decentres professional playing to recover forms such as extemporising, human–animal shows, tumbling, fencing, and dancing, all of which in turn often featured international, female, or more-than-human performance and agency.

Chapter 3 looks at "crowd capacities," using two case studies to examine what it meant to draw a crowd to a site or event of play and the impact venues had on local infrastructure. It focuses on Shoreditch in London and several towns across Lancashire and Cheshire to ask: who went to playhouses? How did they get there? What was the social effect of these recreational acts of mass movement? Shoreditch offers one way of understanding how playhouses altered urban travel. While legal accounts relating to the Theatre have been extensively mined, there has to date been no discussion of fascinating testimony from two women in 1601 who had lived in Shoreditch for well over 70 years. They described the changes brought about by the building of two theatres next to their homes, providing unique details about newly created access routes and gates, including from neighbouring Moorfields. In turn, other depositions referring to the area and Bridewell cases pertaining to surrounding fields create a picture of pedestrian traffic routes created by playhouses. New works in the 1600s saw Moorfields levelled and a series of tree-lined avenues put in that, according to contemporary satirical verse, guided walkers "towards the Curtain." Shoreditch's playhouses therefore physically transformed their surrounding environment, channelling urban traffic towards them: Henry Chettle explained in 1593 that young people flocked not only to playhouses themselves but the areas in which they were located. Playhouse environs were essentially go-to leisure destinations—and not exclusively for the play on offer.

Crowd journeys for commercial leisure elicited concern from authorities, and not only in the large city of London. Records of several sites of play in Cheshire reveal mass gatherings with distinct effects on the local economy but equal moral and social opposition. The north west offers ample evidence for a clash of opinion over playing venues, as religious and political changes met with resistance. An attempted crackdown on "unlawful games" and assemblies in the region offers a useful parallel to periodic calls for "suppression" of London playhouses. For early modern English authorities dealing with plague and possible disorder, crowds were always potentially dangerous, and playhouses represented a locus where recreational assembly could turn into violent affray or mass infection. Yet theatre history has often over-weighted the testimony of antitheatrical and authority voices (being copious sources of detail); this chapter reads these forms in conversation with depositions and non-dramatic contexts to recover a nuanced sense of the playhouse crowd in and out of London. Doing so helps us understand crowds' persistent presence at sites of play. This chapter therefore recounts how playhouses transformed both their physical and social environments; it recognises contemporary anxieties about the drawing power of these venues but acknowledges the affordances of the playhouse crowd for those at all levels of society.

Chapter 4 looks at playhouses as community hubs, and it takes off where the previous one ended to set out a picture of the playhouse as community-facing and community-transforming. It draws on examples across the country where playing venues were central to community cohesion and builds on scholarship about inns, alehouses, and town halls to think about how play offered social, cultural, and political possibilities. It includes three case studies that represent a fundamental sense of playhouse community: the cockpit complex at Congleton, Wine Street in Bristol, and the First Blackfriars playhouse in London. These playing venues prompt the question: what roles did playhouses occupy in the local community?

Communal leisure activity and community-led play has a long history, underpinning medieval traditions of Whitsun plays or mystery cycles, pageantry, and midsummer shows across England. These festivities persisted but were significantly scaled down or suppressed by the 1570s. Congleton provides a fascinating insight into new developments for community "play," as it was home to what might be seen as a council-run sports and leisure facility. Its accounts document regular upkeep, repair, or building on the cockpit site and adjacent baiting ring and archery butts, involving men and women from across the town. Meanwhile, some of these individuals are to be found in court records elsewhere in the county, defending the honour of Congleton when questions of "play" are at stake, such as at a scuffle at a bear-baiting. The town represents a community defined by play, which sat at the heart of local economic and social identities.

Playhouses run by individuals were also at the centre of community action. Documentary evidence from Bristol's Wine Street shows how independent proprietors considered their venture imbricated in craft identity and charity. When cutler and playhouse-proprietor Nicholas Woolfe died in 1615, he left bequests to local charities, to the company of cutlers, and to hospitals on the singular proviso that the playhouse remained *as a playhouse*. This compelling detail guarantees the venue's enmeshment with the social fabric of Bristol—something made even clearer by the fact that alderman and soon-to-be-mayor Henry Yate took over as manager and that Woolfe's bequest payments continued for over a decade. Edward Alleyn followed in Woolfe's footsteps when rebuilding the Fortune, with the actor and bearward insisting on continued play at the venue. These proprietors enshrined in writing a symbiotic relationship between community institutions and the playhouse.

Yet antitheatrical sentiment is also key to understanding the place of the playhouse in the community. Fresh documentary evidence surrounding the First Blackfriars playhouse (1576) points to wider questions about leisure institutions. This chapter closes by building on recent revisionist studies of the petition against James Burbage's Second Blackfriars playhouse plan in 1596, which undermine assumptions about neighbourly antitheatricalism. I move the discussion back to the 1560s and 1570s by presenting fresh documentary evidence that such petitions are part of a longer discussion in the neighbourhood about the desirability of commercial leisure establishments. The Blackfriars was characterised from the 1550s onwards as a site of commercial leisure, home to dancing schools, tennis courts, and bowling alleys. At the same time, it was populated not only by wealthy aristocratic property owners but by artisans of all kinds, including a high proportion of skilled immigrant craftspeople. This chapter sees the First Blackfriars Playhouse as part of this rich wider community, dominated by leisure and craftsmanship— themes abundantly present in the playhouse's repertoire for the 1570s and 1580s. It also presents evidence like Congleton, there was a Blackfriars identity connected to its "liberty" and corresponding attractiveness as a zone of play. This chapter therefore sets out the community benefits of playhouses and their imbrication with neighbouring institutions, crafts, and individuals. It re-evaluates playhouses not as singular entities but as part of the fabric of the early modern parish, liberty, town, or street.

Chapter 5 considers the economic activity behind the playhouse, exploring both the proprietorship of venues and the forms of labour that built and sustained them. It builds on the overlooked early modern work (often by women) that made possible theatre[67] or the book trade[68] and wider socioeconomic production to present playhouses as collaborative businesses. I think again about Henry Walton's commercial stages—a stage proprietor and builder from the 1520s introduced above and considered in Chapter 1—and both London and provincial enterprises to ask: why build a playhouse? The chapter therefore returns to Nicholas Woolfe's will to understand how playhouses sat alongside other personal and business identities, such as his trades of cutler and inn-holder. It also explores how the playhouse business spans different modes of play: like Woolfe, Edward Alleyn was invested in the legacy of his playing empire. This chapter reconsiders the business motivations that linked acting, playhouses, and animal sports. It also, crucially, looks beyond male figures to the preponderance of female playhouse proprietors and so expands our understanding of women's ownership and management. The final sections of the chapter focus on three early modern Marges: Margaret Woolfe in Bristol, Margery Swayne in Congleton, and Margaret Brayne in London. In doing so, I explore women's direct work on playhouse buildings as well as the collaborative nature of playhouse management, moving away from the enduring image of the solo, male entrepreneur to think about other ways in which playhouses were shaped and sustained by various skills, labour, and networks. I finish thinking about Brayne and revisiting the "Esore" question that continues to perplex theatre history: what did Henry Lanman mean when he signed a contract to make the Curtain an "Esore" to the Theatre in 1585? The exact meaning of this word remains unclear; instead, this chapter asks what it means for two neighbouring venues to be in some way connected. I argue the arrangement between the Theatre and Curtain might more rewardingly be read via Margaret Brayne's encounter with it: as John Brayne's widow (co-builder of the Theatre), she claimed after his death half of the profits of *both* playhouses. Conflict and collaboration are united in the complex legal battles fought by Margaret Brayne, who provides a model for revisionist theatre history in fighting to be recognised as a playhouse proprietor and attempting to overturn an assumption of sole male ownership.

The book's final section, its coda, considers the afterlives of playhouses and returns to questions raised in this introduction: why are some spaces considered playhouses and others not, in spite of historical evidence to the contrary? What excludes a playhouse from the canon? I ask what it means to discover the physical remains of a playhouse and think about what interdisciplinary collaboration between archival research and archaeology can do for understanding early modern social spaces. But I also (in line with contemporary archaeological approaches) trouble the idea that physical remains might provide concrete answers. I therefore think about the ephemerality of the early modern playhouse. Contemporaries saw these buildings as continually available for "conversion"—a legal term used in relation to all buildings and applied to numerous playhouses across the period—including the Globe, which is in some sense a "conversion" of the Theatre. At the same time, the materials that comprised playhouses of all stripes are largely organic matter, themselves subject to degradation.

This coda therefore goes on to consider contemporary theories of "decay" and material processes of becoming, looking to the work of Catherine De Silvey, Tim Ingold, and Miles Ogborn. It reads the material decay of physical sites alongside the patchy survival of archival records about playhouses, records that are themselves comprised of organic matter such as skin, rags, and organic compounds. Like playhouses in the period, *histories* of playhouses are in flux and continue to undergo processes of transmutation. True to their contemporary uses, these spaces remain fluid and their boundaries porous. Their afterlives (on the ground and in documents) therefore prompt us to reflect on possible future narratives to be told about these spaces, why we might tell them, and to what evidence we should look. The book's coda asks what new approaches we need to conceive of the period's theatre history, to think about agency and storytelling that looks beyond or differently at the limitations of institutional archives or archaeological artefacts and ecofacts. Playhouses, as the preceding chapters aim to demonstrate, are central test-cases for how historical narratives are shaped and who shapes them.

Notes

1 LC 5/133, p.50, MS, The National Archives, Kew, London.
2 An indicative selection includes: Andrew Gurr, "A New Theatre Historicism," *From Script to Stage in Early Modern England*, eds Peter Holland and Stephen Orgel (Basingstoke: Palgrave MacMillan, 2004): 71–88; Heather Anne Hirschfeld, *Joint Enterprises: Collaborative Drama and the Institutionalization of English Renaissance Theater* (Amherst and Boston: University of Massachusetts Press, 2004); Scott McMillin and Sally-Beth MacLean, *The Queen's Men and their Plays* (Cambridge: Cambridge University Press, 1998); Laurie Maguire and Emma Smith, "'Time's Comic Sparks': The Dramaturgy of And," *The Oxford Handbook of Thomas Middleton*, eds Gary Taylor and Trish Thomas Henley (Oxford: Oxford University Press, 2012) and "On Editing," *Shakespeare* 15.3 (2019): 293–309; Jeffrey Masten, *Textual Intercourse: Collaboration, Authorship, and Sexualities in Renaissance Drama* (Cambridge: Cambridge University Press, 2007); Richard Preiss's *Clowning and Authorship in Early Modern Theatre* (Cambridge: Cambridge University Press, 2014); Tiffany Stern, *Documents of Performance in Early Modern England* (Cambridge: Cambridge University Press, 2009); Tiffany Stern and Simon Palfrey, *Shakespeare in Parts* (Oxford: Oxford University Press, 2007); Robert Weiman, *Author's Pen and Actor's Voice: Playing and Writing in Shakespeare's Theatre* (Cambridge: Cambridge University Press, 2000).
3 Helen Cooper, *The English Romance in Time* (Oxford: Oxford University Press, 2004), p. 8.
4 Herbert Berry, "The First Public Playhouses, Especially the Red Lion," *Shakespeare Quarterly* 40.2 (1989): 133–48; Janette Dillon (referring to "John Rastell's construction of a playhouse") in her "Review of *London Civic Theatre*," *University of Toronto Quarterly* 74.1 (2004/5): 403–4.
5 *Oxford English Dictionary*, "Playhouse, *n.*" 1. See the capaciousness of "plays" in the pages below.
6 John Stockwood, *A Sermon Preached at Paules Crosse on Barthelmew day* (London, 1578), I7v.
7 Andy Kesson, "Playhouses, Plays, and Theater History: Rethinking the 1580s," *Forum*, ed. Andy Kesson, *Shakespeare Studies* 45 (2017): 19–40. p. 20.
8 Kesson, "Playhouses, Plays, and Theater History," p. 27.
9 Kesson, p. 20.
10 Charles William Wallace, *The First London Theatre: Materials for a History* (Lincoln: University of Nebraska Studies, 1913); see Herbert Berry, *The First Public Playhouse: The Theatre in Shoreditch* (Montreal: McGill-Queen's University Press, 1979).
11 Janet S. Loengard, "An Elizabethan Lawsuit: John Brayne, His Carpenter, and the Building of the Red Lion Theatre," *Shakespeare Quarterly* 34.3 (1983): 298–310; Berry, "The First Public Playhouses, Especially the Red Lion," pp. 133–48.
12 E.K. Chambers, *The Elizabethan Stage*, 4 vols (Oxford: Clarendon, 1923).

13 See Kesson for more on the 1590s aesthetic influences on our understanding of drama from the 1580s, as well as of how developments in professional troupe's skew understanding of earlier playing venues.

14 "Playhouses," *Treasures in Full: Shakespeare in Quarto*: www.bl.uk/treasures/shakespeare/playhouses.html. Online. Accessed 26 Oct. 2021.

15 "General Introduction," *The Norton Shakespeare*, ed. Stephen Greenblatt et al. 3rd ed. (London: Norton, 2016): 1–74. pp. 31–2. Holger Schott Syme, "The Theatre of Shakespeare's Time," *The Norton Shakespeare*, ed. Stephen Greenblatt et al. 3rd ed. (London: Norton, 2016): 93–118.

16 Gabriel Egan, "The Theatre in Shoreditch, 1576–1599," *The Oxford Handbook of Early Modern Theatre*, ed. Richard Dutton (Oxford: Oxford University Press, 2010), pp. 168–85. p.172.

17 Ralph Alan Cohen, "The Most Convenient Place: The Second Blackfriars Theater and Its Appeal," *The Oxford Handbook of Early Modern Theatre*, ed. Richard Dutton (Oxford: Oxford University Press, 2010): 209–24. p. 209.

18 For a more sustained discussion of "firstness" and commercial children's playhouses pre-1575, see Callan Davies, "Elizabethan Commercial Playing at St Paul's," *Old St Paul's and Culture*, eds Shanyn Altman and Jonathan Buckner (Basingstoke: Palgrave, 2021): 221–42.

19 See www.beforeshakespeare.com; Callan Davies, Andy Kesson, and Lucy Munro, "London Theatrical Culture, 1560–1590," *Oxford Research Encyclopedia of Literature*. 28 Jun. 2021. Online. Accessed 9 Jul. 2021.

20 David Kathman, "The Rise of Commercial Playing in 1540s London," *Early Theatre* 12.1 (2009): 15–38.

21 Mary Erler, "London Commercial Theatre 1500–1576," *Editing, Performance, Texts: New Practices in Medieval and Early Modern English Drama*, eds Jacqueline Jenkins and Julie Sanders (Basingstoke: Palgrave Macmillan, 2014): 93–106; Meg Twycross, "Felstead of London: Silk-Dyer and Theatrical Entrepreneur," *Medieval English Theatre* 10.1 (1988): 4–25.

22 William Ingram, *The Business of Playing* (Ithaca: Cornell University Press, 1992).

23 Laurie Johnson, *Shakespeare's Lost Playhouse: Eleven Days at Newington Butts* (London: Routledge, 2018).

24 Kesson, pp. 22–3.

25 Kesson, p. 26.

26 For a discussion of "rectangularity" and decentring "roundness," see Holger Syme's blog, "Post-Curtain Theatre History," www.dispositio.net/archives/2262. Online. Accessed 26 Oct. 2021.

27 Kesson, p. 26.

28 Glynne Wickham, Herbert Berry, and William Ingram, *English Professional Theatre, 1530–1660* (Cambridge: Cambridge University Press, 2000).

29 Kesson, p. 26, critiquing John Astington's description of St Paul's in "Why the Theatres Change" *Moving Shakespeare Indoors: Performance and Repertoire in the Jacobean Playhouse*, eds Farah Karim-Cooper and Andrew Gurr (Cambridge: Cambridge University Press, 2014): 15–31. p. 17. For a counternarrative to this de-playhouse-ing of Sebastian Westcott's St Paul's venue, see Davies, "Elizabethan Commercial Playing at St Paul's."

30 Sloane 2530, MS, British Library, London.

31 C 2/328/28, MS, The National Archives, Kew, London.

32 Berry, p. 287.

33 S.P. Cerasano, "The Transitory Playhouse: Theatre, Rose, and Globe," *The Text, the Play, and the Globe: Essays on Literary Influence in Shakespeare's World and his Work in Honor of*

Charles R. Forker, ed. Joseph Candido (Madison: Fairleigh Dickinson University Press, 2016), pp. 95–120.

34 L.b.446 (27 Aug. 1576), MS, Folger Shakespeare Library, Washington DC.

35 *English Professional Theatre*, p. 439.

36 *English Profesional Theatre*, p. 450.

37 Heather Knight, "The Stage Site Bounded by Hearn Street, Curtain Road and Hewett Street, London." Interim post-excavation assessment. (London: MOLA, 2017).

38 Berry, p. 287.

39 TNA, C 24/226/10; Petition to the Privy Council, *c.* 1593, Dulwich College, MSS 1, Article 16.

40 Ingram, pp. 131–46.

41 Ingram, p. 138.

42 Steven Mullaney, *The Place of the Stage: License, Play, and Power in Renaissance England* (Chicago: University of Chicago Press, 1988).

43 See, for instance, *English Professional Theatre*.

44 See the *Engendering the Stage* project for more on female commercial performance (http://engenderingthestage.humanities.mcmaster.ca).

45 David Kathman, "Alice Layston and the Cross Keys," *Medieval and Renaissance Drama in England* 22 (2009): 144–78.

46 Siobhan Keenan, *Travelling Players in Shakespeare's England* (Basingstoke: Palgrave MacMillan, 2002).

47 Keenan, p. 144. Keenan defines such buildings as "exclusively for theatrical use," p. 145, adopting on some of the narrow approaches playhouse definitions queried in this introduction.

48 Elspeth Graham, ed. spec. issue, *Shakespeare Bulletin* 38.3 (2020).

49 Pamela King, "Spatial Semantics and the Medieval Theatre," *The Theatrical Space*, ed. James Redmond (Cambridge: Cambridge University Press, 1987): 45–58; Glynne Wickham, *Early English Stages*, Vol. 2, 1964 (London: Routledge, 2002).

50 Wickham, p. 157.

51 Wickham also emphasises amphitheatricality as a key indicator of the new playhouse, while suggesting rectangular models do not hold sway for the 1570s—a claim that does not hold in light of excavations and research on the Curtain or Newington Butts, or in light of the inn and indoor playhouse models discussed in Chapter 1.

52 Lawrence Clopper, *Drama, Play, and Game: English Festive Culture in the Medieval and Early Modern Period* (Chicago: Chicago University Press, 2001), p. 4.

53 Clopper, p. 19.

54 Clopper, p. 148; p. 168.

55 REPS 7 (microfilm x109/133) fo. 228, fo. 297, COL/CA/01/01/007, MS, London Metropolitan Archives, London.

56 REPS 7 fo. 228 (microfilm x109/133), COL/CA/01/01/007, MS, London Metropolitan Archives, London.

57 See Alexandra Walsham's *The Reformation of the Landscape: Religion, Identity, and Memory in Early Modern Britain and Ireland* (Oxford: Oxford University Press, 2011).

58 Craig Muldrew, *The Economy of Obligation: The Culture of Credit and Social Relations in Early Modern England* (Basingstoke: Macmillan, 1998), p. 1; p. 6.

59 For summaries of and figures on these changes, see Muldrew, pp. 17–30. See also: Bruno Blondè, Peter Stabel, Jon Stobart, and Ilja Van Damme, "Retail Circuits and Practices in Medieval and Early Modern Europe: An Introduction," *Buyers and Sellers: Retail Circuits and Practices in Medieval and Early Modern Europe* (Turnhout, Belgium: Brepols,

2006): 7–30; Tara Hamling and Catherine Richardson, *A Day at Home in Early Modern England: Material Culture and Domestic Life, 1500–1700* (New Haven and London: Yale UP, 2017); Craig Muldrew, "Class and Credit: Social Identity, Wealth, and the Life Course in Early Modern England," *Identity and Agency in England, 1500–1800*, eds Henry French and Jonathan Barry (Basingstoke: Palgrave Macmillan, 2004): 147–77; Mark Overton, Jane Whittle, Darron Dean, and Andrew Hann, *Production and Consumption in English Households, 1600–1750* (London: Routledge, 2004).

60 Robert Tittler, *Architecture and Power: The Town Hall and the English Urban Community, c. 1500–1640* (Oxford: Clarendon, 1991).

61 Phil Withington, "Urbanisation," *A Social History of England 1500–1750*, ed. Keith Wrightson (Cambridge: Cambridge University Press, 2017): 174–98. p. 175.

62 Withington, p. 193; p. 185.

63 Tittler, *Architecture and Power*; Withington, p. 190.

64 "Did the Concept of Race Exist for Shakespeare and His Contemporaries? An Introduction," *Cambridge Companion to Shakespeare and Race*, ed. Ayanna Thompson (Cambridge: Cambridge University Press, 2021): 1–16. pp. 7–8.

65 "Introduction: Culture, Cultural History, and Early Modern Theatre," *A Cultural History of Theatre in the Early Modern Age*, ed. Robert Henke (London: Bloomsbury, 2017): 1–34. p. 2.

66 Clare McManus, "Women and English Renaissance Drama: Making and Unmaking 'The All-Male Stage'" *Literature Compass* 4/3 (2007): 784–96. p. 793.

67 Natasha Korda, *Labors Lost: Women's Work and the Early modern English Stage* (Philadelphia: University of Pennsylvania Press, 2011).

68 *Women's Labour and the History of the Book in Early Modern England*, ed. Valerie Wayne (London: Bloomsbury, 2020).

1

ARCHETYPES

A narrow image of a typical early modern "playhouse" endures in both scholarship and the popular imagination. The iconicity of the Globe, with its thatched roof, polygonal circularity, and timber and white daub, represents today perhaps the apogee of Elizabethan playhouse-ness. The first Globe was built in 1599 on Bankside with the use of some of the materials from the deconstructed timbers of its forebear—the Shoreditch playhouse known as the Theatre. Both these spaces were home to Shakespeare's company, the Lord Chamberlain's Men. The amphitheatrical structure of the Globe has seen reconstructions or homages throughout recent history, from William Poel's abandoned attempt in 1897 to one improbably sitting in the midst of Rome's Villa Borghese gardens. The original Globe's international reach has made it into something of a cipher for Shakespeare's own cultural capital. The playhouse's very name reflects his ostensible global relevance and helps advance (and sometimes contest) a British cultural imperialism.[1] At the same time, these reconstructions are invested in a promise of "authenticity" that situates the Globe of 1599 as the most fitting historical model for a Tudor or Stuart playhouse. The nature and effects of an "authentic" Globe have been widely debated and discussed.[2] Yet a kind of *essential* authenticity lends all reconstructed Globes a unique architectural familiarity. Sometimes that extends to the forensic details of its building materials and processes; sometimes, as with the Australia/New Zealand Pop-Up Globe, it happily rests on a representative structural "globeness."[3] At either extreme, Globe-ness offers a credible nod to the essence of the early modern theatrical past.

Recent reconstructions of other early modern playhouses point beyond the Globe as the sole exemplar of even the "Shakespearean" playhouse (a limiting descriptor that indicates both one particular type of drama as well a historical date range of some mere 20 years: c.1592–c.1612). The American Shakespeare Centre's Blackfriars Playhouse in Staunton, Virginia, USA (opened in 2001) is a reconstruction of what Ralph Alan Cohen claims to be "the first purpose-built (or refitted)

DOI: 10.4324/9781003231127-2

indoor theatre,"[4] while Shakespeare's Globe's Sam Wanamaker Playhouse (opened in 2014) offers audiences and visitors "a *simulacrum*, an *archetype* of an indoor Jacobean playhouse."[5] The initial plans for the Sam Wanamaker Playhouse were motivated by incomplete designs by the seventeenth-century architect John Webb for a theatre that was never built; as such, the stunning indoor building that resulted is not a reconstruction of a singular theatre space but rather a venue attentive to "wider evidence for Jacobean buildings," willing "to draw on examples that contain analogous features."[6] The terms "simulacrum" and "archetype" provide helpful vocabulary beyond discussing the SWP's amalgam reconstruction. They capture how the early modern Globe, the Blackfriars, and more recently John Webb's drawings[7] have come to serve as broadly representative of the early modern playhouse. The Globe suggests a tradition of immersive, outdoor playing and cheap-ticket yardlings, with visually immediate historicity; the Blackfriars and Webb's theatre designs represent the more elite, rarefied, wood and candlelight setting of the kind of smaller indoor venue inhabited by Shakespeare's King's Men after 1609.[8] These historical structures and plans have themselves transcended physical and historical reality to become *archetypal*—metonyms for the early modern past that set up an essential binary of playhouse-ness.

Yet audiences of the period would recognise a vast range of architectural forms and functions in a playhouse. This chapter explores the diverse physical appearance and construction of playhouse buildings across the sixteenth and early seventeenth centuries. Here, I offer very different structural models, each of which present, in their own way, key traits of the playhouse family. I begin by deconstructing the governing notion of the amphitheatre, beginning with the canonical "first" of the Theatre and its related structures from the 1570s onwards, including a "Theatre" carved from a quarry in Shrewsbury used for play and game from at least the 1560s. I then explore other playhouse spaces: outdoor stages and connected structures; indoor halls; single rooms in multi-use buildings; inns, or spaces within or outside inns; alehouses, or spaces within or outside alehouses; bullrings and other animal baiting rings; and adapted alleys and yards.

Such buildings were variously used for commercial recreation and performance across the country, and their architecture reflects overlaps between one form of play and another. These considerations lead us into Chapter 2's exploration of multiform play. They remind us that playhouses never solely or straightforwardly hosted dramatic performance, but *housed*, in every sense, play of all kinds. If we are to find architectural archetypes that unite the early modern playhouse family, they are to be found in these structures—venues whose physical capacities reflect their adaptability and functional capaciousness.

Amphitheatre

The 1570s provide a useful starting point for thinking about the variety of playing spaces across the early modern period: a temporal middle ground that allows us to move between both earlier and later iterations of the playhouse across this period.

While there persists a misleading narrative that the mid-1570s "invented" the playhouse, a myth dismantled in the introduction and further destabilised by this chapter, this decade nonetheless *did* substantially transform the playing landscape of London. It was during these years that amphitheatrical structures or similarly styled venues began to garner significant commentary. This is the architectural model often perceived today as archetypal of the Elizabethan theatre, largely thanks to John Brayne, Margaret Brayne, and James Burbage's building of the influential and influentially named the Theatre.

Vast quantities of legal paperwork survive surrounding the construction and operation of the Theatre in and after 1576. The playhouse was built thanks to a financial and business partnership between the grocer John Brayne and the joiner James Burbage; Brayne had already built a playhouse in Mile End, discussed below, while Burbage was heavily involved in the theatre industry, being himself a player with the Leicester's Men. Burbage leased property in the former priory of Holywell on 13 April 1576, from the landlord Giles Allen. Both the lease itself and later court cases, which continually return to such contractual landmarks, indicate that part of the agreement included taking care of a suite of houses and barns on the location.[9] Eyewitness assessors put the building work done there, separate to the playhouse, at around £240.[10] There was some tension between Allen and Burbage (and later his son Cuthbert) about whether a playhouse were a suitable or acceptable building to construct on the land under the lease arrangements: when the lease was to be extended shortly before its expiration in 1596, Allen insisted that playhouse operations be wound down within five years and the property turned instead to other purposes.[11] Yet Burbage and Brayne put forward from 1576 substantial sums to build the entertainment venue. In court cases, contemporaries who recalled the construction were at odds about the exact figure spent between Burbage and Brayne, or who footed the larger share of the bill, but figures range between £240 and £700.[12] One witness gave a useful ballpark figure of a thousand marks (roughly £666).[13] This is a huge amount of money to construct a building, especially in comparison with the roughly £20 estimated to have been laid out by Brayne just ten years earlier on the stages of an earlier playhouse, the Red Lion.[14] The figure suggests an impressive and perhaps novel scale of playhouse compared to those that had come before—creating a model repeatedly and variously developed over subsequent decades. By the time the similarly styled Fortune was built 24 years later, its builder Peter Streete was assigned £440 for its construction (rising to £520 "for the building" according to Edward Alleyn's memorandum book).[15]

Why did the construction of the Theatre cost over 30 times Brayne's earlier venture in theatre building and come to establish a more grandiose model of playhouse building that continued in London for decades? The question perhaps gets us closer to the nature of its architectural style. Not only do the costs indicate the scale of the building project but they also attest to its splendour—a mixture of classical and vernacular architectural influences designed to suit its Latinate name. Moreover, while all early modern building spaces contain an essential temporariness (captured in discussions about renewing lease on the land, in which the landlord suggested the playhouse might simply be converted into tenement buildings—a fate that befell many playhouses of this period), the level and expense of work expended on its erection indicates the Theatre's purposeful durability, if not its "permanence."

What, then, did it look like? Archaeological excavations have been limited to accessible surviving material: in particular, an inner wall in one of the bays that would have housed bench seating for spectators. Reports from MOLA (Museum of London Archaeology) suggest the Theatre was roughly 22m wide, as a 14-sided polygon (the same layout as the next playhouse built on such a model, the later Rose playhouse). Archaeologists found a drain running across the cobbled surface outside of the playhouse, and they pinpointed a section of the stage (on its west side) with entrances on the east. The Theatre was partially covered with a roof, which left drip marks where water fell into the yard just before the "inner" wall.[16] Outdoor playhouses like the Theatre also had "tiring houses," structures or areas for costuming and backstage business (from the word "attire"), which occupied the backstage area immediately behind the *frons scenae*, or rear wall of the stage. Often, either central and/or flanked entrance doors allowed access onto the stage from such a structure (for actors' entrances and exits), while archaeology shows that other playhouses (like the Curtain) seemingly had passage from the far left and right of the stage.[17]

We can also supplement the archaeological data with information from contemporary manuscript and print sources. Various dramatic references to trapdoors point to an understage cubby hole, possibly with access to the tiring house and the areas beyond the stage, while certain playhouses (such as the second Rose or the Globe) seemingly had winching equipment above that could lower or suspend actors over the stage. Other sources tell us that the Theatre had galleries and upper rooms where pricier seating was available than standing in the cobbled "yard." One employee explains that he was requested

> to go […] to the Theatre upon a play day to stand at the door that goeth up to the galleries of the … Theatre to take and receive … the money that should be given to come up unto the said Galleries at that door.[18]

These galleries were likely subdivided into "rooms," in which spectators could either sit or stand. The Theatre's real estate landlord, Allen, requested, during negotiations for a new lease in 1585, permission for him and his family to "come & take their places" in the building before other audience members and "in some one of the upper rooms to have such convenient place to sit or stand to see such plays as shall be there played freely."[19] William Lambard, writing what is perhaps the earliest English "tour guide," informs readers of the 1590s that "No more than such as go to […] the Theatre […] unless they first pay one penny at the gate, another at the entry of the Scaffold, and the third for a quiet standing."[20] These descriptions evoke not only the physical sense of the Theatre but also the way spectators moved within it, and the hierarchy (of price and perceived status) attendant on different locations within a playhouse.

As well as sketching some of the structural features of the Theatre, contemporaries repeatedly made reference to visual elements not detectable in archaeological excavations. Just a year after it was built, Thomas White called upon audiences and readers of his sermon to "behold the sumptuous Theatre houses," while John Stockwood "discommended" the "gorgeous Playing place erected in the fields."[21] Theatre-ness became a byword from the late 1570s for *sumptuous* design. These elements point to wider domestic design trends that explain something of the architectural ambition of certain playhouses from the 1570s onwards. W.G. Hoskins laid out in 1953 an influential reading of early modern household changes. He saw in the period following the 1550s a "Great Rebuilding," in which medieval houses (often with a large un-ceilinged hall) were made over, enlarged, and reconstructed into almost entirely new houses—often by adding in a ceiling, one or more fireplaces, and employing wainscotting and other decorative features.[22] The notion of a nationwide overhaul of domestic architecture has been critiqued and refined, not least in the context of urban spaces, but the general sense of post-1550 changes in the lived environment testifies to fresh appreciation among early modern builders of the relationship between architecture and "sumptuousness." Indeed, alongside structural redevelopments, scholars have recognised how

> the decoration of interiors was a requirement of status that represented a considerable investment and, as a semi-permanent addition to the fabric of the building, should be considered alongside the creation of ceilings, partition walls and fireplaces as a major intervention in the form and use of a given property.[23]

The Theatre's visual impressiveness, therefore, speaks to the "house" in the term playhouse. Theatre history has long focused on these structures as "unique," but they owe something to wider architectural shifts that visitors and antitheatricalists like White and Stockwood would have recognised in the houses of many of their peers. Reconstructions have looked to the great houses of aristocrats for visual cues, but such changes in decoration and appearance were enjoyed by an increasing number of those in the middle majority of society—established carpenters, brewers, traders, or glovers, for instance. Unimpressed Protestant preachers like White implicitly identified the Theatre's lavishness with domestic spaces, emphasising their house-ness (while also charging them with the hint of visually indulgent, idolatrous popery).[24] Subsequent playhouses in London accordingly echoed such shifts in English interior decoration. The Swan and the Fortune contained impressive features recognised by visitors or built explicitly into their building contracts: the tourist Johannes de Witt praised the "colour of marble" painted on the Swan's columns and its "distinguished" appearance, while the contract to build the Fortune drawn up in 1600 specified wrought plasterwork, including "carved proportions called satyrs to be placed and set on the top of every of the same [stage] posts," with the implication that painting of the ceiling, walls, frame, and gallery rooms would follow its construction.[25] Archaeologists discovered wooden panelling at the Rose playhouse (built 1587; expanded 1592) aligned with wainscotting—carved, decorative panels that perhaps covered the front-facing part of the stage.[26] Each of these so-called "amphitheatrical" playhouses adopted innovative and fashionable interior design choices to confer on play, game, and visual spectacle the status and seriousness advertised by the "modern" houses of the socially secure or the socially mobile. It is no wonder that contemporaries commented as much on the architecture as on the action or performances within.

Reading the features of the Theatre in this way helps us establish a received sense of what the Elizabethan London amphitheatre looked like. Such details have long been regarded as central to theatre historical enquiry for this period: the foundations, in every sense, on which we base our understanding of playwrights, players, and playgoers. Yet "amphitheatricality" is itself a theatre-historical construct. While it helpfully captures a change in design and "sumptuousness" along the lines indicated above, it also elides the important differences between London playhouses as well as the playhouse-ness of other structures both in and outside of the capital. Indeed, "amphitheatre" was not a term widely used in early modern English. The word denotes "an oval or circular building [...] around a central open space or arena."[27] Where "amphitheatre" appears in Elizabethan print, it typically refers to grandiose structures of classical or continental design—distant in time and place from Shoreditch or Bankside.[28] We have already seen, however, that "homely" terms such as "house" or "playing place" were more typically applied to polygonal or rectangular structures in London. The editors of *English Professional Theatre, 1530–1660* (a collection of primary sources) reveal theatre history's "rewriting" of the past at work. They cite a diary entry from the Dutchman Johannes de Witt, upon his visit to London in 1596, in which he remarks that "in London are four amphitheatres of obvious beauty."[29] The four amphitheatres to which he refers are the Rose and Swan in the south in Bankside and the Theatre and Curtain in the north outside Bishopsgate. In the original Dutch, however, "amphitheatre" just reads as "*Theater*."[30] Archaeological excavations have revealed that the Curtain was not "amphitheatrical" at all, at least not in the sense of being "circular." When it was discovered by MOLA in 2016, it turned out to be rectangular. The editors' translation of the capacious Dutch signifier, "theater," into the more prescriptive "amphitheatre" tellingly reveals assumptions about playhouse architecture that new evidence has quite overturned.

In fact, the Theatre, Rose, Swan, and (a little after De Witt's visit) the Globe and the Hope are the only definitively round playhouses in London across the whole of the sixteenth and seventeenth centuries, and there are of course plenty of structures about whose geometry we cannot be sure (a point explored in the following section). Based on these known shapes, circular amphitheatres are outliers rather than archetypes.[31] When the Rose was built in 1587 by Philip Henslowe, it entered a market full of playhouses only one of which—the Theatre—was markedly "round." Before 1596, these two spaces were the only known "amphitheatres" in London. Another way to state this fact is to emphasise that for more than half of the 1590s amphitheatres, strictly defined, were quite simply unusual. This is a decade often regarded as the epicentre of early modern drama: it sees Shakespeare's entry onto the dramatic scene, and by 1596 he had already written most of his histories, *Romeo and Juliet*, and *A Midsummer Night's Dream*. Moreover, crucial innovators and influencers in performance and playwrighting—Richard Tarlton, Christopher Marlowe, Robert Greene, Thomas Kyd—had been dead for several years by the time London saw a third "round" playhouse and would have known their theatrical scene to be dominated by rectangular, room-, or hall-like venues like those discussed below.

The Curtain playhouse is a perfect example of a longstanding non-amphitheatrical structure with elements of amphitheatricality. Long assumed to be round, as the above translation of De Witt indicates, excavations on the playhouse have revealed it to have been built in the rear "courtyard" or "void" of an existing building and to have looked strikingly similar to Spanish theatre spaces, known as *corrales*, such as the surviving example in Almagro (see Fig. 1.1). David Amelang's recent comparative study emphasises the "stand-alone" nature of English playhouses as a marked counterpoint to Iberian examples. Yet the Curtain's striking similarity with this later Spanish space suggests that so-called "Elizabethan amphitheatres" were not entirely distinct from European "courtyard" playhouses[32]—a significance explored below in a discussion of alleys and backsides. Indeed, early modern entertainers

FIGURE 1.1 "Interior appearance of the corral de comedias de Almagro."

Credit: José Manuel Torrejón Ortí. 20 Nov. 2011, 13.22. Attribution-ShareAlike 3.0 Spain (CC BY-SA 3.0 ES).

were arguably more used to performing in rectangular halls or rooms in both London and the provinces, as we will see with other spaces in this chapter.

The very idea of a "freestanding" or "new built" structure is complicated by Elizabethan building practices. Conversion was a commonplace means of repurposing buildings or reusing materials, one that was central to paradigms of playhouse construction. Even the construction of the Globe was described by contemporaries as a "conversion."[33] Meanwhile, the Theatre itself, while it was not converted from existing buildings, was built against and within them—on the foundations of a medieval priory and propped against a pre-existing decayed barn.[34] Such architectural conversion and adaptation helps us appreciate the manifold forms of "playhouse" set out here. They also provide an important qualifier for all commercial amphitheatres. There is a porous line between "new built" and "converted" buildings throughout early modern England, especially when remarkable structures such as the Theatre also made of use of older buildings and may likely have appeared to contemporaries to be, at least in part, an adaptation.[35] Indeed, the medieval brewhouse on the Theatre's north side was remodelled in the sixteenth century, quite possibly for the use or needs of the playhouse. On this evidence, the Theatre seems more like the non-amphitheatrical Curtain, which sat behind an existing tenement fronting onto Curtain Road. These "purpose-built" playhouses were in fact generated by a complex negotiation with their built environment, making use of surrounding structures and blurring the lines between adaptation and what Elizabethan regulations termed "new building."

Although one was rectangular and the other broadly round, the Curtain is regularly coupled with the Theatre in contemporary commentary, leading theatre historians to argue that Elizabethans saw "the two playhouses together as representing all the purpose-built playhouses in and around London."[36] Certainly, the Curtain shared with the Theatre a large outdoor space, a "yard" interior, galleries, and a wooden stage, with coverings over the seated areas.[37] Many of the structural features described above with regards to the Theatre appertain exactly, or equivalently, to the rectangular Curtain. Details are scant, but it is equally likely that the "sumptuousness" of the Theatre applied also to the Curtain—enough so that the two playhouses entered a profit-sharing arrangement in 1585 (a matter discussed in detail in Chapter 5). Crucially, we do not know precisely what date the Curtain was built. It is first mentioned in 1577, but it is possible that this structure was erected *before* the Theatre, as the *Before Shakespeare* project has emphasised,[38] making it an influence on the latter (and hence on other succeeding spaces). Such a line of thinking has rarely been entertained, largely because the Curtain has long been regarded as the poor cousin of its neighbouring space and seen to lack documentation—in pointed contrast to the archive-rich Theatre. Tiffany Stern goes so far as to describe the Curtain as "derivative" and undesirable.[39] Yet it is the longest-lasting of all the London 1570s theatre spaces, undergoing renovation in c. 1611 and hosting plays and players into the mid-1620s.[40] We have no reason to doubt that players and spectators would have regarded the Curtain equally as "sumptuous" and "gorgeous" as its neighbour.

Far from being "derivative," then, the Curtain's mixture of courtyard and amphitheatrical qualities had staying power and influence enough to fly the flag for rectilinear playhouse design. It may well have been an unspoken influence on the building of the rectangular Fortune in 1600. This venture, built by Philip Henslowe and Edward Alleyn, merged amphitheatrical qualities with other spatial features, in particular those of the *courtyard*, the *backside*, the "*booth*" stage, and the *inn*—playhouse models that occupy a significant proportion of the remainder of this chapter. Henslowe and Alleyn cite the Globe playhouse in their building contract as the desired model for the Fortune's stairs, corridors, stage, and finishings ("contrivitions, conveyances, fashions, thing, and things effected, finished and done") except "the frame of the said house to be set square."[41] The most obvious geometrical model for such a building would be the Curtain playhouse, which sat a little to the east of the Fortune's plot, in Shoreditch. The Fortune's own rectangularity has been posited as the blueprint for the "fencing school" and playhouse built in Gdańsk in 1611.[42] The Curtain, however, must be an equal candidate for such an influence.[43] It was likely repaired and re-beautified around this exact date and was famous for hosting fencing prizes (discussed in more detail in Chapter 2). The Curtain therefore provides a series of useful reminders about outdoor commercial playhouses, amphitheatrical or otherwise: all of them vary in their geometric forms; each was influenced by and in turn influenced other kinds of structures (many of which are discussed in this chapter); and each had its idiosyncrasies.

If we accept that even ostensibly similar playhouses differed in architectural design and emerged from mutual relationships with existing environments, then our attention should surely be drawn away from London to perhaps the most truly "amphitheatrical" of playing spaces in sixteenth-century England. Shrewsbury in Shropshire, on the Welsh border, was home to a playing structure that acted as "a place for public services, exercises, or recreations."[44] Writing 11 years after the Theatre was built in London, the poet Thomas Churchyard alludes to the Shoreditch venue when he describes the Shrewsbury structure:

> … behind the walls as chief,
> Where Plays have been, which is most worthy note.
> There is a ground, new made Theatre wise,
> Both deep and high, in goodly ancient guise:
> Where well may sit, ten thousand men at ease…
> […] A space below, to bait both Bull and Bear,
> For Players too, great room and place at will.
> And in the same, a Cock pit wondrous fear,
> Besides where men, may wrestle in their fill
> A ground most apt, and they that sits above,
> At once in view, all this may see for love […].[45]

Churchyard was born in the city in around 1523 and aims in his verse to celebrate Shrewsbury and surrounding Welsh cities, towns, and castles, to a wider readership, drawing on everything from personal experience to historical chronicles. In this section, he powerfully evokes an extraordinary entertainment spot, and he deems it a playhouse by way of comparison with a "Theatre." In doing so, he draws on classical associations with the term, compounded by his recognition that it has "goodly ancient guise," yet it is difficult not to see an allusion to the London playhouse, too. The site is "new made," a generous and useful description that blends the concepts of "converted"/"adapted" and "new built" straddled by London playhouses; it carries the senses of both "remade" and "built anew." In being "new made," the site was not only modified for various forms of "play," but it was also carved from the natural environment and former structures.

Churchyard's phrase is given clarity in subsequent court interrogatories from 1608, in which the venue's precise location is set out: these documents pinpoint it as being in the former Friary of St Augustine in an area previously used by the town to extract stone and clay:

> one parcel of the said close next adjoining [the friary] called the dry quarry from time to time during your remembrance been used and employed [...] for stage plays and Common plays silver games wrestling Running Leaping, and other like activities and recreations.[46]

Its ecclesiastical former life creates an uncanny parallel with the Theatre in Shoreditch, which similarly sat in a former priory (Holywell), and, as we have seen, made use of the canonesses' brewery and bakery buildings. Moreover, Churchyard echoes Thomas White's "sumptuous" description of London playhouses, but more favourably, noting in the margin that the Shropshire venue is a "pleasant and artificial piece of ground."[47] While the form of this particular "Theatre" is very different in location and execution, it shares with the London playhouses described above both a relationship to former monastic space and an appreciation of its goodliness and fairness. Shropshire's quarry-"Theatre" also far outstrips the London venues on scale, accommodating more than tenfold the capacity of the Theatre or Curtain. It seemingly hosted commercial recreation as well as town-sponsored events, given that bearwards, like players, often generated income at the door or on the ground as well as "officially" from town administrations.[48]

This former quarry was not simply a stretch of land on which performances, plays, games, and sports took place. It was "made Theatre wise" by virtue of architectural details and structural additions:

> they as occasion served at their will and pleasure made scaffolds erected booths and [tenements] made stairs and digged and trodden the ground & soil aswell within the compass of the said dry quarry as in other parts of the close above the said quarry for the better beholding and taking the pleasure of the said Common plays and other exercises [...][49]

Those features shared by the Theatre and the Curtain and detected in archaeological excavations were also at the heart of this early modern multiplex in between the English midlands and the north west. The description of these seating structures implies an inherent fluidity and flexibility: not only is the playhouse's multipurposeness at the fore, but its forms, seats, and benches could be recast anew as suited the play medium at hand. Such adaptability would eventually characterise the Hope (1613), the last early modern amphitheatre-style playhouse to be built in London, which itself moved between animal sports and plays and made use of a retractable "stage to be carried or taken away, and to stand upon trestles."[50] Other amphitheatre-style spaces such as Henslowe's Rose playhouse also underwent periods of modification—most notably five years after it was built, in 1592, when its stage and staging capabilities were significantly redesigned.[51]

On the surface, then, nearly 30 acres in an erstwhile friary-turned-quarry that hosted sports, games, and drama on a vast scale might not look or sound like our received notion of an early modern playhouse. Yet the details from court cases and from Churchyard's praise for this patch of repurposed land confirms that the quarry in Shrewsbury "new made Theatre wise" had all the family resemblances of a playhouse. Its scale and the implication of its seating arrangements (with forms and benches placed in an area raised above the performance site) in fact bring it closer to continental and classical "amphitheatres," and so to the term's use by contemporaries, than any London venue. Moreover, one of the deponents to whom interrogatories were posed at the Shrewsbury Guildhall in 1608 was the 63-year-old weaver, Humphrey Leaton. Leaton confirmed that he had known the site to be used for "bearbaitings bullbaitings making Butts and shooting for stage plays and other plays for silver games wrestling Running Leaping and other recreations" for "fifty years and above."[52] At his most conservative estimate, therefore, this (amphi-?)theatre had been operating since the 1560s. This Shropshire quarry does not generally factor into discussions of the English playhouse, yet it exhibits all the features of outdoor playhouses in London from the 1570s onwards.

This brief tour of the Theatre, Curtain, Fortune, and Shrewsbury quarry demonstrates the anachronism of the term "amphitheatre" and its unhelpfulness for grouping or describing playhouses of this period. It was not a term used in this way by contemporaries. Nonetheless, the features associated with these diverse "outdoor" playhouses—to some degree purpose-built with free-standing elements; with some form of "yard" and some form of stage area; and surrounded on some or all sides by galleries, seats, and/or tiring house—do represent a particular playhouse phenomenon remarked upon by contemporaries. Both in London and in Shrewsbury, the boldness of their scale and the impressiveness of their appearance might be summed up in White's contemporaneous adjective, "sumptuous." This term sufficiently conveys the moral disapproval of antitheatricalists who saw these venues as excessive in every respect, while it also recognises the costliness and complexity of "workmanship, construction, [and] decoration."[53] It also conveys these building's classical echoes, most obviously alluded to in the name of Burbage and the Braynes' structure, *theatre*, the term picked up by Churchyard to describe the longstanding quarry venue in Shropshire.

We might therefore recognise amphitheatricality as a "style" or accent if not an architectural blueprint. The Elizabethan writer and poetic theorist George

Puttenham referred to ancient "theatres [...] sumptuously built with marble & square stone in form all round," which "were called Amphitheatres."[54] The implicit link between sumptuousness and classical amphitheatres suggests that, rectangular or round, these buildings conveyed something of what Johannes de Witt described (referring to the Curtain, Theatre, Rose, and Swan) as "the general notion of Roman work."[55] By bringing together Greek and Roman traditions and combining them with English developments in house-building, interior decoration, and existing environmental features, these playhouses blurred (like so many of the performances within them) classical and vernacular styles.

Playhouses with amphitheatrical accents therefore embodied a significant, if overrepresented, element of early modern entertainment venues, even if they do not cohere as a discrete category. Moreover, their origin story remains untold and is perhaps impossible to tell. Scholars have long wondered, for instance, what earlier influences there were for 1570s "amphitheatres." The likes of the Shrewsbury quarry present one indication. Yet the nature of such a question prioritises chronology over variety, and while the remainder of this chapter sets out numerous other models from the first half of the sixteenth century that endured and influenced subsequent playhouse builders, it resolutely does not attempt an evolutionary narrative. Even this narrow cross-section of amphitheatrically accented structures emphasises how the early modern playhouse was governed chiefly by plurality—of history, use, and architectural configuration. Teleological narratives foreclose the crucial overlaps, influences, and contexts shared across time and place by the many spaces discussed across this book. The remainder of this chapter therefore looks further afield at the goodly, fair, and sumptuous range of playing spaces available to early modern players and spectators.

Stage and Scaffold

Play and performance venues in English cities emerged from a variety of architectural traditions, both elite and non-elite. The expansion and endurance of fixed places of play in the sixteenth century onwards to some degree resulted from forms of performance and pageantry long central to the ordinary lives of town and city dwellers. Research into pageantry across England has shown how ludic and theatrical activity occurred on stages of all kinds.[56] They included scaffolds temporarily erected for audiences or performers, or "pageant wagons" that could transport scenes and players to significant locations (like gates, churches, or conduits) as part of pageant or cycle performance. Many of these late medieval English "stages" were sponsored by different social and economic institutions: by the occupational company (such as the Skinners' or the Painters'), by religious guilds, or by local churches or corporations (the latter like a modern town council). Anne Lancashire's copious research has demonstrated that such adaptable staging was central to London culture as well as places like York, Chester, or Coventry; like these cities, the capital also had a thriving theatrical scene dependent on craft-led staging possibilities.[57] S.P. Cerasano has observed how Lancashire's meticulously gathered collection of evidence for civic performance up to 1558 necessitates a "new geography of the city" by drawing attention to infrequent but also routine places of play—the Little Conduit, Leadenhall, various gates, streets, and churchyards which were used as stages or in which stages were erected—dubbing it a "city of stages."[58]

The nature of these stages, in London and elsewhere, often remains unclear. Sometimes they may refer to "booth" stages, easily erected via simple trestles or other wooden arrangements in fairs or marketplaces for a performance.[59] Such arrangements are similar to "pop-up" playhouses today (such as the pop-up Globe in New Zealand and Australia or the Rose in York in the United Kingdom), erected without foundation work and enabling occasional, seasonal, or limited-run performances. While regularity might be one essential family trait for the playhouse, permanence, as the introduction has explained, is not. Transformable, rearrangeable, and flexible: booth stages and other simple scaffold structures were doubtless one important influence on their more structurally substantial cousins. They were also commonly encountered. Towns, cities, and villages across England had a festive rhythm characterised by periodic "church ales" or "wakes," which were a concentrated programme of holiday entertainment (from animal sports to performance). Such ales or wakes generated funds for the repair or enlargement of the parish church, and they were often held in line with the preferred local saints' or feast day—usually after Easter or at Whitsuntide. These entertainments were increasingly frowned upon following the religious changes after the Reformation, but they endured in many parts of the country into the 1560s or 1570s and sometimes beyond. We might therefore see the calendars of both rural and urban England characterised by "pop-up" stages and scaffolds for the types of performance and audience seating required by these festivities. By no means are these *playhouses* in the terms defined here, but they do bear a lightweight architectural resemblance—the playhouse's first cousin once removed.

The range of early stages and scaffolds are only gestured to here, in a book focused on a more defined sense of post-1520 playhouse-ness, but they indicate a developing conceptual and physical relationship between "houses" and play. Across urban medieval and (early) early modern England, pageant machinery and para-phernalia were often kept in "houses" for storage and repair. In 1537, Coventry's Cardmakers and Saddlers sold to the city Corporation its "pageant & pageant House with all & singular their Appurtenances ornaments vestments [...]."[60] Details from 1531 tell us this house contained "playing gear" and other materials.[61] Indeed, such "houses" were where the travelling "stage" used by each company in yearly religious cycle plays was stored, repaired, and erected, alongside other "appurtenances" for performance. Deeds for Coventry's Weavers' pageant house survive from as far back as the early fifteenth century,[62] and R. W. Ingram identifies from various extant documents nine pageant houses of different companies (Weavers, Shearmen and Tailors, Pinners, Cappers, Girdlers, Whittawers, Mercers, Drapers') across the city.[63] While these are hardly "playhouses," then, they are houses for play stages, and they indicate the fluid trajectory between performance structures and the built environment. Evidence from across the country shows that they often returned to public or commercial use in other formats: expenses in Worcester in 1583–4 reveal rents paid by the Weavers for "A tenement where the pageants were"—tenement being broadly a term for a domestic, commercial, or industrial building.[64] Like so many of the period's playhouses, early pageant houses were also transformed for different uses across their lifetimes.

These various examples indicate not only a rich performance tradition but help us understand early concepts of the playhouse, as a commercial venue with regular performance in a specifically designed or adapted structure. While pageant houses might more helpfully be thought of as "garages for stages" (sometimes also storing company administration and other materials) and show no signs of being public or commercial venues, other early stages and scaffolds do align with the concept of the playhouse. Glynne Wickham helpfully recognises *playhouse* has roots in old English as "*Pleg-hus*," a "game-house or play-house."[65] The definition acknowledges the multiplicity and flexibility of the term as set out in this book's introduction. Wickham's example is a venue built in Great Yarmouth in 1539. On the 15th March that year, Robert Copping leased from the town's corporation what is described as a "Game House," with the proviso that he "permit and suffer all such players & their audience to have the pleasure & ease of the said house & gameplace."[66] It seems likely that Copping's motivation for leasing the venue was commercial—like running an alehouse, this Game House could generate income from recreational activities, while the town's terms and conditions ensured that any "officially-sanctioned" entertainer (from the likes of local or visiting players to bearwards) had a guaranteed "house" in which to perform. By extension, the etymological roots of playhouse encourage us to think of any *place for play or game* as part of its extended family, including diverse assemblages or arrangements of stage, scaffold, and/or house.

Indeed, elsewhere, the port town of Lydd in Kent recorded a range of playmaking expenses in the 1550s, and financial documents refer to local man Thomas Godfreye "bringing timber from [the] playing place."[67] James Gibson identifies this simply as an "open area of land,"[68] but we simply do not know what the "playing place" looked like; it may equally well refer to an inside venue. Expenses for timber suggest at the very least that it was more sophisticated than a plain expanse—not least when one considers the local and national playing troupes and bearwards regularly hosted by Lydd. The town also had a tradition of staging its own yearly religious theatrical spectacle, the parish play of St George. Unfortunately, records are irregular and inconsistent when it comes to documenting the costs and labour involved in this entertainment, making it difficult to pinpoint its exact nature or the date at which such performances (and any related structures) faded out.[69] While these were not necessarily regular commercial operations, neighbouring New Romney spent lavishly on performance sites and materials and duly "gathered" at least £11 at their play in 1560 (a bonanza year, thanks to Queen Elizabeth's visit).[70] Both these Kent towns demonstrate investment in playing infrastructure, even if the precise architectural results are now obscured from view. David Dymond has explored the way surviving British place names, including "Playing Place," are toponymic archives of historical sports and leisure locations, being spaces used for "a whole range of recreations."[71] Indeed, the formulation "playing place" in the Lydd accounts equates to Wickham's *pleg-stow*, "a place for play, a gymnasium, wrestling place, amphitheatre,"[72] and this tantalisingly vague description must leave open at least a possibility that this Kentish town, like Great Yarmouth, had something approximating a playhouse along the lines of one or more of the models explored in this chapter.

While there may be some affinities, and even hints at regularity and commercial operation, most early and occasional stages and scaffolds are self-evidently not playhouses. However, a number do take on partially fixed form or regularity as defined venues for play in the early years of the sixteenth century and do, I think, more emphatically qualify as such. The "creative industries" career of Henry Walton, a London mercer, in the 1520s exemplifies how these early sixteenth-century stages and scaffolds expressed many of the key traits of the playhouse family. Walton was at the heart of a flurry of play-related construction, the most researched of which is a stage commissioned and built in the Finsbury garden of printer and playwright John Rastell.[73] The exact purpose and use of the stage remains uncertain. It was likely not an insubstantial structure, based on the lawsuit that gives information about its costs and the labour involved (50 shillings to Walton for building it).[74] That lawsuit came about because Walton refused to return costumes entrusted to him by Rastell while the latter was abroad. Walton hired out these garments "diverse times" during the late 1520s (figures differ, but around 20 times). He appears in this capacity to be not only a "builder" of stages but an early theatrical prospector, who helped to produce and facilitate play performances.

It is unclear what audiences visited Rastell's playhouse or whether they were charged for entry, but Walton's other work that decade is slightly more informative. In 1528, he set about creating a stage for the parish of All Hallows on London Wall. Their account books show that Walton was at the heart of summer entertainment revenues:

> Item Received at the play, clear as it Appears by the gathering book
> --- £5 8s 9d
> […]
> Item harry Walton demands of the parish that he laid out for board --- 7s 6d
> Item harry Walton demands that he laid out for nails—8s […] the one half
> --- 4s[75]

The following year, Walton's claims for the cost of the board were granted:

> Item first paid to henry Walton of old debt of the last year --- 7s 6d.[76]

Walton was keeper of the Mercers' timber-yard ("Surveyor of the Works") from 1525 until 1539.[77] Despite having no formal connection with building trades via a guild, he was in this capacity likely involved in contributing to pageant wagons and shows for London civic entertainments. Like the builders in the entertainment industry later in the century, it is possible Walton capitalised on his existing skills and, given his wider theatrical management experience, helped manage the other labourers recorded by the parish in connection with the stage. These entries are for reasonably small sums, no more than 15 shillings each, though the total amounts to a figure not much shy of the 50 shillings seemingly spent on Rastell's Finsbury stage. The "gathering book" records a decent return on investment, marking an income from playing of £5 8 shillings and 9 pence.

Although the All Hallows stage may well have had a limited lifespan imposed upon its commercial activities, it nonetheless housed regular, seasonal playing: in the year leading up to Walton's construction of the stage, London's Court of Aldermen acknowledged the "Ruin and Decay" of the Church and granted

> license that the parishioners there Shall make a Stage Play there to begin at Easter next and so to continue unto Michaelmas next following, And further it is agreed and granted by this Court that [...] none other parish Shall have like licence during the said term.[78]

Walton's All Hallows structure, seemingly charging audiences for entry and built to host players and spectators for a summer's worth of play, thus presents some of the most copious early evidence for an outside playhouse—one squarely aimed at non-elite audiences. Indeed, the licence grants a monopoly to the parish that permits a sustained period of playing, but it also emphasises fixed place and people connected to that place—especially in its emphasis on the term *there*. Similarly, the phrase "Stage Play" (or "play" in the accounts) could indicate a raft of activities and "wakes" or "ales." The All Hallows' licence and its gathering book therefore raise questions as to what forms of entertainment might have been performed in such early playhouse or playhouse-like spaces—a subject explored in Chapter 2.

Walton's activities as a "builder" are also matched by his role more broadly as a theatrical prospector or impresario able to offer a "total package."[79] In the year that followed Walton's stage-craft at All Hallows, he was involved in managing theatrical activity at another parish, St Botolph's without Aldersgate:

> And of 2s 4d. Received of Walton & his fellows for the hire of the Church yard to play in one [...] of 11s 6d received & gathered at A play in the Churchyard the which play the said Walton by covenant gave unto the Church.[80]

There are no further theatrical clues in these records, but one possibility in line with his exchanges with Rastell and All Hallows above would be that Walton ran a company of players ("fellows") who were in the 1520s and 1530s seeking regular performance venues. Walton had built such a structure the previous year, and here he hired the space (the yard) for the purpose—perhaps setting up a scaffold himself. Again, this particular "play" generated profits for the church and most likely for Walton and his fellows too. Such initiative looks strikingly similar to James

Burbage's interest in finding a home for his own playing company, the Leicester's Men, which resulted in the construction of the Theatre.

The Walton examples cited here suggest that playing was neither purely occasional nor solely for ecclesiastical benefit. There was clearly a substantial market for those involved in play production, costuming, and building within the first decades of the sixteenth century, and Walton's varied business in the 1520s suggests that such activity was by then in full swing in London. "Before the 1570s," in Mary Erler's words, "London had in place not only a lively theatrical community, but a commercially supported one."[81] These examples also give the lie to the idea that the City of London stood in opposition throughout the century to profit-based theatrical performance.[82] Walton's wider contribution to the theatre business in surrounding years points to a commercialised playing industry in action—one that crucially relied on the use of a regular playing venue.

Walton's stages are part of a fluid "family tree" that relates early sixteenth-century pageant wagons, stages, scaffolds, and courtly structures with later enterprises more readily regarded by theatre-historical scholarship as "playhouses." As such, the Red Lion playhouse represents a useful comparison with Walton's earlier activities. While the documented stage for the Red Lion was built some decades later, this playhouse is similarly subject to confusion over its place in sixteenth-century theatre history (occasionally referred to as the "first" playhouse, shifting focus from the Theatre, though sometimes bracketed off as a prototype, temporary structure, or experiment). We hear only of the stage built in 1567 by the grocer John Brayne thanks to two surviving documents that record quibbles over the quality and timeliness of carpentry work on the stage and seating.[83] It was set to open for *at least* a summer of playing, with the only scheduled play performance named as "the story of Sampson."

The limited details in these documents include enough to gather that, at this date, the Red Lion had a stage space, audience seating, and a tall "turret" in the playing area. Rather than debating its status as the "first" playhouse or whether it were an influence on or tester for a later design like the Theatre, co-built by the same John Brayne, perhaps the Red Lion might more helpfully be seen as a space that links the activities of the 1520s and 1530s with the set of playhouses that appeared in the mid-1570s. Like Walton's stages, the Red Lion was assembled from an array of "builder" skills managed by its chief overseer, it appeared for a summer's "play" (perhaps more), and it had links with churchyard theatre in the biblical nature of the only named drama associated with the space. The only difference is that it sits not on church land but on a farm by Mile End.

Indeed, the Red Lion playhouse and its surroundings have now been excavated, and early archaeological analysis points to an assemblage of shifting leisure activity over some hundred years.[84] The playhouse may have sat alongside or transformed into a space for dog-fighting and/or bear-baiting, as well as complementing spaces for drinking and socialising.[85] The significance of its complex- or hub-like set-up positions it as a close parallel to the likes of the Curtain, Newington Butts, or the Bear Gardens on Bankside, as well as to spaces like Canterbury's bullstake—topics picked up in the final sections of this chapter. The stage Brayne built at the Red Lion in 1567 therefore added to a "comprehensive complex,"[86] one continually and perhaps experimentally repurposed for different elements of commercial recreation. It therefore offers a way into understanding earlier such playhouse-like complexes, such as the playhouse in Rastell's garden or seasonal churchyard stages. When Walton built playing venues for All Hallows and St Botolph's, he was supplying one part of a wider expense on play and recreation, and such early sites may well have been seen, in the spirit of church ales or wakes, as miniature "complexes" for seasonal playing activity. Indeed, Chapter 3 explores how such ales brought music, drinking, performance, and animal baiting into commercial playing structures of all kinds across the country, in ways that parallel All Hallows, St Botoloph's, and the Red Lion. Centring Walton's theatrical activities can thereby help reassess not only the early Tudor playing ecology but help refine our narratives about later spaces, too. The Red Lion was quite distinct from a "freestanding" amphitheatre; instead, it appears to have had much in common with the many other multiform spaces discussed across this chapter. When amphitheatricality is no longer privileged as the archetypal or ideal Tudor playhouse form, stages like Walton's begin to seem more naturally in line with the commercial playhouses of the mid-century onwards. These later playhouses show builders and companies adapting to the conditions and spaces available to them for commercial playing purposes, just as Walton had done some 50 years earlier.

Walton's career thus encourages us to see early playhouses as the coming together of elite and courtly architectural projects with vernacular civic, craft, and parish structures. His influences extend from scaffold-stages-cum-playhouses in parish spaces to a bespoke structure for John Rastell's garden, likely to have hosted some of the most influential figures in the country. Walton's work is therefore further proof that spaces like the Theatre did not arise in a vacuum. Gabriel Egan observes that clear influences on or inspirations for the likes of the Theatre elude us (with particular emphasis on its shape); he points to potential antecedents in entertainments like that surrounding Henry VIII's meeting with Emperor Charles V in Calais in 1520—the celebrated Field of the Cloth of Gold, which included a circular banqueting house with stacked galleries. "However," he points out, "these were uncommon structures and it is hard to imagine a route by which their design could influence a grocer and a joiner in London fifty years later."[87] We do not know what Rastell's, the All Hallows, or Botolphs' scaffolds looked like, though we know they were hardly as elaborate as an Henrician royal structure and not nearly as costly as Burbage and the Braynes' later enterprise, but there is no reason to assume they might not be in some ways inspiration for later playhouse builders. Indeed, Walton's work connects elite life with street life. The client for whom he built one of his stages, Rastell, was himself involved with preparations for the Field of the Cloth of Gold in 1520, and Walton was paid for similar workmanship on one of Rastell's court pageants of "hounds, Lions, dragons, & greyhounds" in around 1527.[88] The lines of influence may well be dispersed through Walton onto subsequent commercial models for playing structures such as those at All Hallows and St Botolph. Such influences may be felt further afield, too, in places like Lydd and Great Yarmouth, whose playing places or game houses have left but a faint archival trace.

Hall and Room

Stages, scaffolds, and outdoor structures offer one form of playing venue, but there is an equally long tradition of performance in inside spaces, too. Individual rooms in larger buildings and sizeable halls were among the most popular play venues of Tudor and Stuart England. Many such spaces achieved playhouse-ness in the sixteenth century (and beyond) thanks to proprietors or lessees converting or adapting rooms to suit regular performance before a paying audience—a coming together of theatrically sensitive architectural adaptation and savvy commercial strategy.

There is substantial evidence—perhaps the most plentiful in surviving records—of play and performance taking place in hall or room venues not specifically designed or set aside for public playing but adaptable to it. Such spaces sit on the cusp of this study, influencing the design and use of subsequent playhouses and playhouse-like buildings. Travelling players would have been most familiar with halls or upper rooms across the country that set out an architectural model for playing more like the rectangular Curtain and less like the amphitheatrical structures of the Theatre or Globe. Performances across the period frequently took place in great houses and private residences—large properties and estates owned by aristocrats or wealthy individuals.[89] Barbara D. Palmer has established how these were "central to touring circuits" and suggests they were an extension of the accommodation available pre-dissolution in ecclesiastical playing spaces, such as monasteries.[90] Such houses offered performers lodging and fees. While these venues were not commercial, in the sense that shapes this book's understanding of the playhouse, they did open up to audiences beyond the household. In 1628, Londesborough listed 138 persons at dinner.[91]

Similarly, performance at royal courts—before the King or Queen—intersected with the longstanding tradition across medieval England of performers of all kinds (travelling dramatic troupes, tumblers, jesters) moving between aristocratic halls to halls at court venues (temporary or permanent).[92] However, hall or room playhouses are different: adapted or framed specifically (if not exclusively) with performance in mind and catering to a paying public. Indeed, in the years where performers toured houses, they were also playing inside in popular venues. In 1569, London's Aldermen issued a precept insisting that no area of the city

> suffer any person or persons repairing or Coming to their said houses under the pretence or Colour of hearing or seeing any such Interlude or play to enter into any Chamber or other Close or secret place within their said houses during the time of the said play.[93]

Such restriction followed on from the Common Council precept of the previous year that explained that no "close place" could be open to spectators, with wider entries across the period bemoaning the "multitudes of people" flocking "to hear and see certain Stage plays interludes and other disguisings [...] close pestered together in Small rooms."[94] While these entries sought to proscribe playing in halls or rooms, they evidently reflected a widespread and ongoing practice—one that expanded and continued over the subsequent half century or more. They were matched by limitations on such activity in provincial towns and cities. In both London and elsewhere, many of these "close" venues were likely inns or alehouses (as the next section in this chapter explains). Yet there were also numerous halls and adapted room structures specifically set up for commercial performance and play—an array of indoor, room-based playhouses.

In 1637, a feoffee (or trustee) at the Grammar School at Witton in Cheshire recorded 5 shillings "spent by mr winington & my self when we set the playhouse to be repaired."[95] By this later date, the term had perhaps come into more regular usage; its application here to a building in the school might suggest it had been called a playhouse for many years. Witton was a small township in the parish of Great Budworth. Yet its presence in the region doubtless grew after John Deane (prebendary of Lincoln and a rector at St Bartholomew the Great in Smithfield, London) founded its grammar school in 1557.[96] It is likely entertainments took place at the school from its inception. Performance and theatre were often a part of grammar school activities—sometimes also overlapping with the training of young choristers. In several places across England in the mid-to-late sixteenth century, these performances took on commercial elements, performing before a paying public—sometimes occasionally and sometimes more regularly at fixed spaces, as with companies explored in this section. Such a development was especially acute in London, with companies from the 1570s through to the early seventeenth century performing complex and innovative drama and rivalling adult companies, including Shakespeare's, in popularity. Children were also prominent public performers in other towns and cities. At Bristol in 1570, "Master Turner the schoolmaster of the Bartholomews" was paid for painting pageants and presenting plays, while other Bristol expenses across these years suggest the commercial possibilities of school houses: Bristol schoolmaster Alexander Woodson was paid for "making of Plays at Christmas" in 1595, and the mayor, aldermen, and quite possibly a wider paying public viewed "The Queens Players which tumbled before them at the free school where was tumbling shown also by a Turk upon a Rope, with running on the same" in 1589.[97]

Witton Grammar School may well have hosted such activities in its "playhouse," and entertainment certainly spanned at least drama and music.[98] The 1637 accounting entry lists numerous payments for wood, brick, other materials, and labour on different sides of the playhouse, but it is explicitly framed as *repair* rather than new building. As such, the exact date of the playhouse's erection is obscured by a lack of records and it could well have been built any time during or after 1557. Although we cannot know for certain what commercial activities took place in the venue, there are (as in Bristol) analogous school playhouse spaces from the period that help illuminate what it might have looked like.

Documents in the London Merchant Taylors' court books record the affairs of the guild company as well as its related enterprises, including its grammar school. They gesture to the nature of children's performances and their commercial edge, in particular regarding performance at halls like the Merchant Taylors' and quite possibly at the likes of Witton. In 1573, company bosses complained that

> at our common plays and such Like exercises which be commonly exposed to be seen for money any lewd person thinketh himself (for his penny) worthy of the chief and most commodious place without respect of any other either for age or estimation in the common weal.[99]

These shows need not have been one-offs or occasional events, but could well have been performed as regularly (or "commonly," as their entry puts it) as any plays at other London venues. Indeed, by 1578, the Court of Common Council was prompted to issue a plague-related restriction on "assemblies and shows," from playing to fencing, which made an unusual direct address to "schoolmasters or teachers of youth," who were forbidden from displaying "shows of scholars or children."[100] Here we have a direct example, via regulatory frameworks, of the extent of public-facing children's performance.

The Merchant Taylors' records take us inside the venues in which those plays were performed. They note how the disrespectful behaviour of public attendees prompted "the youth to such an impudent familiarity" with their elders and drew "tumultuous disordered persons […] to see such plays as by our scholars" were performed. These performers were often known as Mulcaster's boys, after their tutor Richard Mulcaster, and they also appear in records of royal court revels in these years. Their popularity extended to a wider audience in the city, with enough spectators willing to pay entry that friends and parents "could not have entertainment and convenient places." Unlike outdoor amphitheatrically accented playhouses, then, there appears to have been no tiered pricing structure at this particular hall playhouse, which likely had a uniform seating level that resulted in something of a free-for-all. In the wake of this theatrical chaos, the company agreed to cease plays in "this our common Hall," although a subsequent entry nonetheless records charges "when as mr Moncasters scholars did play there." Apparently, children's performances were not demure and elite (or courtly or scholarly) affairs, but as rambunctious as any fracases or assemblies associated with venues such as the Theatre and Curtain.[101] The Merchant Taylors' records therefore provide clues to the tenor of commercial children's performance in halls across the country.

Indeed, two of the most successful playhouses across the later sixteenth century emerged from this scholarly-cum-commercial tradition: London's First Blackfriars and St Paul's playhouses. These were small indoor spaces that staged plays entirely performed by child actors. They are typically regarded by theatre historians as more "elite" venues, pricier and catering for a more select audience, although the exact nature of entry prices is uncertain. Reavley Gair suggests (on the basis of evidence from a visitation report in 1598) entry to St Paul's might have been as relatively affordable as a two pence, compared with the penny entry for the amphitheatrical spaces—a point explored in more detail in Chapter 3.[102] By the early- to mid-1570s, the Children of Paul's were performing in London at a venue run by Sebastian Westcote, likely in the Almonry House of the Cathedral.[103] José A. Pérez Díez presents important details about the playhouse's size and shape within the existing outer space of the Almonry and provides key evidence for the capacities of the performance area, discovery space, and tiring house.[104] This small enterprise had all the requisite theatrical architecture needed for ambitious and innovative dramatic performance and lacked nothing of what was available in a larger operation like Burbage and the Braynes' Theatre, built a year later. The commercial nature of the set-up is clear from Westcote's will, which left ten shillings for "Shepard that keepeth the door at plays,"[105] indicating "box office" entry in line with later amphitheatrically accented theatres. Indeed, London's Aldermen emphasised this commercial element when they complained in 1575 about Westcote's practice in keeping plays "and resort of the people to great gain."[106]

Perhaps recognising the profitability of Westcote's enterprise, the deputy choirmaster of the Chapel Royal (and Master of the Choristers of St George's Chapel, Windsor castle), Richard Farrant, leased two rooms from William More in 1576. He proceeded to "pull down one partition and so make of one two rooms one"[107] to create the first playhouse at the Blackfriars—an act of architectural conversion that powerfully demonstrates how demolishing a wall between two rooms in an old medieval building was sufficient structural engineering to make one a builder of playhouses. Where the St Paul's venture utilised the most important religious (and increasingly commercial[108]) site in England, Farrant instead turned to a major former friary and its surroundings, which had already been variously repurposed for domestic accommodation and commercial activity since the 1550s (as explored in Chapter 4). The Blackfriars was thereafter home to both Farrant's Children of Windsor and to his senior chorister-manager William Hunnis's company, the Children of the Chapel Royal. After Farrant died in 1580, his widow Anne Farrant sublet the playhouse, and it was run by a triumvirate of the Earl of Oxford, London scrivener Henry Evans, and playwright John Lyly. It came to an end in the mid-1580s, when its landlord More (and others) disputed the rights of the leasehold and the commercial activity taking place. Indeed, shortly after Farrant's death, More observed disapprovingly how the "room" at the Blackfriars served as "a continual house for plays"—another example of just how flexible was the early modern language of the "playhouse."[109]

An earlier "continual house" for plays sat just up the road in London at Trinity Hall. An account book for the 1550s and 1560s lists numerous instances of hire of the Hall and its surroundings for play and plays.[110] The Hall itself was owned by the fraternity of St Botolph of Aldersgate and sat in the site of a former brewery; following the Chantries Act (which dissolved monastic land in 1547), it was rented from William Harvey, a herald from Somerset, who then handed control back to the parish to be used for their business.[111] Part of that business is recorded in play receipts, which indicate how its rental by players generated commercial income for St Botolph. A "Casual Receipt" from 1568, for instance, details money paid by "diverse persons" for "standing" and "for the hire of Trinity hall for plays and weddings" (with "and other assemblies" struck through but included and preserved in the entries for other years).[112] Here, then, we have evidence of a hall with multiple rooms let out to performers, with the possibility that one or other secondary room acted as a tiring house or as equivalents to some of the other architectural features detectable in the St Paul's Almonry House a decade later. Indeed, the Hall sat in an upper floor alongside two "little chambers," with a buttery and kitchen below (a description that sounds strikingly similar to Farrant's rental of two rooms at the Blackfriars, which also included two cellars below).[113] Eighteenth-century plans preserve the first-floor hall's appearance and its dimensions are recorded in later leases as 54 feet 8 inches east–west by 15 feet 8 inches north–south, with a large stained glass window facing Aldersgate Street that would have cast coloured light over the plays as they were performed. The buttery at the west end had a gallery over the top and the Hall was entered via stairs in Trinity Alley[114]—perhaps the "Box Office" location where money would have been collected for audience entry and maybe doubling as a social or gathering space. Trinity Hall stands out in the regularity of its receipts (in part thanks to the survival of its archival records).[115] As Erler puts it, Trinity Hall was rented regularly by players for ten years, "a long run at what we may call an established part-time neighbourhood theatre"[116]—or, in other words, a playhouse.

Other fraternities, companies, churches, and towns also let out halls for performance across these years. Indeed, church houses and halls like Trinity were familiar places of play across England. The Dorset town of Sherborne and its community made use of the "large room that was 'our part' of the church house for community functions like the church ale," and the "the room and its inventory were also frequently rented out after 1567."[117] The regularity of play in this venue suggests a close parallel to Trinity Hall, offering commercial venues for performance catering to the local community. Moreover, Robert Tittler has demonstrated the regularity with which town halls served as playing spaces. Guildhalls, moot halls, or leet halls, among other names for the central corporate building in a community, were regularly employed for a "wide variety of cultural activities, including ceremony and theatre."[118] As with private residences and aristocratic houses, these venues blurred the lines between commercial recreation and private or corporate functions. Although they were not deliberately built or adapted structures predominantly for play, a feature that helps to narrow this study's conception of playhouses, they were sometimes modified for the purpose on suitable occasions. Moreover, they offered room to accommodate a "large paying audience" in "central, comfortable, and commodious places."[119] Their design clearly shaped and influenced more purposefully adapted or built commercial venues, not least in being amongst the most familiar places for performance of all kinds across England, and their multipurposeness sits in line with the playhouse structures in this book. Certain playhouses even shared

Alehouses also hosted forms of play aside from dramatic performance. There are dozens of examples of alehouses hosting visiting bearwards (individuals who were part of early modern England's widespread animal baiting activities, which are explained in the section below and described in more detail in Chapter 2). The alehouse proprietor Elizabeth Cox chased down the bearwards of Bristol "which had been at [her] house" for her money in 1605.[159] In 1566, the Quarter Sessions in Canterbury presented "William Bery" for "suffering dancing bullbaiting in his house" on the Sabbath, while in Cheshire by the 1630s, a visitor to Henry Massy's alehouse in Hale was so hemmed in by the crowd he "could not stoop in the house to take up any thing that was fallen"—all a result of the fact "the house was so full of people that were come to the bearbeat."[160] As with performances at inns, it is not always clear where exactly such plays and performances would take place, but the butcher and apparent alehouse-keeper Thomas Gleve used his yard.[161] Some of these examples stem from a later period, in which Cheshire courts like the Quarter Sessions were more inclined to prosecute perceived playing infractions than they were the previous century. As such, they indicate belatedly recorded playhouse-like use of the alehouse almost certainly commonplace from at least the 1560s and 1570s.

Indeed, elsewhere in the county, the bearward and bear-seller John Seckerston ran two victualling houses, one fittingly called the Bear, from at least the 1570s. At the time of the Great Fire of Nantwich in 1583, three of his bears escaped during the blaze and ran free about the town.[162] A similar incident occurred in Taunton, Somerset, in 1592, when a rabble of unruly men made directly for the house of George Webb, "which did then keep a bear or bears," to demand "the said Bear keeper to bring out to them his bear" at a ring in the marketplace; when he refused, they violently broke in and unleashed the bear themselves.[163] These various inn or alehouse antics demonstrate how such venues hosted and supported different forms of play—sometimes within the alehouse, sometimes in personal or shared ground outside, and sometimes in nearby public "playhouse" space (as explored below). These are a handful of examples among many across England in which victualling houses served as adaptable venues for commercial play. They help return us to a leisure world in which the conceptual lines between alehouse, inn, and playhouse were porous and permeable.

Ring, Arena, Cockpit

The bears of early modern England introduce us to another arena, literally and figuratively, in which we find the playhouse. Bull- and bear-baiting were enormously popular pastimes, arguably more so than theatre. The nature of these sports is detailed in Chapter 2, but broadly speaking they involved tying a bull or bear to a stake and setting one (or more) dogs on them in a series of "courses." Other entertainments often accompanied this gruesome blood sport. In the early sixteenth century, built venues were established on London's southbank to accommodate regular outings of the bulls, bears, and dogs (and more). Theatre history typically does not regard these or adopted some of the corporate uses of town halls or guildhalls, a topic explored in Chapter 4, suggesting a fundamental relationship in both form and function.

The last venue discussed in this section that exemplifies room or hall playhouses was, fittingly, probably known as *the Playhouse*.[120] This site, located just south of London in Newington Butts, was briefly home to Shakespeare and his company in 1594, though it had a much longer lifespan and significance. Laurie Johnson's detailed research on the venue reveals that it was housed within an existing tenement on land leased near today's Elephant and Castle tube station. Johnson explains that it was "a conversion of an existing structure" and speculates whether it "would have retained the exterior shape while constructing galleries along the interior walls, likely surrounding a stage that filled out the bulk of the central floor plan."[121] Either way, the property would have shared many of the features of other room-based adaptations discussed in this section. Its location, however, offered both drawbacks and advantages. Companies were apparently unimpressed by the "tediousness of the way" to this removed area south of the city.[122] Yet it sat within an enclosure of dwellings and other buildings, surrounded by orchard land and gardens. These provided quite literal shelter from surrounding flood-prone fields.[123] The arrangement also offered its proprietor and landlord possibilities for revenue beyond hosting dramatic performance. With audiences aloof from urban establishments and already gathered in the area for play, the Playhouse at Newington Butts and adjoining venues had market exclusivity for the sale of food, drink, and wider entertainment to a captive audience. Records kept by sewer commissioners at the time (who were responsible for enforcing water drainage and the cleaning and clearance of channels and run-offs and hence tell us a great deal about property names and boundaries) suggest that the name "'the playhouse' referred to the whole enclosure and not just the building."[124] Little is known about most of the Playhouse's decades of existence, but given its longevity, it is quite possible commercial viability was found in a range of leisure offerings, from food and drink to play performance. The speculative idea of such an entertainment complex would align it with the alley models of playhouse-ness discussed in the final section of this chapter.

The intermixture of conviviality with discrete forms of play, from drama to gambling, was central to contemporary ideas of playhouse-ness. Rooms and halls were testament to the fact that venues need not be freestanding or "new built" to have been called or treated as playhouses. They also demonstrate how these sites were not solely the preserve of adult playing companies in London but were sometimes home to other commercial activities. Accordingly, given the affordances of the room and hall, it is perhaps no surprise that inns and alehouses were also well primed to deliver "play" on multiple fronts and were sometimes given, like the establishment at Newington Butts, the name "playhouse."

Inn, Alehouse, House

In 1627, Jacob Abadham was cited in the Quarter Sessions in Suffolk "for keeping a Playhouse" in Ipswich, one name amongst a list of individuals bound by recognisance of £10 "not to play at unlawful games."[125] Two years later, John Payne was bound "not to suffer any playing in his house."[126] These legal citations work directly with and around the term "playhouse" and run with the flexible senses of play set out in Chapter 2. They testify to the capaciousness of its meanings, not least in suggesting that Abadham's venue was home to gambling, dicing, carding, and other activities, as well as (or possibly instead of) forms of performance play, like drama or tumbling. Abadham's playhouse also suggests that the word playhouse could be applied to domestic-adjacent structures of various kinds—commercial, public-facing "houses."

The introduction has shown how "house" applied to a whole range of structures in early modern English, but, as this chapter has shown, its domestic associations were also important to contemporaries' leisure world. The houses of many families above the level of the dependent poor (those on poor relief or in serious economic peril) were sites of social play. Those in the middle ranks of society, in particular, kept "multifunctional houses and spaces," characterised by a "penetration of work and leisure, domestic and commercial production."[127] When it came to entertainment, the overlaps between domesticity and business can trouble the fixed labels typically employed in historical scholarship to describe social and leisure venues, in particular "alehouse" or "inn."

Each of these spaces were themselves "households." Alehouses provide perhaps the most acute example of the household opening up to business, with blurred lines between private and public recreation. Alehouses could only operate with official sanction, and some of the most copious legislation in townships and cities across the country targeted unlicensed alehouses.[128] Indeed, unlike inns, they sat on the wrong side of the law more generally: Mark Hailwood recognises that the national system of alehouse regulation between 1550 and 1630 permitted "recreational sociability" on the condition that venues provided lodging for travellers and victuals to the local poor but proscribed "any forms of recreational drinking."[129] Abadham's Suffolk "Playhouse" implies both an official name for a commonly recognised institution (with its capitalised "P") but also an illicit and unlicenced use of domestic space. Citations for unlicensed "play" in houses of all kinds often indicate the moment at which "play" moves from respectable hosting and socialising in a domestic setting to commercial recreational activity.

There is therefore a close relationship between the "house" open for play and the "alehouse," "tavern," and "inn." Peter Clark rightly warns of the slipperiness between these three terms in early modern English, their deployment being "vague and haphazard": sometimes the term "inn" connoted an alehouse, and sometimes "alehouse" is used more broadly to refer to the more elaborate venue of an inn.[130] Sometimes, commercial food and drink sales or lodging from a household was temporary or ad hoc, taken up for an instance or short period by individuals "though they be not otherwise usually vittailers."[131] Yet, following Clark, it is typical to recognise different "types" of venue despite contemporary imprecision. We might simply soften these fixed categorisations by remembering there was a fluid and flexible vocabulary for all social venues, while acknowledging the important differences in architectural form, fashion, and social status.

Inns, as commonly and legally understood, sat alongside taverns as drinking establishments for the better-off, with alehouses often seen to serve the least well-off in society but in fact accommodating a range of individuals, as Hailwood's study makes clear. Inns supplied food, accommodation, and "parking" (i.e., stables) and so were both a more sophisticated and a more expensive location. Indeed, they were officially acknowledged to be integral to society—perhaps because they typically served a wealthier clientele—and many innholders held important positions within their respective towns and communities.[132] The buildings themselves were also substantial—leaving architectural legacies many centuries after their earliest purposes were through and still recognisable today in towns and cities across England. Their interiors were fashionable and "up-to-date," sometimes including named or signed chambers for lodging.[133] The probate inventory of the wealthy innholder and alderman of Chester, Thomas Thropp, indicates how fashionable such venues could be: one illustrative chamber included wainscotting, glass windows, quality cushions, ceremonial arms and armour, a green and yellow colour scheme running through its upholstered furniture, and numerous pictures, including "oiled work" of "the king's picture the Queen's picture and the prince's picture in frames."[134]

Such locations hosted numerous forms of entertainment (not least dinners for the local political elite), but inns also functioned as performance venues.[135] In such instances, they were sometimes regarded by contemporaries, either explicitly or implicitly, as playhouses. In Bristol, from the early seventeenth century, the cutler Nicholas Woolfe and his wife Margaret Woolfe ran a playhouse from a venue perhaps similar to Thropp's. By at least 1604/5, the Woolfes began to host players performing for a paying public, putting up "certain Comedians whom he suffered to act and play within the said Rooms" for which both he and Margaret "took money"—all in the tenement identified by the complainant in a legal quarrel, Richard Cooke, as a "Common Inn."[136] Margaret testified that her husband held "one house with the appurtenances in wine street within the same city commonly called the playhouse."[137] Her testimony distinguishes the playhouse from the known, named inns of the area, and she also does not "name" the place by a sign or any other distinguishing title or feature beyond "playhouse"; the venue was therefore probably popularly known by this word.

Wine Street helps us picture the physical layout of inn playhouses: multiple chambers let out to different people with a room seemingly regularly set aside for performance, and, like St Paul's or Trinity Hall, with only a single entrance—one "outer street door [...] which is but one and the only way into all the whole house" and used "in Common."[138] Margaret's description of the venue as "commonly" called the playhouse offers a useful analogue for appreciating the imbrication of inn venues with amphitheatrical spaces for early modern audiences—especially those outside of London who would have seen the Woolfes' space as a, perhaps the, default model for a playhouse. Other playhouses in Bristol, seemingly also in similar room spaces, no doubt confirmed this sense of the playhouse-ness of an inn, room, or chamber.[139]

Residents of London might have shared such a view. David Kathman has shown that commercial playing in inns also extends back to at least the 1540s,[140] and by 1557, the Boar's Head by Aldgate was home to a politically controversial play, *A Sackful of News*.[141] Other playhouses in London included the inns the Bull and the Bell, themselves officially listed as two places in which the Queen's Men playing company could play in London in 1583. The Bell clearly had capacities for an elaborate set, as by 1577 the Office of the Revels demanded a prop of a "counterfeit well" be transferred from the venue to court.[142] Indeed, a later legal case involving the Bell's proprietor Henry Houghton indicates something of its layout: a deponent in the court listed as part of the property one cell, one hall, two chambers, a kitchen, and two garretts.[143] It is possible that the hall, or perhaps one of the chambers, was the site for performances. More widely, Kathman explains that while there is some evidence for outside performance of a kind (particularly at the Bull and Bel Savage), it is likely that the Bell and neighbouring Cross Keys inn hosted plays indoors (both having only one yard, which would have been required for "inn business").[144] The Cross Keys was similarly prominent as a playing venue and even drew James Burbage himself down from his own playhouse, the Theatre, in 1579.[145] The venue was still thriving in the mid-1590s, when Lord Hunsdon asked permission from the Mayor to allow his company (including William Shakespeare) to play there as they "have been accustomed."[146] It was seemingly refurbished in the mid-1580s, perhaps bringing it into line with new developments and venues and showing an alignment with fashionable tastes in inn properties, like Thropp's in Chester.[147] The Bel Savage was also a popular venue across these years for plays, fencing, and prose performance. William Lambarde directs visitors to the site in his south-east walking tour of 1576, a recommendation maintained in the second edition 14 years later.[148] As late as the 1630s, William Prynne referred to "*The Belsavage Play-House in Queen* Elizabeth'*s days*."[149] Certainly, then, these were playhouses in the way early modern audiences understood the term.

Alehouses were somewhat distinct from inns and generally did not share sizeable rooms or halls like Houghton's. Nonetheless, they hosted play in similar ways. The rapidly burgeoning market economy of early modern England meant opportunities for economic advancement became ever more limited. The alehouse represented an easy opportunity for those with limited capital: one need invest only in a stock of beer, which could often be bought from a brewer on credit, while any overheads from real estate were already covered by one's household accommodation. Clark points out that "there was nothing purpose-built about the small alehouse."[150] They therefore had a reputation for being significantly less salubrious than an inn or even a tavern, perhaps explaining the claim made by William Fleetwood, the Recorder of London, that in 1575 alone he closed down over 200 unsafe or undesirable drinking holes in London and its suburbs.[151] While they were framed by certain early modern commentators, lawmakers, and political elites as potentially troublesome and undesirable, Hailwood's work has demonstrated that they "were almost universally accepted as a necessary feature of communal infrastructure, albeit one whose role needed to be carefully circumscribed."[152] They had a political culture and were frequented by a range of visitors: "men and women, young and old, married and unmarried, poor and middling sort, servants and masters, apprentices and master craftsmen."[153]

While they may not necessarily be "purpose-built" in the grand sense of a substantial inn, they were, like all other playhouse venues discussed here, adaptable to forms of play. Alehouses were closely associated with the church wakes at which stages and scaffolds were set up. There is also plenty of evidence across England that they acted as venues for play of all kinds—not just music and gaming (with which they are always associated) but also drama and animal baiting. In 1611, during market time in Cheltenham, Richard Clerke and a number of other young artificers and labourers drummed up (literally) interest in a play to be performed at the sign of the Crown, most likely an inn. The town of Cheltenham "disliked" the advertised performance, which they thought was risky at a time when the plague infections were starting to surge in surrounding towns and villages. Despite official suppression, Clerke and his fellows changed the venue from the named Crown and "did endeavour to play […] at the house of one david Powell a victualler."[154] The word "victualler" (alehouse-, tavern-, or inn-keeper) itself denotes the vague and slippery spectrum of language for drinking venues; here it suggests something along the lines of the alehouse—particularly in its pointed contrast to the named and signed venue of the Crown.

Down the road in the same county, in the city of Gloucester, similar restraints were issued by the corporation. By 1580, it issued restrictions "against common Players of Interludes […] for so much as daily experience teacheth and delivereth that the common Players of Interludes and plays Draw away great Sums of money from diverse persons."[155] The precept reminds us of the many misleading silences of the documentary archive, which record only an "official" playing schedule.[156] Clearly there existed a commercial performance market in the city outside of the patronised troupes paid by the chamberlain, even if it left few formal records. Indeed, because this market was not approved by the corporation, we cannot trace performances via the civic payment registers that provide much of what we know about touring professional troupes. We must therefore think beyond these recorded and sanctioned performances to understand regional playing spaces more fully, because the sites that hosted approved performances—often a town hall (known in Gloucester as the Bothall)—were patently not where unsanctioned, or implicitly allowed but unrecorded, commercial play took place.[157] Venues must therefore have existed outside of political institutional buildings, prompting the question, where did these unapproved "common players of interludes" perform? Scott McMillin and Sally-Beth MacLean observe how "records seldom survive from other venues such as inns or churches." They discuss a notable example of the Queen's Men visit to Norwich in 1583 (the year they were formed), when they went on to perform at an inn called the Red Lion. A violent affray erupted that resulted in the performance's entry into the historical record via a lengthy court case and its paperwork.[158] Rare details like this case or Clerke's play from Cheltenham three decades later confirm that alehouses and inns would have been likely destinations for visiting or local players seeking a commercial audience.

so-called baiting arenas as playhouses, and the limited scholarship on this subject has interrogated ways in which they might be superficially similar but are fundamentally different.[164] Oscar Brownstein concludes, in his assessment of whether a "bear garden" on Bankside would have been for Burbage and the Braynes a suitable alternative to their own construction in Shoreditch, that the bear-baiting arena was "a model of a special purpose arena which would be vastly inconvenient for the viewing of plays."[165]

Brownstein's conclusion about the Bankside locations for animal fighting is based on numerous assumptions about both baiting arenas and playhouses. This chapter has already demonstrated how venues for play and performance took on an astounding range of forms in this period. Distinctions between a Bankside bear garden and "proper" playhouses like the Theatre are predicated on a model of professional performance that reifies the stage, tiring house, and galleries most typically associated with amphitheatrically accented spaces. These need not be typical of other playhouses. We simply do not know exactly what the playhouses at Wine Street in Bristol, or Newington Butts, or any of the London inns looked like as performance venues but we know for certain they regularly staged dramatic plays. On the other hand, "the viewing of plays" need not be a barometer for playhouseness—a point proved at length in Chapter 2. Venues like Abadham's in Suffolk that were likely not set up, at least primarily, for theatre were still dubbed "playhouses," while the label itself refers capaciously to a variety of ludic activity, from animal sports to gambling. Bear-baiting and bull-baiting rings and arenas, therefore, were commercial structures that (like alehouses and inns) happily matched the concept and practices of a playhouse.

After all, early modern individuals did not see nice distinctions, in vocabulary or architecture, between theatre and baiting ring. In contemporary maps of London's Bankside, animal rings are both semantically and visually aligned with playhouses. John Norden's 1593 map labels one "the Bear house," suggesting affinities with other linguistic constructions of the term *playhouse*: "house for plays," or its roots in the old-English *pleg-hus*, "game house." Equally tellingly, when Wenceslaus Hollar created his panorama of London in 1647, he confused the labels for the Globe and the Bear Garden. At a glance, while different in many ways, these buildings had plenty of architectural similarities. While large and sensorily dominant presences like kennels and pens mark out one from another, as evident in early maps, there is an equal likelihood that some of the early baiting arenas were not so equipped. Limited evidence about the first three bear gardens built on Bankside suggests that they were enclosed spaces, initially with one and only later with multiple levels of seating. Accordingly, while seating and "performance" arrangements were (in some instances) starkly different to the likes of the Theatre, they had much in common with other playhouses and maintained, like those other spaces, the ability to adapt accordingly.

Animal sports saw Bankside become the home of some of the earliest fixed commercial "arenas" for commercial recreation, dating back to around the 1530s. W.W. Braines's influential scholarship on sixteenth-century Bankside, published in

FIGURE 1.2 Ad Londinvm epitome & ocellvm [1647]. Wenceslaus Hollar. MAP L85c no.29 part 1. The Globe and the Bear-Baiting arena are labelled the wrong way round.

Used by permission of the Folger Shakespeare Library under a Creative Commons Attribution-ShareAlike 4.0 International License.

1924, has fixed the conventions for referring to these baiting arenas, while Sally-Beth MacLean and Stephanie Hovland have lately determined and set out detailed knowledge of the property leases relevant to these various venues.[166] Braines bases much of his assessment on a crucial deposition in Chancery proceedings by a 77-year-old man named John Taylor. Taylor remarked in court

> that he remembereth that the game of bear baiting hath been kept in four several places, vizt. At Mason Stairs on the bankside, near Maid Lane by the Corner of the Pyke Garden, and at the bear garden which was parcel of the possession of William Payne, and the place where they are now kept.[167]

Braines numbers these Bear Gardens 1–4, with number 5 built after the Restoration (and known as Davies's Bear Garden).

Archaeological excavations have added some further clarification to Braines' meticulous work. While little is known of the form or structures of Bear Garden 1 (Mason's Stairs, almost abutting the Thames) and little, too, of Bear Garden 2, the third arena leaves a longer paper trail and has also been subject to some excavation. Anthony Mackinder et al. observe that the entry to the longstanding third arena, sometimes known as Payne's Standings, was entered via an existing property—the Bell and Cock.[168] These properties were known as the "stews" and served as brothels, probably during at least some of the lifetimes of the first three bear gardens. These stews were connected with the victualling trades, too. A proclamation by King Henry VIII in 1546 effectively banned their operation, and it noted that many living in these "Stews" sold victuals and hosted guests for eating, drinking, and lodging. The same year the King licenced Thomas Fluddie, "notwithstanding" this proclamation, to bait and "make pastime" at the stews with his bears, while a few years earlier, a visiting Spanish nobleman observed baiting on the south bank in "an enclosure."[169] The "stew" of the Bell and Cock may therefore have operated like an inn, with passage to a yard housing the bear-baiting venue. Visitors were surrounded by recreational possibilities, many contained within a concentrated space. The wider area was also a sprawling complex of some compelling interest to visitors intrigued by the sights, sounds, smells, and general behaviour of such a large menagerie of dogs, bears, and bulls. The plot of land had "buildings to house young bears and white bears, a bull house and a hay house. There was a pond that was used to wash the bears, and another old pond that served for the disposal of dead dogs."[170] The kennels themselves sat on adjacent land, which also housed an inn called the Unicorn, later purchased by Morgan Pope in a consolidation of land near to the Bear Garden itself.[171] The bear garden arenas did not therefore spring up in an empty plot but emerged from and were physically enclosed by a thriving commercial leisure infrastructure.

Mackinder et al. provide another important update to these playing structures by splitting Bear Garden 3 into two life stages, 3 and 3a. The first structure, 3, collapsed on the 13 January 1583 during a show, killing eight people, including the pursemaker Alice White and the baker William Cockram.[172] The owners rebuilt the arena within five months, producing a structure described as "larger in circuit and compass" and having more than one gallery.[173] This description helps get a sense of the architectural features both of Bear Garden 3a and earlier structures, which presumably had a maximum of one gallery (single-storied), with less capacity, and perhaps less "sumptuous" in design. Mackinder et al. speculate that the new building "was based on the northern playhouses, the Theatre and the Curtain."[174] Such speculation approaches the kind of amphitheatrical-centricity deconstructed at the beginning of this chapter, but the comparison does raise important lessons about changing conceptions of playhouse-ness across the period—not least given that the bear garden arenas themselves had long been posited as inspiration or model for the earliest amphitheatres. Bear gardens and amphitheatres might therefore be seen as circular both in form and influence. More helpfully, we might regard the rebuilt post-1583 Bear Garden as testament to the symbiosis between different playhouse models, moving beyond "firstness" and teleology of design to recognise instead how recreational venues developed via forms of mutual architectural exchange and adaptation.

Scholarship typically overlooks any conceptual joining of venues for sport and theatrical activity in the decades before Edward Alleyn and Philip Henslowe built the Hope playhouse in 1613. Henslowe had acquired the lease of Bear Garden 3a in 1594 (via several real estate deals) and held commercial games at the site for nearly 20 years before he and a partner called Jacob Meade sought to create a venue that was, in Herbert Berry's terms, "a public playhouse and animal baiting house, designed and built to serve as either as its owners chose."[175] The binary or implied "dual-purposeness" of this characterisation is, however, somewhat misleading. The venue was conceived as a singular building and described as a "playhouse," but it had, like almost every other playhouse of the period, multiple functions. What might mark it out as distinct from other amphitheatrically accented spaces is its retractable rolling stage. Yet long before 1613, bear-baiting venues were home to play beyond animal sport, including immersive theatrical entertainments. When Dutchman Lupold von Wedel visited the recently rebuilt Bear Garden 3a in 1584, he described the mass participation of numerous human actors in a "play" discussed in detail in Chapter 2. Henslowe's sense that the Hope could accommodate both professional players and bear-baiting was born out of a conviction that the bear garden was already in some way theatrical. The language of Henslowe and Meade's meticulous contract with carpenter Gilbert Katherens is telling. They requested that he "take down or pull down all that game place or house where bears and bulls have been heretofore usually baited" to "new build, erect and set up again the said playhouse or game place near or upon the said place where the said game place did heretofore stand."[176] The contract then goes onto refer to the Hope variously as "playhouse" and "game place." Henslowe and Meade's phrasing, "set up again the said playhouse," confers on its earlier form a playhouse-ness that clearly did not exactly match the models of the Globe, Swan, or Rose, but that nonetheless shared fundamental similarities with them and with other spaces discussed across this chapter.

Although London might seem to lay claim to some of the earliest commercial arena structures, provincial towns and cities were also dominated by sites for animal sport. Substantial, fixed places for baiting bulls (and, most typically, other animals, too) have a bearing not only on the idea of playhouse-ness as it develops in London but on the way playhouses and places of play would have been understood by those living in outside of the capital, in both urban and rural settings. By national law, all bulls had to be baited before their meat could be sold, making bull-baiting a pragmatic necessity as much as an entertainment, and butchers were regularly fined for selling un-baited flesh. Yet the spaces that arose around this sport—an extension of medieval shambles or flesh-markets—also provided wider entertainment and were in some cases furnished with seating structures in a manner strikingly similar to the amphitheatre in the former quarry at Shrewsbury.

Both Exeter's and Canterbury's bullrings provide useful examples. By the 1450s, baiting bulls in the bullring was considered "ancient custom" in Exeter, and the city had both a substantial ring and an office to match—the Mayor of the Bullring. This extension of civic office seems playful and mocking but was (perhaps at the same time) perfectly serious. Richard Hooker's pamphlet of the *Offices, and duties of every particular sworn Office, of the city of Exeter* (1584) set out the responsibilities of the position:

> First when any bull or bear baiting be appointed, he is first to make the Mayor privy thereof, and no baiting to be used within the city, but that the said Mayor be present or give leave thereunto And he shall see all things to be well done and orderly used at such pastimes [...].[177]

These requirements offer a fascinating insight into the leisure infrastructure of the city, mapped out as part of its political order. Hooker tellingly refers to the baitings as a "pastime," and while bulls were compulsorily baited in line with national ordinances, bears were exclusively employed for recreational sport. This extraordinary office therefore represents something along the lines of an officially sanctioned playhouse proprietor, in charge of a fixed place of play in central Exeter.

Canterbury's bullstake similarly occupied a central position in civic life, both for the butchers as well as for residents looking for recreation. Entries in 1547 record money "paid to a Carpenter for making of diverse forms for the market folks to sit on" alongside "reparations of the Bullstake."[178] Throughout the century, these forms (or benches) were repaired and replaced, as when they were stolen in 1566.[179] Other expenses represent its design and structure. Significant sums were lavished on the paving of the bullstake, for instance, covering over 20 yards.[180] These extended to specially designed seating for the civic elite, such as the "2 Joined Forms for the aldermen to set on at the bullstake" designed and built by Launselot Vandepere in 1580.[181] The location also housed a pump and by 1602 benefited from extensive repairs that alert us to the existence of its sloping roof. This bullstake structure therefore begins to look rather closely related to amphitheatrically accented "playhouses," many of which themselves had sloping roofs over stage and/or seating areas. The Canterbury bullstake also had a weather vane that required polishing and painting, scutcheons (or heraldic images and designs) hung about the space, and a painting of the city's coat of arms.[182] This was a richly arrayed and visually significant structure in many ways similar to the elaborate and deliberate design of "sumptuous" London playhouses. Similarly, just as the various bear gardens on Bankside shifted their structural designs over these years, adding galleries and increasing capacity, so cities and towns outside of the capital adapted, expanded, and decorated their own sites of spectatorship.[183]

Canterbury's expenses on its bullring may, in part, be designed for the upkeep of a much-used and geographically central space for the city, providing seating and beautification of a marketplace area used for an array of economic, legal, and social activity. Yet we know that bull-baiting was widely regarded both as a commercial pastime as well as a legal necessity, drawing audiences, participants, and gamblers. Exeter's Mayor of the Bullring would doubtless also cough and remind us that bear-baiting required a similar if not identical location. When John Blye was presented to the Canterbury Quarter Sessions "for annoying the Queen's high way with the soilage of Two bears" (i.e., for allowing two of his bears to foul on the highways) in 1595, these animals would have been going to or from a baiting.[184] Canterbury even features in the popular culture surrounding bear-baiting in early modern England; one of the country's most famous bears in the early seventeenth century was called Ned of Canterbury.[185] The civic-sponsored bullstake structure would be the most logical location for bear-baiting in a city whose name was conferred on the animals themselves and who regularly paid visiting bearwards to perform.[186] The bullstake also had wider associations with play that can be identified in a thundering epistle to a manuscript book by John Bale in 1561. Bale complained of a "ribald"—a jester or minstrel called Richard Borowes—who "got unto him a drum, with more than a hundred boys at his tail, and commanded a great fire to be made at the Bullstake, where commonly there is most resort of people."[187] The anecdote offers a glimpse into the social practices of a city whose ludic activity centred on the bullstake, conveniently kitted out with substantial seating arrangements.

One final animal sport structure integral to ideas of playhouse-ness is the cockpit. Such sites existed across England throughout the medieval period, but there are signs that these locations were being developed with a new commercial audience in mind. Indeed, there are significant overlaps between playhouses and cockpits. While ostensibly set aside for fighting birds—a largely gendered and gentry-coded sport popular across all counties—certain cockpits developed into more expansive operations. This book is particularly interested in complexes like that at Congleton in Cheshire, which was regularly re-edified throughout the early modern period and that (as Chapter 4 of this book explores) was a substantial and socially important structure within the town. What makes spaces like Congleton's cockpit more playhouse-like, however, is participation in a wider complex of play—a topic explored in Chapters 2 and 4. Not only did the town host local gentry at cockfights, but the cockpit was central to a range of play activities, including bearwards hired "at the time of the great Cockfight," surrounding archery butts, an adjacent paved bullstake, and extending to musicians performing at or near the venue in 1618.[188]

The playhouse qualities of cockpits help us understand the building, development, and adaptation of other playhouses. In nearby Prescot, Richard Harrington built a playhouse just to the west of an existing "Cockpit House," which had operated in the town since at least the 1590s (leased by John Dichfield and then later by his widow). The playhouse's conversion in 1609 "into a house for habitation" implies a life up to that date of commercial "play."[189] It is quite possible this playhouse had something in common with other "house" structures, like Abadham's in Suffolk, and equally possible that the playhouse was inspired by and extended play activities already occurring at the neighbouring cockpit. Indeed, cockpits advertise themselves to human performance, especially given their architectural "ring-like" qualities, which recall in-the-round amphitheatrical spaces. When Christopher Beeston sought a new playhouse for his company, the Queen's Men, in London in 1616, he leased what Berry aptly describes as a "cockfighting enterprise" near Drury Lane—a suite of facilities that included "all that edifices or building called the cockpits and the cockhouses and sheds."[190] Rather than removing these existing cockpits, Beeston adapted them instead to serve his theatrical needs. This elite playhouse did not simply borrow the name "cockpit" but, to some architectural degree, *was* a cockpit. Venues for animal sport therefore offered structural affordances for performance. They remind us that playhouses were never seen to be exclusively for performed drama but "housed" a vast range of commercial recreational activity, within and beyond the bounds of their walls.

Alley and Backside

Walls help provide a bounded sense of the playhouse's scope and structure. Yet not all such venues were defined by built walls. Complexes like Congleton's indicate how playhouses might sometimes be more helpfully seen as play sites, hubs, or centres. Similarly, as we have seen above, stage and scaffold constructions operated like playhouses without necessitating an enclosed building. Other early modern architectural models provide an indication of the porousness of the playhouse "wall" and the types of spaces that bounded or supported, and in some cases formed, the playhouse itself. Most pertinent to the sites of this book are the alley and the backside—two "void" or unbuilt spaces that helped shape the architecture of play.

Broadly speaking, the early modern alley was a narrow lane or passage enclosed by surrounding tenements and buildings (or other forms of cultivated or closed space) and included anything from walkways to places to play sport in. Indeed, bowling was one of the most popular pastimes in medieval and early modern English cities. Bowling alleys were marked out as destinations for both spectatorship and participation—one could enjoy watching the players as well as gambling on them or indeed bowling oneself. They characterised recreational urban space and proliferated, in particular, in the mid to late sixteenth centuries along with the commercial opportunities to be found in the growing service economy. They therefore represent a striking influence on the concept and development of the playhouse; indeed, the word "alley" is often associated in play contexts with "house," making it (like "game house") a semantic relative: in 1573, the London corporation reissued a proclamation against unlawful games that aligned the "common house alley or place of bowling coiting […] half bowl tennis dicing table or carding."[191] The term was fluid when it came to construction in early modern London, however, and the word "alley" encompassed not only sporting venues but sites adapted for residential use. As such, the early modern alley was a contentious space that lay at the centre of a range of building practices and commercial land use in the sixteenth century, from recreation to slum ownership. In the heavily built-up city of London in the 1560s and 1570s, alleys offered a way to exploit a crowded rental market by dividing properties into what we now call "houses of multiple occupancy"—a topic explored in Chapter 5.[192]

A satirical vision of landlords from 1590 indicates how alley space provided a useful commercial complex for its owners or proprietors:

> Some Landlords having turned an old Brew-house, Bake-house, or Dye-house into an Alley of tenements, will either themselves, or some at their appointment, keep tippling in the fore-house (as they call it) and their poor tenants must be enjoined to fetch bread, drink, wood, coal, and such other necessaries, in no other place.[193]

Alleys afforded managers the chance to establish monopolistic micro-markets, which served food and drink and provided other commercial or residential services. In the context of bowling alleys, then, which already offered a range of play options from participation to betting, their wider commercial opportunities position them as blueprints for playing complexes that united food, drink, and entertainment.

The footprint of the alley can be detected in playhouses already discussed in this chapter. The Curtain, for instance, represents a close connection with alley space. It is generally regarded as a "new-built" structure, and illustrations of two playing spaces in Shoreditch depicted in the *View of the City of London from the North towards the South* (c. 1598)—one on the West and one to the East, both with flags[194]—suggest large upright buildings (the Curtain and Theatre). Yet both are flanked and even adjoined by neighbouring structures. Archaeological discoveries have shown the Curtain was in fact constructed in a space nestled between surrounding buildings and behind an existing tenement that fronted onto Curtain Road. Such an arrangement is notably similar to the labelling of the wider enclosure at Newington Butts as "the Playhouse" (rather than one specific edifice).

These play spaces parallel recreational alley complexes established in existing narrow lanes, passages, or enclosures. Contemporaries even identified the Curtain by way of reference to alley space: Richard West described in 1607 how "The garden alleys paled on either side; / If't be too narrow, walking there you slide, / Into a house among a bawdy crew, / Of damned whores; aye there's your whole delight."[195] Even described as garden alleys, the houses adjoining this area of Shoreditch were not characterized as expansive fields, but rather speak to archaeological evidence that the playhouse made use of surrounding properties and was situated within existing structures in much the same way as the city's bowling alleys. It is perhaps most telling that the closest surviving analogue space to the Curtain playhouse, based on archaeological findings, is the Corral de Comedias in Almagro.[196] Such buildings present a powerful similarity with Spanish *corrales*: "spaces left in between buildings that were later recycled for theatrical use."[197] Such a definition would serve the recreational uses of London's alleys, and the likes of the Curtain, equally well.

The Curtain and bear garden can also be understood in line with the amusingly named "backside." Backsides were areas to the rear of a property, sometimes communal and sometimes private, though not always demarcated by walls. Tara Hamling and Catherine Richardson have explored the "particular nature of the permeability of the yard or backside," in early modern England, as spaces that blurred the lines between inside and outside.[198] Yards or backsides were also used for commercial entertainment. Cheshire butcher Thomas Gleve indicates how an alehouse might make use of this rear space by hosting animal sports. He angered justices by "entertaining of an unlicensed belward [bearward] with bears and Causing him to bait his said bears within his backside whereby a multitude of people [...] were gathered."[199] In alehouse contexts, such permeability is especially useful. It helps makes sense of the packed alehouse noted above whose crowds had come to watch a bear-baiting. Similarly, the third Bankside Bear Garden, as we have seen, was entered via an existing tenement and was situated at the "backside" of the Bell and Cock. Builders of both the Curtain and Bear Garden, then, perhaps shared Thomas Gleve's spatial intuitions. Sat at the rear of existing properties, they were likely entered through them or perhaps round them via a connected passage. These were playhouse and backside at once.

Architectural features like the alley or the backside were locations where different play activity came together. Accordingly, they undermine theatre history's enduring fixation on binaries between "indoor" or "outdoor" playhouses. Movement between victualling house and outdoor spectacle on occasions like Gleve's bear-baiting attest to a fluidity between different types of recreation—drinking, spectating, gambling—spread across one or more structures or spaces. Similarly, alley-like set-ups enabled movement between one form of entertainment and another. In the cases of the Curtain and Bear Garden 3, for instance, surrounding space and property offered the chance for socialising away from the "show" at hand. They exemplify the early modern playhouse's dominant characteristic as a flexibly capacious leisure space.

The huge number of spaces surveyed in this chapter demonstrates the elastic nature of the term playhouse and its applicability to a range of architecturally, commercially, and recreationally diverse enterprises across England. I have set out a large family of building "types" that qualified then and so must surely qualify now as playhouses—amphitheatres; stages and scaffolds; rooms and halls; inns and alehouses; rings, arenas, and cockpits—but such a list is hardly exhaustive. Rather, it testifies to the absence of a singular defining model for the playhouse and indicates some of the central architectural strands that applied to the playhouse family. Indeed, many of these different archetypes merged into one another and transcended walls or fixed boundaries: a bear-baiting arena or bullring could be or become a theatre; a backside could transform into an arena; an alley into an amphitheatre; a cockpit into a civic complex. These conversions, adaptations, and shifts are not only a physical rearrangement but reflect the fundamental multiplicity at the heart of early modern *play*—the subject of Chapter 2.

Notes

1 This synergy between London's physically sited Shakespeare's Globe and the world's appetite for Shakespeare is reflected in the Globe to Globe festival that ran under Dominic Dromgoole's artistic directorship in 2012, as part of the UK's "Cultural Olympiad" (dir. Tom Bird).

2 Ania Loomba identifies a "legitimacy of inauthenticity" in the modern Shakespeare industry; in ostensibly "authentic" spaces, productions might be emboldened to worry less about both historical robustness and accurate contemporary cultural representation (such as the representation of extra-European cultures on the London stage), diminishing both past and present cultural differences. See "Shakespeare and Postcolonial Performance," *A Companion to Shakespeare and Performance*, eds Barbara Hodgdon and W.B. Worthen (London: Blackwell, 2005): 121–37. pp. 123–4. W.B. Worthen also recognises that Shakespeare's Globe "restores" an "early modern experience of theatre" by using contemporary modes of history-performance—as much a contemporary fiction or "play" as a past reality, *Shakespeare and the Force of Modern Performance* (Cambridge: Cambridge University Press, 2003), p. 83.

3 For an accessible summary of the historical carpentry practice involved in building Shakespeare's Globe, see Peter McCurdy's comments in Matt Trueman, "Building Shakespeare's Globe," *shakespearesglobe.com*, 12 June 2017.

4 Ralph Alan Cohen, "The Most Convenient Place: The Second Blackfriars Theater and Its Appeal," *The Oxford Handbook of Early Modern Theatre*, ed. Richard Dutton (Oxford: Oxford University Press, 2010): 209–24. p. 209.

5 Jon Greenfield (with assistance from Peter McCurdy), "Practical Evidence for a Reimagined Indoor Jacobean Theatre," *Moving Shakespeare Indoors: Performance and Repertoire in the Jacobean Playhouse*, eds Andrew Gurr and Farah Karim-Cooper (Cambridge: Cambridge University Press, 2014): 32–64. p. 37.

6 Oliver Jones, "Documentary Evidence for an Indoor Jacobean Theatre," *Moving Shakespeare Indoors: Performance and Repertoire in the Jacobean Playhouse*, eds Andrew Gurr and Farah Karim-Cooper (Cambridge: Cambridge University Press, 2014): 65–78. p. 78.

7 These drawings are also important for the reimagined seventeenth-century theatre at Prescot, Lancashire. See Elspeth Graham, ed. *Shakespeare Bulletin* 38.3 (2020).

8 For discussion of Shakespeare's companies (the Chamberlain's Men and the King's Men) at both these spaces, see Sarah Dustagheer, *Shakespeare's Two Playhouses: Repertory and Theatre Space at the Globe and Blackfriars, 1599–1613* (Cambridge: Cambridge University Press, 2017).

9 REQ 2/87/74; REQ 2/184/45, MSS, The National Archives, Kew, London.

10 C24/226/11 (testimony of Richard Hudson, bricklayer), MS, The National Archives, Kew, London.

11 REQ 2/184/45, MS, The National Archives, Kew, London.

12 C24/226/10; C24/226/11, MSS, The National Archives, Kew, London.

13 STAC5/A12/35, MS, The National Archives, Kew, London.

14 Herbert Berry, "The First Public Playhouses, Especially the Red Lion," *Shakespeare Quarterly* 40.2 (1989): 136–7.

15 *English Professional Theatre*, eds Glynne Wickham, Herbert Berry, and William Ingram (Cambridge: Cambridge University Press, 2000), pp. 536–7; MSS 8, MS, Dulwich College Archive, Dulwich, London; fo. 6v ("What the Fortune Cost Me"). Alleyn and Henslowe spent significantly more on land leases, including down Whitecross Street and Golding Lane, totalling £1,320). Equivalent figures are not available for the Theatre, but the Fortune expenses suggest a model of playhouse construction in line with Burbage and the Braynes approach to recreational buildings.

16 "4-6 New Inn Broadway, London, EC2A 3PR, Post-Excavation Assessment [Site code NIN08]," March 2013 (London: MOLA, 2013), pp. 12–3.

17 Heather Knight, "The Stage Site Bounded by Hearn Street, Curtain Road and Hewett Street, London." Interim post-excavation assessment. (London: MOLA, 2017).

18 C24/228/10 (Nicholas Byshop's deposition), MS, The National Archives, Kew, London.

19 K.B.27/1362/m.587, MS, The National Archives, Kew, London: a lawsuit in which land-lord Giles Allen sued Peter Street for dismantling and carrying away the Theatre struc-ture, deeming it worth £700. The transcription is taken from Charles William Wallace, *The First London Theatre* (Nebraska: University of Nebraska Press, 1913), pp. 177–8. See also: Herbert Berry, "Design and Use of the First Public Playhouse," *The First Public Playhouse: The Theatre in Shoreditch* (Montreal: McGill-Queen's University Press, 1979): 29–45. p. 36; Gabriel Egan, "The Theatre in Shoreditch, 1576–1599," *The Oxford Handbook of Early Modern Theatre*, ed. Richard Dutton (Oxford: Oxford University Press, 2010): 168–85. p. 172; Tiffany Stern, "'You That Walk I'th Galleries': Standing and Walking in the Galleries of the Globe Theatre," *Shakespeare Quarterly* 51.2 (2000): 211–15. p. 212.

20 William Lambard, *Perambulation of Kent* (London, 1596), Q2r.

21 Thomas White, *A Sermon Preached at Pawles crosse*" (London, 1577), C8r; John Stockwood, *A Sermon Preached at Paules Crosse* (London, 1578), J7v.

22 W.G. Hoskins, "The Rebuilding of Rural England, 1570–1640," *Past and Present* 4 (1953): 44–59.

23 Tara Hamling and Catherine Richardson, *A Day at Home in Early Modern England: Material Culture and Domestic Life, 1500–1700* (New Haven: Yale University Press, 2017), p. 14.

24 Non-didactic or non-spiritual decoration sits partly at odds with Reformist aesthetics, though scholarship has importantly shown that Protestant households were nonethe-less themselves highly decorated spaces: see, for instance, Tara Hamling, *Decorating the Godly Household: Religious Art in Post-Reformation Britain* (New Haven: Yale University Press, 2011).

25 *English Professional Theatre*, p. 441; p. 535.

26 Julian Bowsher and Pat Miller, *The Rose and the Globe: Playhouses of Tudor Bankside* (London: MOLA, 2009), p. 48.

27 OED "Amphitheatre," 2; stemming from "double" theatre, based on the semicircularity of classical theatres structures.

28 John Eliot's guide to France, published in 1592, firmly aligns it with the past, noting that the town of Bourges had a large house once "otherwise called the Arenes, in old time an Amphitheatre," while the popular *Theatre of Gods Judgements* (1597) tells a damning story of 50,000 fencers in ancient Rome "hurt and maimed at one time by the Amphitheatre that fell upon them." John Eliot, *The Survay or Topographical Description of France* (London, 1592), E2r; *Theatre of Gods Judgements* (London, 1597), V1r-v.

29 *English Professional Theatre*, p. 441.

30 Karl Theodor Gaedertz, *Zur Kenntnis der Altenglischen bühne nebst andern beiträgen zur Shakespeare* (Bremen, 1888), p. 7.
31 See Holger Syme's blog, "Post-Curtain Theatre History," www.dispositio.net/archives/2262. Online. Accessed 26 Oct. 2021.
32 David Amelang, "Comparing the Commercial Theatres of Early Modern London and Madrid," *Renaissance Quarterly* 71.2 (2018): 610–44.
33 See various testimonies in REQ 2/184/45, MS, The National Archives, Kew, London.
34 "4-6 New Inn Broadway, London, EC2A 3PR, Post-Excavation Assessment [Site code NIN08]," March 2013 (London: MOLA, 2013).
35 REQ 2/184/45, MS, The National Archives, Kew, London.
36 *English Professional Theatre*, pp. 405–6.
37 Knight, "The Stage Site."
38 See Andy Kesson's discussion of opening dates in "Playhouses, Plays, and Theater History: Rethinking the 1580s," Forum, ed. Andy Kesson, *Shakespeare Studies* 45 (2017): 19–40. pp. 29–31.
39 Tiffany Stern, "The Curtain Is Yours," *Locating the Queen's Men: Material Practices and Conditions of Playing*, eds Helen Ostovich, Holger Schott Syme, and Andrew Griffin (Farnham: Ashgate, 2009): 77–96.
40 See the acquisition of the property by Thomas Greene this year at C54/2075/17.
41 *English Professional Theatre*, pp. 534–5.
42 Jerzy Limon, "The City and the 'Problem' of Theatre Reconstructions: 'Shakespearean' Theatres in London and Gdańsk," *Actes des congrès de la Société française Shakespeare* 28 (2011): 159–83. p. 178.
43 I am grateful to Heather Knight for this observation.
44 *Records of Early English Drama: Shropshire*, Vol. 1, ed. J. Alan B. Somerset (Toronto: University of Toronto Press, 1994), p. 294.
45 Thomas Churchyard, *The Worthines of Wales* (London, 1587), L1r.
46 *REED Shropshire,* Vol. 1, p. 295.
47 Churchyard, L1r.
48 See receipts in a travelling bearward's memorandum book at MSS 2 010, MS, Dulwich College Archive, Dulwich, London.
49 *REED Shropshire,* Vol. 1, p. 295.
50 *English Professional Theatre*, p. 598.
51 Julian Bowsher and Pat Miller, *The Rose and the Globe: Playhouses of Tudor Bankside* (London: MOLA, 2009).
52 *REED Shropshire,* Vol. 1, p. 298.
53 OED "sumptuous, adj." 1.a-b, 2.
54 George Puttenham, *The Arte of English Poesie* (London, 1589), F3r.
55 *English Professional Theatre*, p. 441.
56 Various possibilities exist, for instance, for performing "cycle" plays: A.C. Cawley, *Medieval Drama* (London: Methuen, 1983); Pamela King, "Spatial Semantics and the Medieval Theatre," *The Theatrical Space*, ed. James Redmond (Cambridge: Cambridge University Press, 1987): 45–58; Christine Richardson and Jackie Johnston, *Medieval Drama* (London: Macmillan, 1991); Glynne Wickham, *Early English Stages,* Vol. 2, 1964 (London: Routledge, 2002). For an insight into early modern pageantry in London, see Tracey Hill, *Pageantry and Power: A Cultural History of the Early Modern Lord Mayor's Show, 1585–1639* (Manchester: Manchester University Press, 2010).
57 *Records of Early English Drama: Civic London to 1558*, ed, Anne Lancashire, 3 vols, (Toronto: University of Toronto Press, 2015); Anne Lancashire, *London Civic Theatre: City Drama and Pageantry from Roman Times to 1558* (Cambridge: Cambridge University Press, 2002).

58 S.P. Cerasano, "A City of Stages," *Medieval and Renaissance Drama in England* 30 (2017): 202–12. pp. 210–11.

59 Cerasano, "A City of Stages."

60 *Records of Early English Drama: Coventry*, ed. R.W. Ingram (Toronto: University of Toronto Press, 1981), p. 145.

61 *REED Coventry*, p. 131.

62 *REED Coventry*, p. xlii.

63 *REED Coventry*, p. lii.

64 *Records of Early English Drama: Herefordshire and Worcestershire*, ed. David N. Klausner (Toronto: University of Toronto Press, 1990), p. 447.

65 Glynne Wickham, *Early English Stages*, Vol. 2, 1963 (Abingdon: Routledge, 2002), p. 166.

66 Wickham, p. 166.

67 *Records of Early English Drama: Kent*, ed. James M. Gibson, Vol. 2 (Toronto: University of Toronto Press, 2002), p. 694.

68 *REED Kent*, Vol. 1, p. lxvii.

69 *REED Kent*, Vol. 1, p. lix.

70 *REED Kent*, Vol. 2, p. 785.

71 In a discussion of the football-like sport of "camping" in East Anglia; David Dymond, "Place-Names as Evidence for Recreation," *Journal of the English Place-Name Society* 15 (1992): 12–8. p. 15.

72 Wickham, p. 166.

73 Janette Dillon "John Rastell's Stage," *Medieval Theatre* 18 (1996): 15–45 and "John Rastell vs Henry Walton," *Leeds Studies in English* n.s. 28 (1997): 57–75; David Kathman "The Rise of Commercial Playing in 1540s London," *Early Theatre* 12.1 (2009): 15–38; Maura Giles Watson "John Rastell's London Stage: Reconstructing Repertory and Collaborative Practice," *Early Theatre* 16.2 (2014): 171–84. C.R. Baskervill, "John Rastell's Dramatic Activities," *Modern Philology* 12 (1916): 557–60, was the first to treat this at length.

74 REQ 2/8/14 (interrogatory for Nicholas Sayer), MS, The National Archives, Kew, London.

75 MS 05090/1 fo. 41*, MS, London Metropolitan Archives, London.

76 MS 05090/1 fo. 43v, MS, London Metropolitan Archives, London.

77 See *Acts of Court of the Mercers' Company, 1453–1527* (Cambridge: Cambridge University Press, 1936) and Anne F. Sutton, *The Mercery of London: Trade, Goods, and People, 1130–1578* (Aldershot: Aldgate, 2005).

78 REPS 7 fo. 228 (microfilm x109/133), COL/CA/01/01/022, MS, London Metropolitan Archives, London.

79 Meg Twycross, "Felsted of London: Silk-Dyer and Theatrical Entrpereneur," *Medieval English Theatre* 10.1 (1988): 4–25. See also: John C. Coldewey, "That Enterprising Property Player," *Theatre Notebook* 33.1 (1977): 5–12; Kathman, pp. 15–38.

80 MS 01454/47 sheet 4*, MS, London Metropolitan Archives, London.

81 Mary Erler, "London Commercial Theatre, 1500–1576," *Editing, Performance, Texts: New Practices in Medieval and Early Modern English Drama*, eds Jacqueline Jenkins and Julie Sanders (Basingstoke: Palgrave Macmillan, 2014): 93–106. p. 94.

82 There was a host of regulatory policies designed to capitalise upon playing throughout the later sixteenth century.

83 K.B. 27/1229 m.30, MS, The National Archives, Kew, London; MS 4329/1 fo. 128v, MS, Guildhall Library, London. See also Janet S. Loengard, "An Elizabethan Lawsuit: John Brayne, His Carpenter, and the Building of the Red Lion Theatre," *Shakespeare Quarterly* 34.3 (1983): 298–310.

84 Stephen White, "Finding the Red Lion: The Latest on the Earliest Playhouse Found in Whitechapel," *London Archaeologist* 16.2 (2020): 44–6.

85 Archaeology South-East, "Archaeological Excavations at Whitechapel Central, 85 Stepney Way: A Post-Excavation Assessment and Updated Project Design Report" (London: Archaeology South-East, 2020).

86 White, p. 46.

87 Gabriel Egan, "The Theatre in Shoreditch, 1576–1599," p. 172.

88 E36/227 fos 31v-32r, MS, The National Archives, Kew, London.

89 One entertaining and informative way into this performance tradition is via Henry Medwall's meta-theatrical play, *Fulgens and Lucres*, which Clare Wright explores in the contexts of both its setting and performance in a great hall, "Fulgens and Lucres," *The Oxford Handbook of Tudor Drama*, eds Thomas Betteridge and Greg Walker (Oxford: Oxford University Press, 2012): 177–91.

90 Barbara D. Palmer, "Early Modern Mobility: Players, Payments, and Patrons," *Shakespeare Quarterly* 56.3 (2005): 259–305. p. 272.

91 Palmer, p. 276.

92 For an overview and starting point for this history as it bears on the Elizabethan period, see John Astington, *English Court Theatre, 1558–1642* (Cambridge: Cambridge University Press, 1999).

93 REPS 16 fo. 138 (Feb. 1569), COL/CA/01/01/018, MS, London Metropolitan Archives, London.

94 JORS 19 fo. 143v (3 February 1568) and fo. 168 (30 May 1569), COL/CC/01/01/019, MS, London Metropolitan Archives, London.

95 *Records of Early English Drama: Cheshire (including Chester)*, Vol. 2, eds Elizabeth Baldwin, Laurence M. Clopper, and David Mills (Toronto: University of Toronto Press, 2007), p. 800.

96 See statutes at *REED Cheshire*, Vol. 2, p. 797.

97 *Records of Early English Drama: Bristol*, ed. Mark C. Pilkington (Toronto: University of Toronto Press, 1997), p. 78; p. 147; pp. 135–6.

98 *REED Cheshire*, Vol. 2, p. 798.

99 MS 34010/001 fo. 699, MS, Guildhall Library, London.

100 JORS 20 fo. 432, COL/CC/01/01/020-21, MS, London Metropolitan Archives, London.

101 The disorderliness of outdoor playhouse attendance is cited several times in the Middlesex Sessions (see, for instance, recognisances against James Burbage and John Brayne in April 1580, MJ/SR/0225/4, London Metropolitan Archives, London.

102 Reavley Gair, *The Children of Paul's: The Story of a Theatre Company, 1553–1608* (Cambridge: Cambridge University Press, 1982), p. 10.

103 For scholarly reassessments and overview of this space, its location, and its architecture, see Callan Davies, "Elizabethan Playing at St Paul's," *Old St Paul's and Culture*, eds Shanyn Altman and Jonathan Buckner (Basingstoke: Palgrave, 2021): 221–42; José A. Pérez Díez, "The 'Playhouse' at St Paul's: What We Know of the Theatre in the Almonry," *Old St Paul's and Culture*, eds Shanyn Altman and Jonathan Buckner (Basinsstoke: Palgrave, 2021): 197–220; Roze Hentschell, *St Paul's Cathedral Precinct in Early Modern Literature and Culture* (Oxford: Oxford University Press, 2020), pp. 153–4.

104 Díez, "The 'Playhouse' at St Paul's."

105 PROB 11/64/142 (14 April 1582), The National Archives, Kew, London.

106 REPS 19 fo. 18 (8 Dec. 1575), COL/CA/01/01/021, MS, London Metropolitan Archives, London.

107 L.b.446 (27 August 1576), MS, Folger Shakespeare Library, Washington DC.

108 See Roze Hentschell's account in *St Paul's Cathedral Precinct in Early Modern Literature and Culture.*

109 Quoted in Irwin Smith, *Shakespeare's Blackfriars Playhouse: Its History and Its Design*, (New York: New York University Press, 1964), p. 467. See discussion of "playhouse" in Before Shakespeare work, including on the website and in Kesson, "Playhouses, Plays, and Theater History: Rethinking the 1580s," Forum, ed. Andy Kesson, *Shakespeare Studies* 45 (2017): 19–40. See also the introduction for more discussion of this work.

110 See *Records of Early English Drama: Ecclesiastical London*, ed. Mary Erler (Toronto: University of Toronto Press, 2008), p. xliii.

111 "Introduction," *Parish Fraternity Register: The Fraternity of the Holy Trinity and SS. Fabian and Sebastian Parish of St Botoloph without Aldersgate*, ed. Patricia Basing (London: London Record Society, 1982), pp. vii–xxviii.

112 MS 01454/71, MS, London Metropolitan Archives, London.

113 LR 2/241, MS, The National Archives, Kew, London.

114 Record No. 6989 "Trinity Hall" by John Carter (1782) (p5350302), *London Picture Archive*, online. Accessed 10 Jan. 2021. Print reference at p5350302, MS, London Metropolitan Archives, London (formerly Maps and Plans 591/TRI, Guildhall Library); MSS 10907, 10907A (1666), MS, Guildhall Library, London. See Basing, "Introduction," *Parish Fraternity Register*, pp. vii–xxviii.

115 For more detail on comparative halls, see Erler's introduction in *REED Ecclesiastical London*, p. xliii.

116 "London Commercial Theatre, 1500–1576," p. 102.

117 *Records of Early English Drama: Dorset and Cornwall*, eds. Rosalind Conklin Hays and C.E. McGee (Toronto: University of Toronto Press, 1999), pp. 40–1.

118 Robert Tittler, *Architecture and Power: The Town Hall and the English Urban Community, c. 1500–1640* (Oxford: Clarendon, 1991), p. 139.

119 Tittler, p. 141.

120 Laurie Johnson, *Shakespeare's Lost Playhouse: Eleven Days at Newington Butts* (Abingdon: Routledge, 2018), p. 78.

121 Johnson, p. 79.

122 As phrased by the Privy Council, MS 1, Article 018 (c.1590), Dulwich College Archive, Dulwich, London. There is a rhetorical manoeuvre at play, too, in this description, as the Lord Strange's Men desired to return to their "home" venue of the Rose. For more, see Johnson, *Shakespeare's Lost Playhouse*; Lawrence Manley and Sally-Beth MacLean, *The Lord Strange's Men and Their Plays* (New Haven: Yale University Press, 2018), p. 51. Alan Nelson's evidence necessitating the revised date for this document of 1590 is cited by Manley and MacLean.

123 Johnson, p. 87.

124 Johnson, p. 78.

125 C/2/9/1/1/8 p. 178, MS, Suffolk Archives, Ipswich.

126 C/2/9/1/1/8 p. 198, MS, Suffolk Archives, Ipswich.

127 Tara Hamling and Catherine Richardson, *A Day at Home in Early Modern England: Material Culture and Domestic Life, 1500–1700* (New Haven and London, 2017), p. 266.

128 Phil Withington sees this as a growth of civic regulation aiming to "profit from the burgeoning trade in intoxicants while alleviating market pressures." See "Intoxicants and the Early Modern City," *Remaking English Society: Social Relations and Social Change in Early Modern England* (Woodbridge: Boydell P, 2013): 135–63. p. 156.

129 Mark Hailwood, *Alehouses and Good Fellowship in Early Modern England* (Woodbridge: Boydell P, 2014), p. 223.

130 Peter Clark, *The English Alehouse: A Social History, 1200–1830* (London: Longman, 1983), p. 5.

131 See Mayor William Blanke's letter to Lord Burghley in 1582, which complains of houses capitalising on the start of the legal term by renting out rooms or selling food and drink; Lansdowne 37 fo. 8, MS, British Library, London.

132 See Withington, "Intoxicants," for the example of York.

133 Clark, p. 4.

134 Thomas Thropp, Inventory, 1621, MS, Chester Archives and Local Studies, Chester.

135 Palmer queries widespread use of inns as venues by professional touring players, but inns could serve as playhouses aside from hosting travelling troupes, while also being models for or sites of provincial playhouses, as discussed here. See Palmer, "Early Modern Mobility,".

136 REQ 2/296/80, MS, The National Archives, Kew, London. Cooke complained about a break in the terms of his tenancy and argued that, having moved out, Woolfe rented out and used his rooms and neglected to return Cooke's money.
    C2/328/28, MS, The National Archives, Kew, London.

137 C2/328/28, MS, The National Archives, Kew, London. See the final portion of the article below for more details on Woolfe's two hired Wine Street properties (one from Christ Church and one from the Bristol Corporation).

138 REQ 2/296/80, MS, The National Archives, Kew, London.

139 See Siobhan Keenan, *Travelling Players in Shakespeare's England* (Basingstoke: Palgrave MacMillan, 2002).

140 Kathman, pp. 15–38. See also Lawrence Manley, "Why Did London Inns Function as Theatres?" *Huntington Library Quarterly* 71.1 (2008): 181–97.

141 Privy Council Minutes 2/7, p. 695.

142 AO3/907/5 p. 272, MS, The National Archives, Kew, London.

143 C2/Eliz/B24/63, MS, The National Archives, Kew, London. See also Kathman, "London Inns as Playing Venues for the Queen's Men," *Locating the Queen's Men: Material Practices and the Conditions of Playing*, eds Helen Ostovich, Holger Schott Syme, and Andrew Griffin (Farnham: Ashgate, 2009): 65–76.

144 Kathman, "London Inns as Playing Venues for the Queen's Men," p. 72.

145 C24/226/10, MS, The National Archives, Kew, London.

146 Remembrancia II 33, COL/RMD/PA/01/002, MS, London Metropolitan Archives, London.

147 C2/Eliz F8/52, MS, The National Archives, Kew, London. See Kathman, "Alice Layston and the Cross Keys," *Medieval and Renaissance Drama in England* 22 (2009): 144–78.

148 William Lambard, *Perambulation of Kent* (London, 1576), Aa2r.

149 William Prynne, *Histriomastix* (London, 1633), p. 556.

150 Clark, *The English Alehouse*, p. 65.

151 Lansdowne 20 fo. 20r., MS, British Library, London.

152 Hailwood, *Alehouses and Good Fellowship*, p. 54.

153 Hailwood, *Alehouse and Good Fellowship*, p. 226.

154 *Records of Early English Drama: Cumberland, Westmorland, Gloucestershire*, eds Audrey Douglas and Peter Greenfield (Toronto: University of Toronto Press, 1986) pp. 288–9.

155 *REED Cumberland, Westmorland, Gloucestershire*, pp. 306–7.

156 For patronised troupes in regard to this order, see Sally-Beth MacLean, "Adult Playing Companies, 1583–1593," *The Oxford Handbook of Early Modern Theatre*, ed. Richard Dutton (Oxford: Oxford University Press, 2010): 39–55; p. 51.

157 Similar such licensing questions apply to York, which in 1582 explained that approved "players of Interludes" could play in the city twice at the "common hall"—once before

the Mayor and once before the "commons," *Records of Early English Drama: York*, Vol. 1, eds Alexandra F. Johnston and Margaret Rogerson, (Toronto: University of Toronto Press, 1979), p. 399. This playing arrangement did not necessarily apply to other towns or cities (or necessarily consistently for York) and does not account for incidents when players performed without permission (doubtless common, as suggested here, beyond the written record). For a sample list of playing troupe infractions in various locations, see the "players and playing" section in *EPT* 250–9.

158 For a summary, see Sally-Beth MacLean and Lawrence Manley, *The Queen's Men and their Plays* (Cambridge: Cambridge University Press, 1998), pp. 42–3.

159 *REED Bristol*, p. 165.

160 *REED Kent*, Vol. 1, p. 195; *REED Cheshire*, Vol. 2, pp. 682–3.

161 *REED Cheshire*, Vol. 2, pp. 693–4.

162 *REED Cheshire*, Vol. 2, p. 734. See also Elizabeth Baldwin, "John Seckerston: The Earl of Derby's Bearward," *Medieval English Theatre* 20 (1998): 95–103.

163 *Records of Early English Drama: Somerset*, Vol. 1, ed. James Stokes (Toronto: University of Toronto Press, 1996), pp. 218–19.

164 For conceptual similarities, see Andreas Höfele, *Stage, Stake, and Scaffold: Humans and Animals in Shakespeare's Theatre* (Oxford: Oxford University Press, 2011).

165 Oscar Brownstein, "Why Didn't Burbage Lease the Beargarden? A Study in Comparative Architecture," *The First Public Playhouse: The Theatre in Shoreditch, 1576–1598*, ed. Herbert Berry (Montreal: McGill-Queens' University Press, 1979): 81–96. p. 89.

166 See the *REED Online* edition for *The Bear Gardens and Hope Playhouse*, with associated chapters on their property ownership, entertainment history, and Henslowe and Alleyn. I am grateful to Sally-Beth MacLean for sharing her Shakespeare Association of America 2020 paper on early baiting arenas, "Early Bear Garden Entertainment Records: Tracing the Evidence."

167 E 134/18JasI/Mich10, m. 5, MS, The National Archives, Kew, London. Qtd. in W.W. Braines, *The Site of the Globe Playhouse, Southwark* (London: Hodder and Stoughton, 1924), p. 87.

168 Anthony Mackinder with Lyn Blackmore, Julian Bowsher, and Christopher Phillpotts. *The Hope Playhouse, Animal Baiting and Later Industrial Activity at Bear Gardens on Bankside: Excavations at Riverside House and New Globe Walk, Southwark, 1999–2000* (London: MOLA, 2013), pp. 11–2.

169 Again, I am thankful to Sally-Beth MacLean for transcriptions of these documents, discussed in "Early Bear Garden Entertainment Records."

170 Mackinder et al., p. 11. See E 134/18JasI/Mich10 ms 3, 4, 5, MS, The National Archives, Kew, London.

171 Mackinder et al., p. 11; Walter W. Greg, *Henslowe's Diary: Part II* (London: A.H. Bullen, 1908), p. 26; MacLean, "Early Bear Garden Entertainment Records," p. 10.

172 Lansdowne 37 fo.8r, MS, British Library, London; John Field, *A Godly Exhortation* (London, 1583).

173 See testimony at E 134/18JasI/Mich10, cited in Braines.

174 Mackinder et al., p 13.

175 *English Professional Theatre*, p. 595.

176 *English Professional Theatre*, p. 598.

177 *A pamphlet of the offices, and duties of euerie particular sworne officer, of the citie of Excester* (London, 1584), I1r.

178 *REED Kent*, Vol. 1, p. 167.

179 *REED Kent*, Vol. 1, p. 194.

180 *REED Kent*, Vol. 1, p. 194.

181 *REED Kent*, Vol. 1, p. 198.

182 *REED Kent*, Vol. 1, p. 199; pp. 241–2; p. 277.

183 Other regional places offer limited information in the record but present tantalising glimpses of similar structures. Elsewhere in Kent, for instance, Thomas Cooke was paid for paving 148 yards of ground "at the place commonly called the bere stake" in Maidstone in 1574, in *REED Kent*, Vol. 1, p. 715.

184 *REED Kent*, Vol. 1, p. 233.

185 John Taylor, *Bull, Bear, and Horse, Cut, Curtaile, and Longtaile* (London, 1638), D9r.

186 See *REED Kent*, Vol. 1, p. 171; p. 187; p. 193; p. 195.

187 *REED Kent*, Vol. 1, pp. 187–8.

188 *REED Cheshire*, Vol. 2, p. 644. See Chapter 4 for more detailed discussion of the complex.

189 *Records of Early English Drama: Lancashire*, ed. David George (Toronto: University of Toronto Press, 1991), pp. 77–84.

190 *English Professional Theatre*, p. 623; p. 626.

191 JORS 20 fo. 127v, COL/CC/01/01/020–21, MS, London Metropolitan Archives, London.

192 For a detailed discussion of the relationship between bowling alleys and playhouses in the period, see Callan Davies, "Bowling Alleys and Playhouses, 1560–1590," *Early Theatre* 22.4 (2019): 39–66.

193 Henry Chettle, *Kind-Harts Dream* (London, 1593), F1v-2r.

194 On dating and discussion of possible identification of these buildings, see: Herbert Berry, "The View of London from the North and the Playhouses in Holywell," *Shakespeare Survey* (2000): 196–212.

195 Richard West, *The Court of Conscience* (London, 1607), D3v.

196 Heather Knight, "The Curtain Rises," talk given at Hackney House, 21 July 2018. See also, Knight, e-mail messages to the author, September 2018.

197 Amelang, p. 65.

198 *A Day at Home*, p. 67.

199 *REED Cheshire*, Vol. 2, pp. 693–4.

2
MULTIPURPOSE SPACES

The architectural diversity of playhouses reflects the activities that took place inside and around them. These were always multipurpose spaces. Chapter 1 emphasised how conversion and adaptation brought playhouses into being and continued to reshape them, and this chapter proceeds to explore their functional mutability. Why did a bullring in Canterbury morph into a theatre? What did Shoreditch's Curtain have in common with cloisters in a former London friary used as a bowling alley? These questions remind us that "playhouse" meant not simply "theatre" in our contemporary sense of the word, but rather indicated a space of *play* in its fullest early modern meanings.

The commercial activities that took place in playhouses therefore included but extended beyond drama. This chapter aims to recover something of what the word meant to residents of, for instance, sixteenth-century or early seventeenth-century Bristol, Canterbury, Cheshire, London, or Norwich. Doing so requires moving beyond the well-researched professional playing industry—which centred on (but was not limited to) the onstage performance of scripted drama—to think about the other forms of performance, sport, and game that sat alongside it: fencing and wrestling, animal sports and performance; tumbling and gymnastic displays; extemporising (a linguistically witty form of improvisation); music and dancing; and other, sometimes stubbornly enigmatic, "shows" or "displays." One could have paid to see these modes in playhouses across England, and any one playhouse accommodated more than one such activity. Many of these non-dramatic play forms featured foreign, female, or more-than-human performers and creators, in a picture quite different from the hackneyed idea of the Elizabethan "all-male stage."[1] Indeed, playhouses were not always dominated by troupes of "professional" English men. They could be and often were eclectic and cosmopolitan venues.

Playhouses were also multipurpose spaces in ways other than performance. My account of the multipurpose playhouse accordingly leads into Chapter 3 by

DOI: 10.4324/9781003231127-3

asking: what else drew visitors to these sites? Other play forms included drinking, eating, socialising, and gaming—participatory leisure acts that complemented or competed with audience-demanding spectacles. We have already seen how distinctions between theatrical spaces and inns or alehouses were not always clear-cut. Varied forms of consumption were an important part of the playgoing experience. I therefore consider what it might have been like to visit a venue that accommodated different interests simultaneously—catering (literally and figuratively) for different tastes via specific commercial, aesthetic, and architectural configurations. Not everyone visiting the Theatre or the Globe cared a great deal about the performance of *Romeo and Juliet* or *Hamlet* taking place on the stage. Plenty came to drink or gossip or enjoy the jig at the close of the show. This was a recreational world where attention could happily be divided, in which neither play nor plays necessitated quiet, singular, or linear engagement.

Vocabulary of Play

In 1600, a weaver from London called John Wheately travelled to Norwich and "did show a Licence made by Edmond Tylney esquire Master of the Revels for the showing of a beast called A Basehooke."[2] The clerk noting this down in the Mayor's Court Books added in the margin, as shorthand, "a strange beast shown." This enigmatic account reflects one element of early modern English entertainment culture, the display of unusual or non-normative bodies—both human and animal. As Trinculo remarks in Shakespeare's *The Tempest*, in his dehumanising description of Caliban, "A strange fish. Were I in England now, as once I was, and had but this fish painted, not a holiday fool there but would give a piece of silver."[3] Such instances indicate the violent and voyeuristic race-making at work in early modern culture.[4] They also indicate how "play" itself was a flexible concept (always in need of critical analysis) and how obfuscations and absences in archival records of performance can sometimes obscure the racial components of early modern performances—particularly those outside of the drama performed by professional companies. It remains unclear what exactly Wheately's "Basehooke" was,[5] but the fact that Tilney had issued a licence for its "showing" testifies to the broad range of commercial recreational displays and the individuals (human, "beast," or otherwise) involved.

Tilney was the Master of the Revels, and the latter word in this title can be read as a synonym for play. His royal patent, issued in 1581, conferred on him the power to "authorise license and command" everything to do with the Office of the Revels, which provided entertainment for the royal court; it also included the power

> to Warn command and appoint in all places within this our Realm of England as well within Franchises and liberties as without all and any player or players with their playmakers either belonging to the noble man or otherwise bearing the name or names of using the faculty of playmakers or players of Comedies Tragedies Interludes or what other shows soever from time to

time and at times to appear before him with all such plays tragedies Comedies
or shows as they shall have in readiness or mean to set forth [...].[6]

The typical legalese of the document does nothing to dispel the capaciousness of
the idea of play. By the time Tilney issued Wheately's licence for his "Basehooke"
18 years later, the Master of the Revels was evidently generating income from
anything that might fit under the vocabulary employed in his patent. Theatre
historian Richard Dutton reads this as Tilney "exploiting powers in his 1581
patent to licence non-theatrical entertainments":"He may have been doing it for
some time around London, but the first mention of it (and most frequent subsequent references) are to be found in Norwich," Wheately's Basehooke being
the debut example.[7] Yet the Office of the Revels was always responsible for all
sorts of entertainment at court. Moreover, the patent's liberal use of "or" clearly
encouraged Tilney to think about the multiplicity of commercial play beyond the
noted dramatic types (comedies, tragedies, interludes) and extended most open-
endedly to "what other shows [what]soever". The "faculty of playmakers" is a
wonderful turn of phrase that most obviously refers in this context to authors of
dramatic plays but that could, elastically, describe any of the purveyors of entertainment discussed here.[8]

Tilney's interpretation of his powers reflects the way "play" was employed
in early modern English to refer to a range of non-dramatic activities, both as
a noun and a verb. A few years after the Basehooke's appearance in Norwich,
the bearward John Moore was given "leave to play with his Bears."[9] This verbal
formulation might sound childish today, recalling a teddy bear's picnic, but it
connoted a whole recreational sub-industry—that of bear-baiting. Similarly, one
of the most popular early modern pastimes alongside bear-baiting was bowling—
a term for a range of games played in bowling alleys and (presumably like bear-
baiting) often bet upon by spectators. Contemporaries used the noun "play" to
describe these activities, as when a landlord in London's Blackfriars bemoaned
Henry Naylor's new bowling alleys:

> [he] hath of late set up within the said precinct three common bowling
> Alleys: an alley for play Commonly called nine holes & a place as it is
> reported provided for a game called black and white or else for a Dicing
> house To which plays there resort in great number as well apprentices and
> servants as others [...] who there spend and consume their time & very
> much money.[10]

Going to see a play need not mean watching a five act tragedy; it could, these details
show, mean having a flutter in a bowling alley built in the cloisters of a former friary.
With this in mind, we can revisit Henry Walton's 1520s London stages, discussed
in Chapter 1, one of which recorded money "Received at the play."[11] The noun is
today often fixed to refer to a linear dramatic performance (usually with a script or
text in mind), but throughout the period covered by this book it could equally well

indicate a raft of entertainments (extending, in Walton's early period, to church ales or wakes that comprised a range of festive activities).[12]

The scope of the term "play" insists on relationships between, rather than a separation of, different forms of recreation. Glynne Wickham explains how "the two words 'recreation' and 'pastyme' supply the key to the ambiguity transferred into English from *ludus* and extending outwards into both 'play' and 'game'."[13] These issues directly come to bear on playhouses themselves, which hosted more than one type of activity. Commercial dramatic performance was inflected by these other, related types of pastime, game, or recreation. Erika Lin has demonstrated how commercial theatre was "fully imbricated in the representationally porous and generically hybrid forms of entertainment that characterized seasonal events," such as the church ales or wakes discussed in Chapter 1's exploration of scaffolds and perhaps "played" upon Walton's stages; these included May Games, morris dances, and Robin Hood plays.[14] The very category of "theatre" that we use today developed as a "negotiation" (in Lin's terms) with other forms of entertainment. We must accordingly recover the semantic significance of the terms "play" and "player," and perhaps even Tilney's "playmaker," in order to understand early modern culture. Tom Bishop has detected a slow historical shift from "player" to "actor" over the period, which has gone on to eclipse the way theatre was more accurately regarded by contemporaries as "a form of play or an event which include[d] various kinds of games or play-routines."[15] These discursive contexts reinforce how playhouses hosted multiple forms of play within their defined physical space.

The early modern vocabulary for play perhaps explains why spaces like the Hope playhouse were not seen as particularly outlandish. The Hope was deliberately designed to accommodate both animal sport and professional drama (which in turn included other forms of play described below)—a commercial recreational institution not limited to one subset of "play." Along the same lines, we saw in Chapter 1 how the bullstake at Canterbury acted as a ludic centrepoint for the city. It is perhaps no surprise that this space was formally converted into a playhouse in the 1660s.[16] Such a transformation fits with the architectural adaptability of playhouses, but it is also testament to their multipurposeness. While Canterbury's indoor hall playhouse was a post-Restoration development, the centuries-long use of the bullstake for play of all kinds demonstrates a long theatrical trajectory; its conversion in the later part of the seventeenth century built, quite literally, on existing uses and conceptions of the site.

This chapter explores the many uses of a playhouse via some of the most prominent entertainment activities available to spectators and participants. The categorised subheadings help to organise the chapter, but they are resolutely not intended to sharpen and fix play into tidy sub-genres. They should rather indicate the multiplicity of mode and media that sustained the early modern leisure industry. Just as the architectural forms of playhouses overlapped, shifted, and blended into one another, so each of the play forms discussed here were connected and sometimes united. Here, then, is a glimpse into the doings of those "using the faculty of playmakers."

Drama

Perhaps the most obvious thing to see at a playhouse, from our perspective today, would be a commercial dramatic play, like those performed by adult professional companies. Drama, as conventionally understood, is not the central focus of this book, which encourages readers to look beyond the well-researched theatrical activities of the period, and sustained studies of this topic can be found elsewhere. But it was a crucial feature of the spaces in question and warrants a brief overview as part of this chapter, not least to gesture to the many ways it overlapped with other play elements explored below.

When *Romeo and Juliet* was first published in 1597, the text's title page noted how it had "been often (with great applause) plaid publicly," but did not mention any specific venues.[17] By the time of a later reprint, in 1609, its title page brandished the name of a Bankside playhouse: "As it hath been sundry times publicly acted, by the Kings Majesty's Servants at the Globe."[18] Playhouses are notoriously difficult to find on title pages of printed plays, which often advertise other "selling" features (such as company, court performance, or, later on, authorship).[19] As such, many longstanding playhouses never appear on printed plays, including the Theatre—the likely opening night location for Shakespeare's play. The idea of printing a commercial play was still reasonably new in the 1590s, when *Romeo and Juliet* was first printed. There are also very few references to playhouses themselves on the front pages of printed drama (where performance history is advertised), making it difficult to know for certain what play appeared in what venue, when, how, and with what frequency or variation. It also poses an historical challenge, because our access to the live play activities of the period is almost always mediated through printed records, which are often misleading, impartial, or incomplete. As Aaron Pratt puts it, "most 1580s plays were not available to [print] readers in the 1580s," and when some few of them were eventually printed, they often reflected a later performance iteration of that play.[20]

Scholarship has looked to the London playing companies and their repertories to reconstruct what playhouses showcased what.[21] The earliest recoverable repertory for a commercial playhouse in England can be found at the First Blackfriars playhouse in London, where drama was performed by the resident children's company. Although they operated at the venue from 1576, no plays survive (at least in unrevised form) from the first four to five years. Yet some of the plays produced in the following decade do announce their association with the venue via prologues, such as John Lyly's *Campaspe*, printed in 1584 with a "Prologue at the Blackfriars." The Blackfriars company in question, the Children of the Chapel Royal, also appear in court payments where plays were sometimes listed, while plays like George Peele's *The Arraignment of Paris* name the company on its title page. The Blackfriars therefore offers a relatively early example of a company resident at a single playhouse, a selection of whose plays found their way to the print market and even advertised their association with the venue. We can accordingly establish a First Blackfriars Playhouse repertory (as attested by Martin Wiggins's *British Drama* catalogue): *The*

Wars of Cyrus (late 1570s/early 1580s?),[22] Anthony Munday's *Fedele and Fortunio* (c.1579–84), Lyly's *Campaspe* (1583) and *Sapho and Phao* (1584), and Peele's *The Arraignment of Paris* (1581–4). These plays demonstrate the investment of children's drama in playhouse performance and their surrounding environs, a subject explored in depth in Chapter 4.

Establishing resident companies and their repertories is trickier when it comes to regional playing venues. Surviving details of provincial performance do not often include the play performed, while there is rarely evidence of a "resident" company at most spaces or even in most towns or cities. Bristol, however, offers an exception to this rule. It was home to the Children of the Royal Chamber, ratified in 1615 by the Master of the Revels under the Queen's patronage and led by John Daniel (whose brother, Samuel, was a poet and playwright). Their licence permitted them "to use and exercise the art and quality of playing Comedies histories Interludes morals pastorals Stage plays […] in such usual houses as themselves shall provide, as in other convenient places."[23] The company offers a further example of both the formal and generic range of play performed in "houses" across the country, even if we cannot say exactly what these playmakers produced.

Performance in "usual houses" does, however, provide one way of understanding how drama sustained playhouses and was sustained by them. London shared this approach and language when it came to professional troupes based regularly or permanently in the capital. Two 1570s London spaces were built by individuals with firm connections to professional playing troupes—James Burbage at the Theatre was a member of the Leicester's Men and Jerome Savage of Newington Butts was named in royal court payments as a leader of the Warwick's Men.[24] By the 1580s, particular playing companies were further associated with one or more specific spaces across the capital: the Queen's Men licence, as recorded by London's Aldermen in 1583, explained they were "permitted to use the exercise of playing at the Signs of the Bull in Bishopsgatestreet, and the sign of the Bell in gratiousstreet and nowhere else […]."[25] Scholars have also emphasised the importance of commercial developments spearheaded by the Lord Strange's Men, perhaps the earliest "large-scale company in extended London residence," thanks to their spells in 1590 and beyond at the Rose playhouse.[26] The language of "usual" houses applies to many of these spaces. In spring of 1586, the Privy Council restricted playing in London "in respect of the heat of the year now drawing on" to avoid plague, while restricting "the ordinary assemblies of the people" to "public places" of play, with the Theatre and Newington Butts named.[27] Another restriction, aimed at preventing breaches of the peace following a riot, ordered London to "take order that there be no plays used in any place near thereabouts as the Theater, Curtain or other usual places there where the same are Commonly used."[28] The vocabulary of "common," "usual," and "ordinary" sat parallel to the idea of the playhouse, marking out play venues for popular audiences.

Yet the lines between "professional" troupes and other performances of drama in usual playhouses were not always clear-cut. The city of Gloucester's order in 1580 against "common Players of Interludes" (discussed in Chapter 1) testifies to the range of spaces in which players (seemingly without patronage) performed. Similarly, neighbouring Cheltenham witnessed young artificers and labourers putting on a play in 1611 at a victualler's house.[29] Commercial dramatic performance was by no means the preserve of royally or aristocratically sanctioned groups, even if regulation very often sought to proscribe those without powerful patrons. Equally,

> it is possible to make too sharp a divide between "nonprofessional" or "nonplayhouse" plays and their supposed opposites. *Gammer Gurton's Needle*, for example, was staged at Christ's College, Cambridge sometime in the early 1550s, but is later recorded as having been performed by a professional company, possibly the Admiral's Men, in Frankfurt in 1592, and was therefore part of a professional company repertory."[30]

These examples testify to the diversity of both performers of drama and the nature of drama itself. The "medley" theatre identified by Scott McMillin and Sally-Beth MacLean, which was central to the Queen's Men company, is an especially useful example of the fact that "drama" in the early modern period may well have looked very different to many Shakespearean productions today. Medley describes a "predominantly visual" performance style, which focussed attention on "objects, costumes, the gestures of actors, and patterns of stage movement" in which "spoken language tends to be subordinate."[31] This popular and influential dramatic approach (which reached across almost all areas of the country via their concerted touring energy) reminds us of the multiple registers of theatricality simultaneously present in playhouses in the 1580s and beyond.

Drama in playhouses also took on other forms that challenge our categorisations today. The theatre-maker turned theatre-hater Stephen Gosson wrote approvingly in 1579 of "The two prose books played at the Bel Savage, where you shall find never a word without wit, never a line without pith, never a letter placed in vain."[32] The idea of "playing" a prose book raises a fascinating possibility of a much-expanded dramatic scene. Here, linguistic complexities of written text are matched with oratorical skill, generating a performance at the Bel Savage playhouse that sits on the borderline between early modern audiobook and theatre show. Gosson's phrase could more simply signify dramatic plays written not in verse but in prose, but emphasis on the term "book" suggests a more explicit physical text. Dramatic performance in playhouses also developed from other non-professional traditions, not least in schools across the country. Chapter 1 has shown how school houses or rooms across England were sometimes described as playhouses. The drama that survives from well-documented children's performance traditions, like the Children of the Chapel Royal and the Children of Paul's in the 1580s and 1590s, can provide models by which we understand children's performances in other parts of the country at other times. These particular performers were "pioneers not only of theater music but also of tragic form and emotional expression."[33]

Accordingly, scripted dialogue, from which we still teach, learn, and perform the period's drama today, was not always the given medium for structuring commercial performance in playhouses. Other elements—song, visual representation, prose books—often had equal billing, along with many of the elements discussed here in subsequent sections. Richard Preiss has importantly resisted the "organising agency" of playtexts, noting that "texts were the medium by which theatre preserved itself, and whenever we reconstruct it, we do so through their logic."[34] Preiss calls for the restoration of the clown—as improvisatory comic force—to the construction of theatrical events. Certainly, early modern visitors to the playhouse came for a range of reasons and, like any spectator today, engaged with or enjoyed different elements of playgoing. Some were doubtless there, like Stephen Gosson at the Bel Savage, to appreciate the literary skill of a well-placed letter or a well-measured line. Others may have had different ideas of quality.

Indeed, there is ample evidence that many audience members did not engage with dramatic plays in playhouses in the linear and holistic sense implied by printed playtexts (with chronological plot and scenes and bounded beginnings and ends). This is not to suggest that individuals never enjoyed plays in their totality or that narrative and language did not matter to early modern spectators: they clearly did. But not always, not consistently, and not for all types of drama. Playtexts (and thinking and discussion about them) have reified certain value judgements about drama of the period, prioritising and canonising narrative cohesion and rhetorical sophistication (typically in the model of Shakespeare). As we have already seen, not all drama conformed to such a pattern, and accordingly not all audience members engaged with it as a total and cohesive aesthetic experience.

Individuals frequently came and went during dramatic productions. Richard Madox noted in his diary in 1582 how he and his fellows, unimpressed with the "matter" of one offering at the Theatre, simply walked out.[35] A later seventeenth-century writer reflected on his younger days out at playhouses in the 1600s and recalled how, on certain rowdy occasions,

> the Players have been appointed, notwithstanding their bills to the contrary, to act that [which] the major part of the company [ie audience] had a mind to; sometimes *Tamburlaine*, sometimes *Jagurth*, sometimes the *Jew of Malta*, and sometimes parts of all those, and at last, none of the three taking, they were forced to undress and put off their Tragic habits, and conclude the day with the merry milkmaids.[36]

This fanciful recollection must be taken with a pinch of salt, but its image of playgoing shows how dramatic performance could resist the idea of linearity and instead revel in skits, sketches, and excerpts like a variety show. Anecdotes about crowds shouting for "Friars" in around 1612 at the Curtain also suggest that the audience's opinion on play choices was indeed occasionally expressed and was quite possibly heeded.[37]

S.P. Cerasano observes how

> there was a fair amount of movement into and out of the audience throughout a performance; and also [...] the audience was altogether more openly

responsive than modern audiences. The famous 'nut-cracking Elizabethans' shouted at players, responded to jokes with wisecracks of their own, and (metaphorically) nipped at the heels of the actors standing close to the edge of the stage. Yet [...] there was some sense of etiquette involved in playhouse attendance.[38]

There clearly were expected behavioural norms, often rehearsed by exasperated playwrights in pleading prologues. Cerasano paints a picture of two extremes of audience response: extreme detachment (by exiting and entering) or extreme engagement (by bantering and responding to actors). Yet it is possible many individuals were somewhere in the middle: for instance, one might enjoy improvised clowning but not care much for long rehearsed dialogues; in turn, one may have enjoyed the physical dexterity of a fight scene, but not engaged so much with another plot strand of the play. Others were doubtless rapt by the rhetorical sensibilities of the playwright and the oratorical and physical skills of the actor. Thomas Nashe evoked the power of embodied representation when he described the effects of Talbot in the newly staged *1 Henry VI* in 1592:

> How would it have joyed brave Talbot (the terror of the French) to think that after he had laid two hundred year in his Tomb, he should triumph again on the stage, and have his bones new embalmed with the tears of ten thousand spectators at least, (at several times) who in the Tragedian that represents his person, imagine they behold him fresh bleeding.[39]

Many dramatic plays themselves accommodate the multipurposeness of the playhouse, not only by integrating music, combat, dancing, and other play elements into the drama but by allowing for wandering attentions. Plays with regular choric or interlude interventions particularly lend themselves to punctuated viewing experiences, as they offer useful updates to audiences who may have disregarded one particular plot. Robert Greene, a dramatist of the 1580s and 1590s, provides especially helpful examples:

> each of Greene's plays is organised around a specific spectacle or attraction, which functions as a distilled unit of impression, which carries profound thematic implications for the work as a whole, but which also retains its significance outside of that particular representational context.[40]

In this, they align with individual pageants within the wider contexts of a Lord Mayor's Show and to their equivalent centrality on visual devices.[41] Greene's work is structured around set-pieces, often visual ones, that allow audiences to enjoy, say, talking brazen heads, thunderbolts, mirrors, or songs and dances as discrete elements while also allowing them to be part of the narrative whole of a play.

Other dramatic examples show us playwrights recapping things for audiences. Even a play as structured around "story" and around revenge—what John

Kerrigan sees as one of the most fundamental units of dramatic "exchange"[42]—as Shakespeare's *Hamlet* offers its audiences updates on the play's progression. Each of Hamlet's soliloquies essentially assures spectators that no action has yet taken place: they have not missed anything. They are updates on inaction. While in literary and philosophical terms they draw readers and spectators to the extremes of existential contemplation, they also serve dramatic functions—and one of those functions is to punctuate the "narrative" and retune its audiences. "Here's what you missed in the last half hour of *Hamlet*…". We might detect a similar pattern in the lengthy and seemingly superfluous "recognition" scene at the end of *Cymbeline* (c. 1610), which laboriously reiterates all the plot points of the past four acts. John Lyly models the structural benefits of episodic narrative in *The Woman in the Moon* (c. 1590), a play whose main character, Pandora, is governed by different celestial deities across successive acts. Each planet, when in the ascendent, offers updates on the play's overarching narrative as they alert us to the mood of their instalment. Numerous plays of the period—Elizabethan and Jacobean—are punctuated with these "updates." They provide anchor points for spectators reengaging with the narrative having been diverted by set-pieces or spectacles or momentary lack of interest or by the playhouse's other attractions.[43]

It is perhaps telling, then, that although we struggle to find the Theatre on the title page of any dramatic play and its neighbouring Curtain, the longest-lasting London playhouse, appears on only one (*Hector of Germany*, 1615), the print market does recognise the latter Shoreditch playhouse via a different kind of performance. The clown Robert Armin joined Shakespeare's Lord Chamberlain's Men some time early in the seventeenth century. Around this date, perhaps before or after joining, he released a jest-book of his stand-up comedy called *Quips upon Questions*.[44] The title page describes him in cod-Latin as "Clunnico de Curtanio Snuff," the Clown of the Curtain, Snuff. Here, the playhouse is used to advertise not the dramatic output of Armin's colleague Shakespeare but "play" of a different kind—clowning and improvisatory skits. The remainder of this chapter explores the way playhouses accommodated a wide range of such attractions for audiences, sometimes as discrete events and sometimes simultaneously.

Combat

In 1609, Thomas Dekker wrote a guide for "gallants," those who might be regarded as early modern "hipsters": young, fashionably dressed, and with disposable income; what Dekker elsewhere calls a "spangle-baby."[45] The satirical advice includes how one should "behave" in a playhouse. His instructions list an array of largely objectionable behaviour: manspreading on a stool on the stage, interrupting the actors, laughing in the middle of the most sombre tragedy. Although this tongue-in-cheek insight into playhouse behaviour is presumably exaggerated, it does (like all satire) reflect something of true practice. Individuals most certainly did sit on the stage and behave questionably, as dramatic prologues from the period make clear.[46]

One of the more telling rhetorical flourishes in Dekker's guide concerns activity that takes place within the playhouse. He tells receptive gallants, "Before the Play begins, fall to cards, you may win or lose (as *Fencers* do in a prize) and beat one another by confederacy."[47] This brief vignette gives a lively example of what you might see if you turned up to a playhouse half an hour or so before a dramatic play began. It also indicates the multiple forms of play that took place, sometimes simultaneously: *the* Play is one entertainment among other plays, including gambling at cards. Just as tellingly, Dekker's fencing analogy is not only, or in fact not at all, metaphorical. "Prize" is the name for a match played at fencing, and such prizes typically took place in playhouses. In one brief sentence, then, Dekker compasses three different forms of play equally at home in the fashionable gallant's playhouse.

Fencing is one of the most explicitly documented playhouse activities from the 1560s and 1570s to around 1590. A surviving manuscript book kept by the Masters of Defence (the society in charge of "approving" fencing qualifications) details numerous prizes played various venues—some in large outside areas such as Leadenhall or Greyfriars, and plenty of others at playhouses:

> Vallentyne Long played his provost's prize at the Curtain in Holywell the fifth day of August at three weapons: the long sword, the back sword and the sword and buckler. There played with him two Provosts, vid[elicet] Robert blisse and Androwe Bellow, And John Dewell who had a Provost's licence for that time. And so the said Valentine Long was admitted provost under Gregorye Grene / Master. 1582.
>
> [...]
>
> John Goodwen played his Master's prize the eighteenth day of May at the Bull in Bishopsgate street at three kind[s] of weapons [...]. 1579. [...]
>
> James Cranydge played his master's prize the 21 of November 1587 At the bellsavage without Ludgate [...].
>
> Edward Harvie played his provost's prize the five and twentieth day of August at the Theatre at three weapons [...][48]

There was a hierarchy of admission into the Masters of Defence, which began with the Scholar's Prize, moved up to the Provost's, and then to full admission (with the ability to train an apprentice) after the Master's prize.

Not only did these prizes take place in playhouses, but there were significant overlaps between fencing and other recreational pastimes and professions. Henry Naylor, master fencer and proprietor of three bowling alleys in the cloisters of the Blackfriars in the 1570s, went on to train the famous clown Richard Tarlton: an entry in 1587 recorded, "Mr tarlton was allowed a master the 22nd of October under henry nayllore in 1587," where he is described (as member of the playing company the Queen's Men) as "ordinary groom of her majesty's chamber."[49] Overlaps between fencing and acting or other dramatic performance are hardly surprising given the nature of dramatic performance on stage. Even most canonical and "classical" of dramatic plays from the period depended upon skill at game and sport, as well as on audience ability to recognise the intricacies of such skill. *Hamlet's* closing scenes hinge almost entirely upon a fencing match, for instance, a play form that gestures outside the drama to other playhouse attractions that often took place in the same space. Shakespeare emphasises how Hamlet's opponent Laertes had been trained in France, most likely in continental Italian fencing style, in which long rapiers and thrusting movements contrasted the older-fashioned English play (which tended towards heavier broad swords and play at sword and buckler).[50] Even dramatic performance, then, encompassed and necessitated other forms of expertise and relied on an audience's ability to "read" other play forms.

Fencing clearly drew crowds to playhouses, and orders from the London corporation sought to regulate the sport just as they regulated dramatic playing, especially during periods of plague: "no Fencers shall make any open Fences assemblies for playing of prizes or other like gathering together of the Queen's people."[51] The regulation of fencing points to both similarities and differences between playhouses in early modern England. Authorities recognised the differences between an outdoor playhouse and an indoor one and the concomitant dangers when it came to spreading infection. In 1582, the London corporation found itself in a "match" of its own with the nobleman Ambrose Warwick, after they forestalled his servant James Croft from playing a fencing prize at the Bull in Gracious Street (an inn playhouse that hosted playing and fencing, as noted in Chapter 1). The Mayor was concerned with the Bull as a venue, deeming it "somewhat too close for infection." He suggested Croft might instead fence in a space like the Leadenhall, or "lawfully [...] play at the Theatre or other open place out of the City."[52] It is difficult to read too much into these distinctions, but there is a clear implication that the Bull was a "close" and probably an indoor or very crowded sheltered space. The Theatre offered better hygiene as an open-air amphitheatre-style space. While these differences sharpen distinctions between indoor and outdoor playhouses when it comes to plague, perhaps the most salient point is that Warwick's servant *wanted* to play at the indoor venue, in the way so many of those entering the Masters of Defence had done before him. Indeed, just two years later, London's Alderman approved Valentine Long (recorded in the citation above at the Curtain for his earlier prize) "to play his Fence prize at the Sign of the Bull."[53] For individuals like Long, just as for his peers in the acting profession, moving between venues like the Curtain and the Bull was simply part of London's leisure industry: both were sites "to play," if in this instance at a different pastime than acting.

Playhouse combat was by no means, however, an exclusively London pastime. The Society of the Masters of Defence record several prizes taking place elsewhere, including Stamford (Lincolnshire) and Hertford (Hertfordshire),[54] as well as in Kent:

> 1568 [...] John Wootton played a certain prize at Canterbury in Kent with certain scholars / he did agree with the masters and so was admitted a Provost. [...]

> Willyam Mathewes played his master's prize at Canterbury the fifth day of
> June at four kind of weapons That is to say the long sword the back sword the
> sword and buckler and the rapier and dagger [...] 1583.[55]

There is no precise venue recorded for these performances, but given that spaces
such as the Leadenhall were sometimes used in London, one possibility would be
Canterbury's bullstake, discussed in Chapter 1 and above, which was large, paved,
draped with escutcheons, and ready with standings. Alternatively, prizes could have
taken place in a range of inns or yards, as we have seen. Examples from across the
country suggest that inns or alehouses were habitually used for combat. When King
James visited Lincoln in 1616, he went to an inn at the sign of the George "to see
a Cocking there." After the cockfight, the King went to another inn or alehouse
called "the Spreadeagle to see a Prize played there by a fencer of the City." After
the initial prize was fought, a member of the royal court challenged Lincoln's own
at the game, in which "the fencer & scholars of the City had the better [...]." The
rivalry resulted in a minor affray, seemingly at the encouragement of the King himself.[56] These regional examples suggest a similar combat culture to London, taking
place at drinking establishments and/or open market or gathering spaces.

Fencing exemplifies the way early modern play went beyond English professional dramatic companies. In London in the Elizabethan period, the sport was
markedly cosmopolitan. Fencers like Vincentio Saviolo and Rocco Bonetti were
well-known names, and when George Silver published his fencing manual in 1599,
he claimed to have known "three Italian Teachers of Offence in my time."[57] Bonetti
had opened a fencing school in Warwick Lane in around the 1570s, moving to a
new venue in the Blackfriars in the 1580s. The growing popularity of Italian fencing in England sparked controversy, debate, and even violence, rooted in nation-
alism. Silver relates an incident in which a man named Austen Bagger, "not standing
much upon his skill, but carrying the valiant hart of an Englishman," went upon a
joke with friends to fight Bonetti at "his house in the *Blackfriars*"; Bonetti "looking
out at a window, perceiving him in the street to stand ready [...] with all speed ran
into the street."[58] Bagger grievously injured the Italian, tripping and treading upon
him, and left him lying injured in the road. The fight contrasts Bonetti's refined foreign style and "two hand sword" to the "valiant" English heart—part of the contrast
between new delicate continental fencing styles and the heavy English approach.
The spectacular nature of this combat sport is therefore one touchpoint for issues
of immigration and national identity, played out, quite literally, in playhouses across
the country.

Fencing also raised questions about gender and masculinity, as Bagger's "valiant"
braggery makes abundantly clear. Sword-wearing was a badge of (generally gentlemanly or aristocratic) masculinity. It was circumscribed by so-called "sumptuary
laws," which restricted the length of a sword and dictated by degrees (such as
knight, baron, etc) who was permitted to own gilded rapiers or daggers. Early
modern society also defined appropriate clothing by gender, and swords were not
associated with female dress. Yet one prominent figure of early modern London

FIGURE 2.1 *The roaring girle. Or Moll Cut-Purse* (London, 1611). STC 17908.

Used by permission of the Folger Shakespeare Library under a Creative Commons Attribution-ShareAlike 4.0 International License.

flouted the sumptuary laws that circumscribed dress and appearance and remains even today visually aligned with the sword.

Mary Frith, also known as Moll Frith or Moll Cutpurse, was described in the period as a woman who dressed as a man. However, Moll's sexual identity and gender presentation was and is complex.[59] What is certain is the prejudice that attended such a perceived breach of decorum. Moll's supposed cross-dressing was the subject not only of gossip but of legal prosecution, going cap in hand with other criminal misdemeanours, including theft and burglary.[60] Moll was famous enough for Thomas Dekker and Thomas Middleton to write an eponymous play, *The Roaring Girl* (1611), in which the rapier-wielding Moll skilfully dresses down a leering man hoping for a tryst in Grey's Inn Fields. This astonishing scene captures one means of combatting (quite literally) early modern misogyny, accompanied by a *tour de force* speech. The ensuing fight prompts Moll's opponent, Laxton, to remark (perhaps knowing the skill of the actor), "Heart, I think I fight with a familiar, or the ghost of a fencer! She's wounded me gallantly."[61] "Ghost" was a synonym for an actor (and "familiar" acts here as another possible synonym, for both "performer" and for "ghost," as in a witch's familiar). This brief gloss on Moll's martial prowess therefore proves a metatheatrical nod to the overlaps between player, fencer, and performer. Is Laxton fighting an actor or a trained fencer or both? Laxton also recognises those moments of jeopardy and contest that attend almost any attempt to play-act violent sport, in which choreography threatens to slip into genuine competition. Playhouses, which hosted both serious prizes and fictional drama, doubtless blurred the lines between such distinctions for early modern audiences.

Moll's playhouse presence itself collapsed fiction and reality. During one performance in 1612, the real Moll Frith appeared on stage "in the public view of all the people there present in man's apparel & played upon her lute & sang a song."[62] Moll was in fact popularly and legally associated with such spaces; London's Consistory Court noted how Moll "frequented all or most of the disorderly and licentious places in the City as namely she hath usually in the habit of a man resorted to alehouses Taverns Tobacco shops & also to play houses."[63] Part of that "habit" included, at least in the popular and print imagination, swords or blades of some form—not only to pursue trade as a "cutpurse" but as part of the visual presentation that associates "the roaring girl" with the playhouse world. The famous woodcut image of Moll presents the sword as a phallic symbol of cross-dressing and a visual emblem of transgression.

FIGURE 2.2 *Paradoxes of defence*, by George Silver (London, 1599). STC 22554.

Fencing accordingly represents a key element of playhouse culture. Many early modern playhouse-goers visited the Theatre, the Curtain, or the Spreadeagle in Lincoln to watch a fencing prize. This may have been some people's primary engagement with these venues. Our framing of many early modern playhouse spaces has typically been via the playtext—itself distanced from the play event but recording in some way a small proportion of the drama that took place on stage. Fencing, like many other forms of combat, does not leave such textual afterlives. The records we have of them are indirect and partial—the book of the Society of the Masters of Defence, for instance, does not go far beyond 1590. Yet the Swan and the Rose were used for fencing prizes as late as the 1620s, even when these venues were no longer hosting dramatic plays.[64] These facts should trouble our sense that the playhouse was always or necessarily or primarily for drama. Valentine Long would have had a different understanding of what it meant "to play."

Animals

Ben Jonson's *Bartholomew Fair* (1614) was one of the earliest plays performed at the Hope playhouse. Its induction revels in its theatrical location, thanks to a terse exchange between a book-holder, carrying the playbook; a scrivener, equipped with Jonson's message to the audience; and the playhouse's Stage-Keeper. The latter is dismissed as one good "for what? Sweeping the stage? Or gathering up the broken apples for the bears within?", making explicit reference to the Hope's more-than-human performers.[65] The stage may be set for a stage play but animals are never far from the audience; the stage-direction vocabulary "within" playfully implies their presence just behind the tiring house or under the stage. Certainly, this was a playhouse designed from the outset to accommodate both human and animal players, with its stage-on-wheels retracting to allow space for bear-baitings. Jonson makes further reference to this multipurposeness by referring to its smell: "the place being as dirty as Smithfield," where the play is set, "and as stinking every whit."[66] As we have seen, the Hope sat on a spot home to three previous bear gardens, with kennels and animal pens in close proximity to its south. While the playhouse is unique among surviving evidence in explicitly building the activities of drama and animal blood sports into its architectural design, the combination of the two is not especially unusual. We have already seen how numerous playhouses of the period accommodated animal performance or sport. Moreover, the Globe, Rose, and Swan playhouses would also have shared the smells and sounds of the nearby animal pens. Contemporaries did not always see a fine distinction between theatrical playhouse and animal baiting arena, as the architectural affinities noted in Chapter 1 indicate. Animals were accordingly features of the playhouse family, both for performance and sport.

Bear-baiting and bull-baiting were games in which one or more dogs are set upon a bear or a bull chained to a post, in front of spectators, some of whom may also have had some form of allegiance or investment—like supporting a side or identifying with a local bear, bull, or dog.[67] Bull-baiting had long been a legal

FIGURE 2.3 Londinum florentissima Britanniae urbs, by Claes Visscher. GA795.L6.V5 1625 Cage.

Used by permission of the Folger Shakespeare Library under a Creative Commons Attribution-ShareAlike 4.0 International License.

requirement for butchers wishing to sell any meat, which had to be tenderised by baiting before it could enter the market for any use. However, the sport quickly became a leisure activity, especially when combined with bears, and by the early sixteenth century there was a nationwide appetite for baiting of both animals as commercial entertainment. The practice had spanned the country since at least the fourteenth century, and it also compassed all social standings. Everyone from field worker to prince would have known both bulls and bears well, lived beside them, and perhaps had some emotional or local connection to them. Angry neighbours issued lawsuits and complaints, in which they objected to frightening ursine movement across their private pathways or expressed irritation at the mundane "soiling" of public streets.[68] By the sixteenth century bears were an important part of national and regional identity. Many were famous: Harry Hunks, George Stone, Sackerson (who is referenced in Shakespeare's *Merry Wives of Windsor*). Many were also closely associated with particular English locations, such as Judith of Cambridge or Ned of Canterbury. These toponymic soubriquets suggest early regional fan cultures, explored at length in Chapter 4.

Thomas Dekker evokes the cruelty involved in baiting itself in his account of such an entertainment at Bankside in 1609. In his telling, the bear garden is a version of hell, in which "the bear (dragged to the stake) showed like a black rugged soul, that was Damned, and newly committed to the infernal Charle [churl?], the *Dogs* like so many *Devils*, inflicting torments upon it." Dekker reads in the spectacle an allegory for the poor man going to war against the rich (the dogs up against the "mighty" bear), but he also responds in a humane way to the cruelty, feeling sorry for the subsequent spectacle of "a blind *Bear* [...] tied to the stake," whipped by men "til the blood ran down his old shoulders." For Dekker, the sight prompted "pity," and recalled the "poor starved wretches," often homeless people, whipped as they were tied to posts in London "when they had more need to be relieved with food." Dekker's account finishes with the entrance of "an old Ape dressed up in a coat of changeable cullers (on horseback)," who rode around the "circuit with a couple of curs muzzled," barking at and chasing him.[69]

Dekker's analogies alone testify to the multiple elements involved in bear-baiting, particularly when concentrated in a playing space with a discrete audience. Even in this brief account there are three distinct activities: baiting, whipping of the blind bear, and then the ape on horseback. Such variation in animal cruelty (dressed up as sport) is confirmed by the only surviving playbill for bear-baiting on Bankside, dating from some time in the early seventeenth century (and quite possibly referring to the Hope):

> Tomorrow being Thursday shall be seen at the Beargarden on bankside a great Match played by the Gamesters of Essex who hath challenged all comers whatsoever to play 5 dogs at the single bear for 5 pounds and also to weary a bull dead at the stake and for your better content shall have pleasant sport with the horse and ape [and] whipping of the blind bear.
>
> *Viuat Rex*[70]

This public poster sets out the way the sport was advertised in London as well as giving insight into the practicalities involved—a "challenge" by a collective of Essex players, matches against both bears and bulls, and an ape and blind bear. The advertisement demonstrates the close affinity between baiting and playing, which was similarly advertised through public playbills. It also emphasises the combination of regionality and travel involved in the game: the "Gamesters of Essex" are important enough to be flagged by way of their home location, perhaps stoking London competition, while they have seemingly travelled south to get to the Bankside bear garden.

Although the game was widespread and popular, it is surprisingly difficult to find accounts of how exactly it was conducted. Evidence from Cheshire suggests that spectators held "staves" or staffs that they used to pull the dogs off the bear as appropriate.[71] Thomas Crosfield's diary entry from 1635 offers more systematic detail as to the procedures of baiting. He watched in the churchyard of St Clement, Oxford, which seemingly had a temporary playhouse structure that included chambers; his account therefore indicates something of the practice in playhouses or temporary arenas of all kinds:

> Seen a bull baiting in St Clement's where the manner is thus:
>
> 1. 1d a piece for every person that goes in & 2d in a chamber
> 2. the Bull master may strike the dogs if two set on at a time
>   1. The Dogs. 10. or 12 are brought chained into the yard, where tied their anger or courage such as to bite or break the chains they are tied with.
>   2. The Bull brought in with horns buttoned, & tied to the stake, walks about, the dogs one at once set on: if he catch him above collar, chiefly by the nose accounted victor./ after all have played over round they commonly have a second bout -.
>   3. In the throwing or tossing of the dogs often they are killed or maimed, but that to save them men run & catch them in the fall. & keep them back from the fierceness & eager onset, whereby otherwise they would be quite quashed, maimed or slain by the Bull that watcheth their onset.
>   4. If the bull be cunning he will never run away, but warily watch the very first onset of the dog, & he receives encouragement from his masters stroking of him.[72]

The prices set out by Crosfield match attendance at popular plays, which typically cost one pence entry with another pence for a chamber or private standing. His description also indicates the number of animals involved and the way the event was policed by the bear- or (in this case) bull-keeper, also known as bearwards or bullwards. In Dekker's description, those involved in setting forth and managing the game have an inherent theatricality; when men come on to whip the blind bear in Bankside, Dekker sees them as "a company of creatures" who "took the office of Beadles upon them."[73] Not only does their cruelty approximate that of the local officer with responsibility for the workhouse, but Dekker frames them as assuming an identity like actors in a performance.

Indeed, the baiting proper was occasionally accompanied by other ludic activities. Such moments remind us that animal baiting arenas and playhouses were often interchangeable and sometimes combined both theatrical and animal shows at the same time. German tourist Leopold von Wedel wrote probably the fullest description of a sixteenth-century performance at a bear-baiting arena. He recounts a visit in 1584 to Bankside, in which he vividly, if enigmatically, describes the multiple forms of play on offer:

> These dogs were made to fight singly with three bears, the second bear being larger than the first and the third larger than the second. After this a horse was brought in and chased by the dogs, and at last a bull, who defended himself

FIGURE 2.4 Woodcut from *Antibossicon*, by William Lilly. (London, 1521). STC 15606. Used by permission of the Folger Shakespeare Library under a Creative Commons Attribution-ShareAlike 4.0 International License.

bravely. The next was that a number of men and women came forward from a separate compartment, dancing, conversing and fighting with each other: also a man who threw some white bread among the crowd, that scrambled for it. Right over the middle of the place a rose was fixed, this rose being set on fire by a rocket: suddenly lots of apples and pears fell out of it down upon the people standing below. Whilst the people were scrambling for the apples, some rockets were made to fall down upon them out of the rose, which caused a great fright but amused the spectators. After this, rockets and other fireworks came flying out of all corners, and that was the end of the play.[74]

Von Wedel's summary raises questions about translation as well as of how to parse an unfamiliar culture and its practices. Yet his description is thorough if not entirely clear, and powerfully relates the dynamic, multimedia activities on display at these animal baiting arenas. His visit came the year after the previous bear garden had collapsed, resulting in several deaths and some public condemnations of the pastime in sermons.[75] He was therefore in a shiny new playing place, built as we saw in Chapter 1 with extra galleries and enlarged in a model related to the likes of the Curtain or the Theatre playhouses in Shoreditch.

In the absence of pretty much any other evidence of visitor experience in bear-baiting playing places, von Wedel's account defamiliarises "playing" for us today. His description and its translation beg the question, what exactly *was* a "play"? The event comprises not only a traditional baiting, but a performance made up of multiple participants, human and more-than-human, male and female. It was also furnished with extraordinarily elaborate props: a giant flower exploded by a firework, flying fruit, and audience involvement. The event sets out a radically participatory model of performance that makes no distinction between those involved in the "play" and those in the audience. This may well have been typical; we simply do not know exactly how often such shows occurred at animal baitings. It may be that dramatic activity (scripted or unscripted, immersive or presentational) was a standard part of animal sport.

Accordingly, von Wedel's account of Bankside in 1584 suggests a different reality for commercial playing spaces in London than that found in histories of Shakespearean playing companies. Performers need not belong to a male professional troupe. Here, for instance, "humans and animals are equivalent performers."[76] Indeed, from the visiting German's perspective, animal sport was in S.P. Cerasano's words "a choreographed, 'theatrical' event," that "changes quite radically our sense of the aesthetic orientation that drew the crowds to the Paris Garden."[77] In turn, not only are animals here afforded performative agency, but Clare McManus sees in the account a frank acknowledgement of female performance: "von Wedel's matter-of-fact description of his theatrical women does not suggest that they are exceptional [...] He simply accepts and notes their presence." The professional dramatic stage is an exception in wider early modern performance culture in its exclusion of female performers: "is it not 'the all-male stage' which is the real anomaly, the exception rather than the theatrical rule?"[78]

Animal performance helps break down the idea of the self-contained professional "theatre" itself, pointing beyond the amphitheatrical space deconstructed in Chapter 1 to a range of playing venues within the playhouse family. It was not only baiting that featured more-than-human performance. A collection of anecdotes and jokes relating to the career of Richard Tarlton preserves (doubtless with fictional flourishes) elements of the period's performance culture that go beyond staged drama. One such encounter at the Cross Keys playhouse and inn was with "a horse of strange qualities" owned by a man called Bankes. Tarlton had been playing with the Queen's Men at the Bell and entered the Cross Keys "to see fashions"; Banks told his horse, "go fetch me the veriest fool in the company," and the horse walked straight to Tarlton. In response, Tarlton asked Bankes to request of his horse, "bring me the veriest whore-master in the company." The horse promptly led his owner Bankes over to Tarlton.[79] The jest perhaps requires an Elizabethan sense of humour to appreciate fully, leaning on the moral disparagement and misogyny of the term "whoremaster," but the horse represents a distinguished actor in the skit. Its "strange qualities" recall the "Basehooke" of Norwich, also a performing creature. Seen through the "strange qualities" of animals, the Cross Keys playhouse becomes a site for improvised and more-than-human creativity, centring the agency of non-professional actors like Bankes and his horse.

The relationship between human and animal performance erodes distinctions between one type of playing space and another, pointing us to similarities rather than differences between theatrical and theatrically adjacent play venues. Edmund Gayton's recollections about the entertainment scene of early seventeenth-century London emphasise such erosion. In Gayton's picture of a lively play day, dissatisfied playgoers riot and almost dismantle the playhouse, before heading

> to the Bawdy houses [...] and instantly to the Banks side, where the poor Bears must conclude the riot, and fight twenty dogs at a time beside the Butchers, which sometimes fell into the service; this performed, and the Horse and Jack-an-Apes for a jig, they had sport enough that day for nothing.[80]

While this vision is satirical and hyperbolic, it does emphasise the fluidity of early modern leisure practices. The spectators' play journey collapses the walls between the playhouse and the bear-baiting arena and incorporates animals and humans in a fashion closely aligned with the eyewitness accounts of bear-baiting spectacles noted above. Rather than seeing activity in the bear garden as quite distinct from that of the "professional" playhouse, Gayton's memories, Bankes's horse, and von Wedel's eyewitness account use human–animal performance to emphasise the playhouse-ness of a range of sometimes overlapping venues. In each of these locations, drama and more-than-human play (and cruelty) sat alongside one another.

Tumbling

One of the earliest surviving dramatic plays associated with the commercial London playing companies, *The Rare Triumphs of Love and Fortune*, was performed at court before New Year in 1582 by the Lord Derby's Men.[81] Alongside it, "Sundry feats of Tumbling and activity were showed before her Majesty on New Year's Day at night by the Lord Strange his servants."[82] Lord Derby and Lord Strange were father and son, both part of the Stanley family. During this period, Strange patronised a company of tumblers or acrobats and his father a dramatic troupe. Just a few years later, Strange gave his name to a slightly different company, also focused on dramatic acting, which became one of the first long-term resident companies at a single play-house during their stint at the Rose in London. The Stanley family moved between dramatic acting and gymnastics both within a matter of days (at court) and over several years (in the life of Strange as a patron). Their court appearance in 1582 emphasises how "the faculty of playmakers" under the remit of the Master of the Revels Edmund Tilney was by no means solely theatrical. Historians have observed of the earlier sixteenth century that "playing" spanned a range of meanings and "might have included dancing, tumbling, clowning, juggling, fencing, mime and minstrelsy along with (or sometimes instead of) the declaiming of lines."[83] We have already seen, however, how such fluidity endured into and beyond the later Elizabethan period. A playing company was not always a dramatic troupe.

Inevitably (as with any playmaking under Tilney's authority) overlaps between acrobatics and drama were not confined to the court. Companies like Strange's and others, such as the Peadles (regularly paid by the royal treasurer in the early seventeenth century), performed publicly at defined playing places. The Stanley family were based in the northwest and had close connections to the city of Chester. The year after Strange's acrobats appeared at court, the churchman Christopher Goodman complained in a letter to the family about public performances of tumblers in the city (alongside bear-baitings and dramatic performance), noting that they played regularly.[84] It is not always easy to determine the precise location in which performances like these took place, but a surviving advertisement from Bristol in the 1630s suggests that inn or alehouse locations served as well for gymnastics as they did for plays and bear-baitings. This Bristol playbill was printed but preserved a blank space, in which someone penned in the venue for performance:

> At the *Rose in winestreet* this present day shall be shown rare dancing on the Ropes, Acted by his Majesty's servants, Wherein an Irish boy of eight years old doth vault on the high rope, the like was never seen: And one Maid of fifteen years of age, and another Girl of four years of age, do dance on the low Rope; And the said Girl of four years of age doth turn on the stage [...].[85]

These acrobatics took place in a venue just along from the inn called "the playhouse" on Wine Street, and the two locations may have been perceived in similar terms. This rare surviving example of a commercial tumbling advertisement with a named playing place situates tumbling and rope dancing in popular venues. It suggests that these play activities were as at home there as at court. More significantly, this instance proves beyond doubt the presence of women and girls on commercial stages showcasing extraordinary playing skills. Clare McManus identifies such rope-dancing displays as central to conceptions of femininity and bodily deportment; they find their way onto the commercial stage via boy actors' impersonations, and accordingly these activities were not and are not "rigidly gendered."[86] As with other modes of play discussed here, then, there were productive overlaps and exchanges between one performance genre and another.

Tumbling represents a significant influence from continental and Ottoman performance. By 1575, the Mayor of London Thomas Norton made unfavourable reference to the "unchaste, shameless, and unnatural tumbling of the Italian women" who were touring the country, along with male compatriots,[87] suggesting something of the conjunction of female and foreign performance. Lord Strange's interest in his own troupe of tumblers may have been "shaped at court and by the Kenilworth festivities in 1575, and Leicester's promotion of tumbling by touring Italians may also have influenced Ferdinando's [Strange's] patronage of acrobatic performers in his first troupe."[88] Indeed, numerous French, Italian, and Turkish performers toured England across the early modern period, bringing with them extraordinary skills and displaying inventive tricks. The French acrobat Peter Bromvill was awarded licence to perform at the Swan playhouse in 1600, granting him royal favour to show (in a typical phrasing) "feats of activity" at the venue.[89] More widely across England, Philip Butterworth observes,

> not only is 'an hongarian' recorded at Shrewsbury but French, Italian, and Turkish dancers on the rope are cited at Edinburgh, Newcastle, Norwich, and Bristol while Turkish, French, and Dutch tumblers and vaulters are recorded at Ipswich, Dover, and London.[90]

Such labelling is always down to an element of uncertainty, not least in a period when national or racial descriptors were often applied creatively. "Turk," for instance, "was a mutable word in early modern England, difficult to untangle from a range of associations with Muslims, the Ottoman imperial state, and English converts to Islam."[91] Its application would have evoked a range of associations for English spectators, from "military might and commercial potential" to the expectation of visual difference: "bodily modification and the turban" were "some of the primary markers of the 'Turk' in early modern England."[92] It is therefore "not inconceivable that such designations might have been adopted by some of the performers themselves in order to strengthen the perceived mysteriousness or publicity value of their performed feats."[93] In turn, however, McManus emphasises how such feats and attendant mystery or exoticism shaped early modern England's intertwined perceptions of femininity, performance, and race.[94]

Tumbling and acrobatics were also part of a wider popular investment in forms of "convivial entertainment, noise, spectacle and colour."[95] The curious example of an "Olympic Games" held in Cotswold, the brain child of a man called Robert Dover, initiated in 1612, demonstrates the broad appeal of games and gymnastics across the social scale. The Cotswold Games involved a range of sports and play, from throwing the sledge, to dancing, to musical playing, all under the banner of "Public merriments."[96] These activities explicitly involved "every sort of men, age, sex, degree," including "Country lasses […] rural Swains […] Lords, Ladies, Shepherds, Country people all."[97] This vibrant festival of sports and games testifies to a popular performance culture transcending (at least according to published poetic paeans) class and gender that endured throughout the sixteenth and seventeenth centuries. These games were politically charged, and the publication of a poetic collection celebrating them in the 1630s implicitly supported King Charles's programme of reviving traditional celebrations against those calling (in crude terms) for a more puritanical approach to festivity.

Nonetheless, the games were not merely a political experiment. They represent longstanding skills in and appetites for physical performance across the country. Dover's Olympics may, in turn, indicate some of the popular activities that occurred at the amphitheatrical playhouse in Shrewsbury's former quarry from the 1560s onwards, discussed in Chapter 1. Others also attempted to copy the model. In 1619, one John Adamson had built a playing place in the Gogmagog hills near Cambridge,

FIGURE 2.5 Second frontis picture of Cotswold Games from *Annalia Dubrensia* (London, 1636). STC 24954 copy 3.

in which he "purposed to have exhibited & used […] games for three weeks' space." However, authorities disliked the idea of the public gathering, and he was ordered to dismantle "all his booths which he hath builded."[98] Adamson's pop-up standings were designed for a range of sporting activities. His booths present parallels with Shrewsbury's "Theatre" and possibly suggest something of the built infrastructure of the Cotswold Olympics. The frontispiece to the poetic homage to the games depicts a range of built or erected structures, including tents and a castle-like edifice. These rural venues housed play of a different model to professional-drama-orientated London playhouses, but they invited spectatorship of and participation in a huge array of physical play. In such instances, tumbling and sporting endeavours were not limited by social status, gender, or notions of professionalism: playhouses for the people.

Improv

On 7 October 1614, crowds gathered at the Hope playhouse on Bankside to hear a "trial of wit."[99] The poet John Taylor (often known as the Water-poet, as he was by profession a Thames ferryman) had agreed to meet William Fennor (who called himself "The King's Majesty's Rhyming Poet") on the stage to exchange repartees in prose and verse: "[Taylor] to play a Scene in Prose, and [Fennor] to answer him in Verse."[100] The event did not go ahead as planned. "When the day came that the Play should have been performed, the house being filled with a great Audience, who had all spent their moneys extraordinarily," Fennor "Ran away & left [Taylor] for a *Fool*, amongst thousands of critical Censurers […] in a greater puzzle then the blind *Bear* in the midst of all her whip broath [broth]."[101] Both men had put down money for the event, and Taylor claimed he had lost a sizeable outlay of £20. The reason the show fell through depends on whom you ask. Taylor insisted that he lost face and reputation, left stuck alone on the stage, because Fennor simply failed to show up. Fennor, however, claimed he was blindsided, and that the rules of this exchange of wits were unfair: Taylor promised to advertise his "Challenge" to Fennor beforehand, but then went and published it in so "braving" a manner that the battle of wordplay was stacked in his favour. Fennor maintained, in any case, that he had been called away to visit his sick father. Both men call this planned but abortive rhyming challenge a "Play."

Their challenge at the Hope is another popular element of early modern entertainment at home in the playhouse: events made up of improvisation and extemporisation. Improvisation was a key part of any play, dramatic or otherwise, which frequently gave performers (especially comic ones) licence to adapt or react in the moment. The phrase "extempore performance" describes speeches given without preparation or pre-written composition. Early modern audiences were thrilled by those who were particularly talented at delivering witty and rhetorically sophisticated (and often bawdy or humorous) ad libbed performances. We have already encountered one of the most famous stage presences of the period, Richard Tarlton, who was known for such flights of fancy. Posthumously published "jest" books commemorated his talents at wordplay for many years after his death. Taylor's "challenge" at the Hope was modelled on the structure of such extemporisation, which sometimes positioned the clown as "an audience adversary," requiring, in turn, a series of themes or oppositional topics. One such set-up, for instance, "involved the clown's extemporal versification on a question or proposition, tending overwhelmingly toward the insult of specific spectators."[102]

Such improvisational wordplay was often a chief attraction of the playhouse and was even said to take up equal amounts of stage time to scripted drama. Richard Preiss's study of the clown emphasises its popularity by pointing to a range of examples in which spectators focused chiefly on extemporal performance.[103] Anthony Munday's "blast" against "theatres" in 1580 grouped "common plays, usual jesting, and rhyming extempore" in seemingly equal billing.[104] Preiss records how a spectator in Bristol noted in his commonplace book (a running notebook where individuals recorded quotations of moral or rhetorical interest) how:

> One Kendal a fool in a stage play in Bristol being merry acting the part of the vice, spoke extempore as followeth, in dispraise of the noble Britains:
>
> > if thou art a Britain born
> > it fits thee to wear the horn
>
> John Brittan, a prentice of one Thomas Dean of Bristol, his reply to Kendall: twice: as followeth:
>
> > A Britain's name I truly bear
> > I leave the horn for thee to wear:
> > The horn becomes the Saxons best
> > I kissed thy wife; suppose the rest.[105]

The improvisation on display here not only records an offhand exploration of national identity and historical mythology, alongside typical sexual innuendo; it also emphasises popular audience participation in extemporal entertainment. Like crowds at a bear garden absorbed into an immersive performance, spectators here engage the verbally inventive clown directly and in this case even better him with a withering and triumphantly patriotic riposte.

Improvisation need not be limited, however, to wordplay. Other audience engagement points to a range of ways in which either stage players or audience members performed extemporally. In Gloucester in 1602, the audience member John Wylmott

> present[ed] himself upon the […] stage, and said […] he could play better than any of those stage players, and offered to go upon the same stage and to take one of the same players instruments out of their hands and to have played upon it himself.[106]

(Perhaps predictably, the deponent in the court case relating this affair "did Judge the said Mr John wylmot to be overtaken with drink at that time [...].")[107]

A similar attempt to usurp professional players or musicians reached court in Cheshire in 1593, after the clerk William Hicock aggressively asked to borrow a treble violin outside of John Stil's tavern in Chester. The musician Richard Preston duly obliged, and the clerk "played very excellent well thereon."[108] In popular performances of music and songs that took place in streets, marketplaces, or drinking venues across England, including "rounds" or ballads (such as those found in cheaply printed and widely available broadsides), collective or group participation was central. The soundscape of early modern England's leisure industry was therefore also punctuated by (sometimes skilful) improvisation. The practice may even have been built into more formal musical performance, like those discussed in the following section, if we are to accept that "the most salient characteristics" of early music "were improvisation and spontaneity."[109]

Many of these instances blur the lines between "professional" performer and the observer or even what we might now call the amateur. Certain forms of improvisation depended not only on playfully adversarial relationships between performer and audience but actively transformed audience members into performers. At the Bull playhouse in London, for instance, Tarlton was in the midst of performing on stage when an audience member in the gallery threw an apple at him. The fruity interruption prompted Tarlton to reel off a witty rhyme at heckler's expense.[110] The apple-thrower seated in a gallery or Hicock's musical performance in and outside a tavern in Chester break down boundaries between spectator and spectacle. Clowning depended upon the overlapping of these areas, as did the likes of animal performance on the Bankside, where audience member and performer became (in von Wedel's eyes) indistinguishable. At the same time, improvisational events like Taylor and Fennor's failed "Challenge" demonstrate an appetite not just for impromptu action but also for planned extemporising. Both such forms position the playhouse as a space of structured but unscripted performance.

Improvisation therefore opens play up beyond the boundaries of the professional performer, and in doing so it provided platforms for those excluded from English dramatic companies. "Heckling" or interrupting performers initiated an improvisatory exchange that allowed any audience member, man, woman, or child, to shape a performance event. More structured improvisation, as recorded in texts, often depended on female performance. *Tarlton's Jests* records numerous instances in which the clown's wife initiated or organised the extemporising:

> *Tarlton* being merrily disposed, as his wife and he sat together, he said unto her, *Kate* answer me to one question without a lie, and take this crown of gold: which she took on condition, that if she lost, to restore it back again. Quoth *Tarlton,* am I a Cuckold or no *Kate?* Whereat she answered not a word, but stood silent: notwithstanding he urged her many ways: *Tarlton* seeing she would not speak, asked his gold again: why quoth she, have I made any lye?

no, says *Tarlton:* why then, goodman fool, I have won the wager: *Tarlton* mad with anger, made this Rhyme:

> As women in speech can revile a man,
> So can they in silence beguile a man.[111]

Tarlton and his wife ran an inn in London, and the numerous references to her behaviour suggest a deliberate outward show that situates her as an equal performer. In this anecdote, they are sat together (quite possibly in an inn), and the compiler of the jest book frames Kate's contribution as of equal wit to her husband's. Her performance extends beyond spoken improvisation, depending on the bodily pose of "standing" silent, while her punchline combines the physical and rhetorical comedy associated with professional Elizabethan clowns. Indeed, elsewhere in the collection, Kate is instrumental as a foil for Tarlton, prompting or setting up jokes as though in a double act. The ad hoc nature of improvisational performances both in and out of the playhouse—from a mystical horse to marital jests—depended upon theatrical agency and invention beyond the professional male performer.

As well as discrete improvisatory events, playhouses accommodated ad hoc invention within and around scripted dramatic performance. Rarely, but occasionally, these were preserved in published playtexts themselves. *The Rare Triumphs of Love and Fortune* records the dramatic licence extended to its clownish character, Lentulo:

> Enter Lentulo with a Ring in his mouth, a Marigold in his hand, and a fair suit of apparel on his back: after he hath a while made some dumb show, Penulo cometh running in with two or three other.[112]

This fascinating stage direction indicates the extratextual play required of performers. It is difficult to tell whether or not this describes what has already been seen on stage or whether it records instructions directed at the actor—an issue that attends almost all early modern stage directions, which are usually limited and sometimes seem directed at a subsequent reader rather than the playhouse performer.[113] Either way, Lentulo's dumb show sets up an improvisatory scene in the midst of the play, structured by the surrounding narrative and most immediately by the physical props used to guide the actor's performance. Other examples of actorly licence are detectable in printed "etceteras"; Christopher Marlowe's *Doctor Faustus* provides a well-known example:

> ROBIN. I, a goblet? Rafe, I, a goblet? I scorn you, and you are but a etc.[114]

Such moments appear in other texts, too, where they act as what Stephen Purcell calls "textual cues for improvisation."[115] Laurie Maguire describes the etcetera as a mark or cipher that "can embody the body and the bawdy," and while it may record omissions (for reasons of censorship, for instance), it also serves to "invite the actor to supply his own dialogue or noise," as "a textual moment which gestures beyond the text—whether in prose or in performance."[116] Each of these instances is complicated by its recording as and via text. Scholars have noted how improvisation seems to become increasingly textualised and scripted over the later sixteenth and early seventeenth centuries, transmuting extemporisation into textual prescription.[117] But these moments nonetheless do record a commonplace element of early modern play: "remembering," as well as "simulating" (in Purcell's formulation), improvisation.[118]

In all these examples, play in the playhouse goes beyond the playtext. Improvisation characterises all forms of performance, but it also appealed to audiences in its own right, drawing thousands (in Taylor's estimate) to a playhouse. Actorly extemporisation in these moments comes close to fencing or animal baiting; it contains elements of choreography, but is always subject to the unknown, the ad hoc, the interruption, or the unexpected outburst. The parallels between combat and early modern improvisation extend to its adversarial nature. Competition on stage and friction between audience and performer was crucial to bravura displays of wit or jokes at another's expense. Taylor tellingly calls the planned event at the Hope a "*Bear-garden* banquet of dainty conceits,"[119] while his initial provocation to Fennor is described as a "challenge"—the precise word used in the surviving bear garden advertisement to those brave enough to compete. Taylor's metaphor refers not only to the playhouse's equal function as an animal arena but draws actorly improvisation into line with combative sport. Here, scripted drama is put aside to accommodate what Taylor and Fennor identify as a different kind of "Play," which unites many of the ludic elements described in earlier sections of this chapter—a coming together of wordplay and swordplay, clause and claws.

Music and Dancing

In 1612, the Middlesex General Sessions of the Peace issued an order "for Suppressing of Jigs at the end of the Plays":

> by reason of certain lewd jigs, songs and dances used and accustomed at the playhouse called The Fortune in Goulding Lane, diverse cutpurses and other lewd and ill-disposed persons in great multitudes do resort thither at the end of every play, many times causing tumults and outrages.[120]

This order presents a fascinating picture of audience-goers flocking to the playhouse, not to hear *Hamlet* or *Doctor Faustus* but to enjoy the dance that rounded out the entertainment (which was itself characterised by improvisation). It raises as many questions as it answers: did these "lewd and ill-disposed persons" pay for entry to the playhouse simply to enjoy these songs and dances, or was it free to get in once the dramatic show had come to a close? Where might they have been drinking before they arrived at the playhouse? These are issues picked up in Chapter 3, but here it is important to note how popular "jigs, songs and dances" were among audiences "accustomed" to seeing them at the playhouse. Like improvisation, and as an expression of it, they provided attraction in their own right as well as furnishing staged drama with added forms of play.

Each of the playhouse types explored in Chapter 1 habitually hosted music and dance in a variety of formats. Amphitheatrically styled spaces in London like the Fortune, as well as touring spots in the country visited by professional troupes, generally combined dramatic performance with musical accompaniment, not least as part of plays themselves. Drummers and trumpeters found regular employment in such companies, while dramatic plays frequently call for music or instrumental accompaniment in stage directions or by characters' speech.[121] Theatrical music developed along with the practices of different early modern commercial playhouses: while adult companies typically used the jig to conclude plays, indoor-performing children's companies often used "instrumental and vocal interludes before and during performances," and "inter-act music was also gradually adopted by the adults after 1608."[122] These elements were present not only in London playhouses but across the country—both when companies from the capital went on tour and also within a variety of local performance spaces (as evidenced by the audience member in Gloucester attempting to wrest an instrument from a player's hand in the early 1600s). Playhouses were necessarily multimedia, and music and dance were fundamental elements of any play-goer's experience.

Recent studies have argued for the importance of music in structuring and making sense of the drama itself, suggesting playing companies used it as a tool to shape audience responses and prompt active participation.[123] Moreover, some commercial playing traditions were especially associated with musicality, not least children's companies, whose skill sets brought together choir singing and acting. For instance, early London companies like the Children of the Chapel Royal and the Children of Paul's were "shaped by the practices of continental European theater, and insular ballad and song traditions."[124] As with other forms of play that can escape the textual record, surviving evidence of playhouse musicality is patchy (even in printed plays); often, song lyrics or music circulated separate to the play itself.[125] Their textual-physical detachment suggests something of the way music and drama were so often united as live play forms, but it also indicates that they were equally appreciated separately. Play forms in the playhouse operated interchangeably and simultaneously, but their manifold sub-elements also had cultural currency of their own within and beyond the playhouse.

Outside of the professional dramatic company, many towns and cities sponsored a company of "waits," or musicians (named after the oboe-like instrument that used to be central to their music-making). They too were "players" in the properly capacious sense of the term. While they performed at the houses of nobility or at civic functions and events, they also appeared in popular commercial venues. Canterbury's Chequers Inn (made famous by Chaucer's pilgrims) and Crown Inn, for instance, were home to performances by the city's waits in the early seventeenth century.[126] As early as 1505, the Red Lion Inn on the High Street was host to the King's minstrels.[127] Musical performance thereby accompanied both entertainment of and by the city elite, but it also enlivened more accessible alehouse spaces. Elsewhere in Kent, for instance, the alehouse keeper Tymothie Ingester was punished for keeping a garland "with a minstrel playing" during sermon time in 1600.[128] Bristol offers particularly rich evidence for the musicality of such commercial playing spaces. Christopher Marsh's study of the social place of music in early modern England notes that the city had a remarkably high rate of instrument ownership, including examples as early as 1550 in which an inventory records viols in the possession of an innkeeper.[129] By the time the playhouse in Wine Street was in operation in the following century, its proprietor Nicholas Woolfe owned two virginals. In his manor of Dulwich near London, the actor and play entrepreneur Edward Alleyn himself owned and repaired numerous lutes, recorded in his account book over a decade or so from 1617. These examples from men deeply invested in playhouses and their legacy evidence an alignment of theatrical and musical cultures (further explored in Chapter 5).

The kind of jigs sometimes performed at the end of staged drama were also matched by a popular dancing culture across England. As with fencing, the pastime generated a sub-industry of instruction and performance. A pamphlet written in 1579 described what it might be like to visit a dancing school in London for the first time:

> When we were come into the school: the Musicians were playing and one dancing of a Galliard, and even at our entering he was beginning a trick as I remember of sixteens or seventeens, I do not very well remember but wonderfully he leaped, flung and took on.[130]

Such a dancing school could be found among the bowling alleys, fencing school, and playhouse of the Blackfriars (discussed at length in the Chapter 4). But one need not visit London to see the commercial profits made from dance. Waits like those described above sometimes expanded beyond music to dance instruction. Chester provides some of the richest evidence about popular singing and dancing in commercial contexts thanks to the lively Cally family—a dynasty of popular musicians and dancers, eventually employed as the city's official musicians. One of the family, Robert, was up until four in the morning one day in April 1612, teaching Margery Waterson to dance, and they "stayed dancing one hour."[131]

Very often playing venues hosted a general combination of such music, dance, and celebration. We hear of them most typically when they do so at illicit hours (such as late at night or during sermon time) and so become subject to local policing, thereby surviving in the period's plentiful legal records. They indicate where the likes of Robert Cally and Margery Waterson might strut their stuff: in Cheshire, alehouse keepers like William Tomson were punished for keeping piping, dancing, and general revelling in their venues.[132] Legal citations for these activities underpinned a generalised sense of play experienced at the many houses of leisure, in the broadest sense, that characterised the recreational world of early modern England.

Play beyond Performance

The topics discussed above broadly concern types of performative play encountered by early modern playhouse-goers. Yet playhouses were not exclusively concerned with performance. Thomas Dekker indicates the wider gaming environments of the playhouse when he refers to play at cards taking place on the stage by spectators. Provincial venues like Jacob Abadham's in Suffolk, discussed in Chapter 1, were described as "playhouses" because they (like numerous others cited in the county's Quarter Sessions) hosted "playing & suffer[ed] playing" in their houses.[133] These indictments typically refer to tabling (like backgammon), carding, or dicing and indicate a widespread culture of participatory recreation that centred on gambling. The well-travelled William Sampson, who had lived at London, Bristol, and Wolverhampton, moved to Chester in the 1580s, where his testimony at a Quarter Session's hearing in 1585 maps one way in which alehouses served as playhouses. He told the court he dined with his wife at five o'clock before departing to Widow Warmingham's alehouse "to pass away the time." While there, he ate and then "fell to play and then [...] [Mr] Ince and he played at the cards for ale and apples for 2 hours space."[134]

The commercial playing industry was therefore framed and received in legal terms by overlaps between different types of public leisure: "pro- and antitheatrical debates of the time were similar to the general debates about which games should be lawful and which should not,"[135] including proclamations dating back to Henry VIII's reign and earlier on activities including bowling and tennis playing. But conceptual relationships between performance and gaming were not limited to top-down restrictions and regulation. Gina Bloom argues that playhouses were "built right next to gaming establishments," making them geographically related.[136] Indeed, in his "survey" of the city of London (describing its historical and present character) first published in 1598, John Stowe characterises areas by their clustering of various "play" venues. The area north of Moorgate, which led to Shoreditch playhouses, was by the turn of the century "of late years inhabited (for the most part) by Bowyers, Fletchers, Bow-string makers and such like, now little occupied; Archery giving place to a number of bowling Allies, and Dicing houses, which in all places are increased, and too much frequented."[137] Yet as we have seen, venues were not always neatly distinguished by their specific offerings. Theatres often hosted cardplay, just as taverns sometimes hosted dramatic performance.

Evidence for every playing venue in this period speaks to their wider commercial place within the service and leisure industries. For instance, amphitheatre to tavern supplied visitors with food and drink. In bear-baiting arenas, "fruits, such as apples pears and nuts, according to the season, are carried about to be sold, as well as ale and wine."[138] Archaeological digs in London confirm that this contemporary tourist's observation was true of all the theatrical sites of Bankside and Shoreditch.[139] The Theatre was adjoined by a former brewhouse of some ongoing new use (perhaps for selling goods or food), Henslowe's Rose was related to his erstwhile partner John Cholmeley's drinking establishment, and inn playing spaces were connected by their very nature to the food and drink industry. Alongside food and drink, hawkers sold other items, such as books or ballads, while visitors were offered other paid services, including sex work.[140] Indeed, while playhouses were not (despite the protestations of antitheatrical preachers and pamphlet writers) defined by their criminality, they were clearly sites that facilitated a range of both licensed and unlicensed commerce. These, then, were sites of extensive business possibility—a point explored in more depth in Chapter 5.

The uses of "play" to describe activity in the many commercial leisure spaces across England emphasises the fluidity of the early modern English playhouse, which hosted a multitude of recreational possibilities. A play could describe a game of bowling, a "course" at bear-baiting, or an extemporal battle of wits. These venues were therefore not solely the homes of aristocratically or royally patronised professional theatre troupes. By looking beyond the male company actor, we see the many elements of commercial play dependent on the skill and agency of performing women, on the exploitation and unpredictability of animals, or on the internationalism and cosmopolitanism that influenced and underpinned England's entertainment scene.

Perhaps unsurprisingly, the forms described in this chapter are not exhaustive. The period had a vibrant puppetry scene, for instance, and enjoyed displays of ingenious technological curiosities.[141] Yet the subheadings in this chapter indicate the range of activity regularly offered in commercial play venues, not as an "add-on" to dramatic performance but often as an end in itself. The public regulation issued by Middlesex in 1612 states that numerous visitors flocked to the playhouse after the drama was finished to enjoy jigs. When put into context with the other activities discussed here, this order should remind us that early modern society did not see playhouses through the lens of the print market (with printed plays as their predominant surviving textual witnesses), nor always through more modern interests in "literary" or "theatrical" expression. These were always vibrant, multipurpose sites, which drew people to them for a multitude of reasons. Chapter 3 explores some of the other draws to these venues and their environs and the journeys that accompanied them.

Notes

1 See Clare McManus's emphasis on the "broad, varied world of performance," and observation "that Renaissance theatrical culture was populated by both men and women" (p. 785) in her critique of the "All-Male Stage," "Women and English Renaissance Drama: Making and Unmaking 'The All-Male Stage,'" *Literature Compass* 4/3 (2007): 784–96. See also: Clare McManus, *Women on the Renaissance Stage: Anna of Denmark and Female Masquing in the Stuart Court* (Manchester: Manchester University Press, 2002); Sophie Tomlinson, *Women on Stage in Stuart Drama* (Cambridge: Cambridge University Press, 2005).

2 David Galloway, *Records of Early English Drama: Norwich*, ed. David Galloway (Toronto: University of Toronto Press, 1984), p. 115.

3 2.2.27–30. *The Tempest, The Norton Shakespeare*, eds Stephen Greenblatt et al., 3rd ed. (London: Norton, 2016): 3215–66. For race and postcolonial readings, see the helpful

critical overviews in: Brinda Charry, "Recent Perspectives on *The Tempest*," *The Tempest: A Critical Reader*, eds Alden T. Vaughan and Virginia Mason Vaughan (London: Bloomsbury, 2014): 61–92; and Virginia Mason Vaughan, "The Critical Backstory: "What's Past Is Prologue,'" *The Tempest: A Critical Reader*, eds Alden T. Vaughan and Virginia Mason Vaughan (London: Bloomsbury, 2014): 13–38.

4 See, as a selection of works, Surekha Davies, *Renaissance Ethnography and the Invention of the Human: New Worlds, Maps and Monsters* (Cambridge: Cambridge University Press, 2016); Kim F. Hall, *Things of Darkness: Economies of Race and Gender in Early Modern England* (Ithaca: Cornell University Press, 1998); Ania Loomba, *Shakespeare, Race, and Colonialism* (Oxford: Oxford University Press, 2002); Ania Loomba and Jonathon Burton eds, *Race in Early Modern England: A Documentary Companion* (Basingstoke: Palgrave Macmillan, 2007); Arthur L. Little, *Shakespeare Jungle Fever: National-Imperial Re-Visions of Race, Rape, and Sacrifice* (Stanford: Stanford University Press, 2000); Joyce Green MacDonald, *Women and Race in Early Modern Texts* (Cambridge: Cambridge University Press, 2010); Ayanna Thompson, ed., *The Cambridge Companion to Shakespeare and Race* (Cambridge: Cambridge University Press, 2021); Sydnee Wagner, "Racing Gender to the Edge of the World: Decoding the Transmasculine Amazon Cannibal in Early Modern Travel Writing," *Journal for Early Modern Cultural Studies* (spec. issue on Early Modern Trans Studies, eds Simone Chess, Colby Gordon, and Will Fisher) 19.4 (2019): 137–55.

5 Laurie Johnson has suggested, in a Twitter exchange, it might refer to "bay shuck," with "shuck" meaning "devil" or "dog." Others pointed out the "bay" is a description of horse colour coat "(Brandon Christopher), that "shough" is used in Macbeth in reference to a dog or cur (James Wallace), and that it could be a twisted form of the term "basilisk" (Derek Dunne). Twitter.com; @callanjd March 22 2021, 10.48AM and replies.

6 C66/1606 m.34, n.4, MS, The National Archives, Kew, London.

7 Richard Dutton, *Mastering the Revels: The Regulation and Censorship of English Renaissance Drama* (Basingstoke: Macmillan, 1991), p. 116.

8 Callan Davies, Andy Kesson, and Lucy Munro. "London Theatrical Culture, 1560–1590," *Oxford Research Encyclopedia of Literature*, 28 Jun. 2021. Online. Accessed 9 Jul. 2021.

9 *REED Norwich*, p. 165.

10 LM 413/1-414, c.1580s, MS, Surrey Historical Centre, Woking, UK.

11 MS 05090/1 fo. 41★, MS, London Metropolitan Archives, London.

12 Richard Preiss has queried the idea that a play is synonymous with text by exploring other forms of "organizing agency of the theatrical event", *Clowning and Authorship in Early Modern Theatre* (Cambridge: Cambridge University Press, 2014), pp. 5–6.

13 Glynne Wickham, *Early English Stages*, Vol. 2. 1963 (London: Routledge, 2002): 32. Lawrence Clopper has shown how play encompassed a range of activities drawn together by the flexibility of the term from the medieval period onwards, in *Drama, Play, and Game: English Festive Culture in the Medieval and Early Modern Period* (Chicago: University of Chicago Press, 2001).

14 Erika Lin, "Festivity," *Early Modern Theatricality*, ed. Henry S. Turner (Oxford: Oxford University Press, 2013): 212–29.

15 Tom Bishop, "Shakespeare's Theater Games," *Journal of Medieval and Early Modern Studies* 40.1 (2010): 66.

16 David Lewis, "Buttermarket," *Canterbury Historical and Archaeological Society*, www.canterbury-archaeology.org.uk/buttermkt/4590809461. Online. Accessed 11 Jun. 2021. See also David Shaw, "A Military Guard for the Canterbury Playhouse in 1744," https://djshaw.blog/2017/10/29/a-military-guard-for-the-canterbury-playhouse-in-1744/. Online. Accessed 11 Jun. 2021.

17 William Shakespeare, *An excellent conceited tragedie of Romeo and Iuliet* (London, 1597).

18 Shakespeare, *The most excellent and lamentable tragedie of Romeo and Iuliet* (London, 1609).

19 For discussion of plays in print, see (as a selection) Lukas Erne, *Shakespeare and the Book Trade* (Cambridge: Cambridge University Press, 2013); Alan B. Farmer and Zachary Lesser, "The Popularity of Playbooks Revisited," *Shakespeare Quarterly* 56 (2005); Andy Kesson and Emma Smith eds, *The Elizabethan Top Ten: Defining Print Popularity in Early Modern England* (Farnham: Ashgate, 2013).

20 Aaron Pratt, "Printed Playbooks, Performance, and the 1580s Lag," *Forum*, ed. Andy Kesson, *Shakespeare Studies* 45 (2017): 51–9. p. 53. See also Andy Kesson, "Playhouses, Plays, and Theater History: Rethinking the 1580s", Forum, ed. Andy Kesson, *Shakespeare Studies* 45 (2017): 19–40. p. 22.

21 For an overview of repertory analysis, see wider special issue and Tom Rutter, "Introduction: The Repertory-Based Approach," *Early Theatre* 13.2 (2010): 121–32.

22 See Chapter 4.

23 Quoted in Siobhan Keenan, *Travelling Players in Shakespeare's England* (Basingstoke: Palgrave MacMillan, 2002), p. 149.

24 For more on professional player connections to their playhouses, see William Ingram, *The Business of Playing* (Ithaca: Cornell University Press, 1992).

25 REPS 21 fo 10r, COL/CA/01/01/023, MS, London Metropolitan Archives, London.

26 Lawrence Manley and Sally-Beth MacLean, *The Lord Strange's Men and Their Plays* (New Haven: Yale University Press, 2014), p. 63.

27 PC 2/14, 11 May 1586, pp. 83–4, MS, The National Archives, Kew, London.

28 PC 2/19, 23 June 1592, pp. 414–5, MS, The National Archives, Kew, London.

29 *Records of Early English Drama: Cumberland, Westmorland, Gloucestershire*, eds Audrey Douglas and Peter Greenfield (Toronto: University of Toronto Press, 1986), pp. 306–7; pp. 288–9.

30 Callan Davies, Andy Kesson, and Lucy Munro. "London Theatrical Culture, 1560–1590," *Oxford Research Encyclopedia of Literature*, 28 Jun. 2021. Online. Accessed 9 Jul. 2021.

31 Scott McMillin and Sally-Beth MacLean, *The Queen's Men and their Plays* (Cambridge: Cambridge University Press, 1998), p. 125.

32 Stephen Gosson, *School of Abuses* (London, 1579), C7v.

33 Lucy Munro, "Children's Companies and the Long 1580s," Forum, ed. Andy Kesson, *Shakespeare Studies* 45 (2017): 97–105. p. 104.

34 Richard Preiss, *Clowning and Authorship in Early Modern Theatre* (Cambridge: Cambridge University Press, 2014), p. 3.

35 *English Professional Theatre, 1530–1660*, eds Glynne Wickham, Herbert Berry, and William Ingram (Cambridge: Cambridge University Press, 2000), p. 343.

36 Edmund Gayton, *Pleasant Notes upon Don Quixote* (London, 1654), Mmm3r.

37 Jenny Sager, *The Aesthetics of Spectacle in Early Modern Drama and Modern Cinema: Robert Greene's Theatre of Attractions* (Basingstoke: Palgrave MacMillan, 2013), p. 141.

38 S. P. Cerasano, "Must the Devil Appear? Audiences, Actors, Stage Business," *A Companion to Renaissance Drama*, ed. Arthur Kinney (Oxford: Blackwell, 2004): 193–211. p. 198.

39 Thomas Nashe, *Pierce Penilesse his supplicacion to the diuell* (London, 1592), H2r.

40 Sager, *The Aesthetics of Spectacle*, p. 9.

41 See Tracey Hill, *Pageantry and Power: A Cultural History of the Early Modern Lord Mayor's Show* (Manchester: Manchester University Press, 2010).

42 John Kerrigan, *Revenge Tragedy: Aeschylus to Armageddon* (Oxford: Oxford University Press, 1996), p. 4.

43 These ideas were first set out on the Before Shakespeare website: Callan Davies, "Losing the Plot: Audiences, Scraps of Performance, and Selective Participation," 6 April 2018 (www.BeforeShakespeare.com). Online. Accessed 10 Nov. 2021.

44 *Quips upon Questions* (London, 1600).

45 Thomas Dekker, *The guls horne-booke* (London, 1609), E2r; *Satiromastix* (London, 1602), E3r.

46 The prologue to Ben Jonson's *The Devil Is an Asse* bemoans those who force actors to "act, / Incompasse of a cheese-trencher," i.e. in a very small circle, and "knocke us o'the elbowes," and plead for "room" and attention (disapproving of exactly the behaviour lampooned by Dekker). *The Devil Is an Asse* (printed with *Bartholomew fayre*) (London, 1631), N2r.

47 Dekker, E4r.

48 Sloane 2530 fo. 12r; fo. 3r; fo. 7r; fo. 11r, MS, British Library, London.

49 Sloane 2530, 6r.

50 For more on these styles, see Ian Borden, "The Blackfriars Gladiators: Masters of Fence, Playing a Prize, and the Elizabethan Stuart Theater," *Inside Shakespeare: Essays on the Blackfriars Stage*, ed. Paul Menzer (Selingsgrove: Susquehanna University Press, 2006): 132–55.

51 "A proclamacion to auoyde assemblies this tyme of infection," 1578, at JORS 20, 07 Nov. 1572–1 Aug. 1579. MS. COL/CC/01/01/020–21. London Metropolitan Archives, London, fo. 432.

52 24 July 1582; Remembrancia 1, COL/RMD/PA/01/001, London Metropolitan Archives, London, 384.

53 REPS 21, 05 Nov. 1583–22 Oct. 1588. MS. COL/CA/01/01/023, London Metropolitan Archives, London, f.111v.

54 Sloane 2530, 9r, 10r.

55 British Library Sloane MS 2530, fo. 9r; fo. 3r.

56 *Records of Early English Drama: Lincolnshire*, Vol. 1, ed. James Stokes (Toronto: University of Toronto Press, 2009), pp. 213–4.

57 George Silver, *Paradoxes of Defence* (London, 1599), I4v.

58 Silver, *Paradoxes*, K1r.

59 For exploration of trans identity and Moll Cutpurse in performance, see the *Engendering the Stage* project (http://engenderingthestage.humanities.mcmaster.ca).

60 See the summary of Mary Frith's life and its relationship to her fictional persona by Lauren Liebe at "Mary Frith, Moll Cutpurse, and the Development of an Early Modern Criminal Celebrity," *Journal of Early Modern Studies* 10 (2021): 233–48.

61 *The Roaring Girl*, 3.1.125–6. *English Renaissance Drama: A Norton Anthology*, eds David Bevington et al. (London: Norton, 2002): 1371–451.

62 Paul Mulholland, "The Date of *The Roaring Girl*," *Review of English Studies*, n.s., 28 (1977): 18–31. p. 31.

63 Mulholland, p. 31.

64 *English Professional Theatre*, p. 435; p. 450 (see records in Sir Henry Herbert's office book, now lost but noted by Edmond Malone).

65 *Bartholomew Fair*, Induction ll. 50–1, *English Renaissance Drama: A Norton Anthology*, eds David Bevington et al. (London: Norton, 2002): 969–1065.

66 Induction ll. 157–8.

67 See the Box Office Bears project (www.boxofficebears.com) for research on the game, its wide social reach, and different forms of historical analysis (from documents to animal DNA). For background and wider reading on bear-baiting, see Erica Fudge, *Perceiving*

Animals: Humans and Beasts in Early Modern English Culture (Basingstoke: Macmillan, 2000); Andreas Höfele, *Stage, Stake, and Scaffold: Humans and Animals in Shakespeare's Theatre* (Oxford: Oxford University Press, 2011).

68 *Records of Early English Drama: Lancashire*, ed. David George (Toronto: University of Toronto Press, 1991), pp. 97–8; *Records of Early English Drama: Kent*, ed. James M. Gibson, Vol. 1 (Toronto: University of Toronto Press, 2002), p. 233.

69 Thomas Dekker, *Worke for armorours* (London, 1609), B1v-2r.

70 MSS 2, Article 041, Dulwich College Archive, Dulwich, London.

71 *Records of Early English Drama: Cheshire (including Chester)*, Vol. 1, eds Elizabeth Baldwin, Laurence M. Clopper, and David Mills (Toronto: University of Toronto Press, 2007), p. 20.

72 *Records of Early English Drama: Oxford*, Vol. 1, eds John R. Elliott Jr, Alan H. Nelson, Alexandra F. Johnston, and Diana Wyatt, (Toronto: University of Toronto Press, 2004), p. 535.

73 Dekker, B2r.

74 Gotfried von Bülow. "Journey through England and Scotland Made by Lupold von Wedel in the Years 1584 and 1585," *Transactions of the Royal History Society* n.s. 9 (1895): 223–70. p. 230.

75 John Field, *A Godly Exhortation* (London, 1583).

76 McManus, "Women and English Renaissance Drama," p. 786.

77 S.P. Cerasano, "The Master of the Bears in Art and Enterprise," *Medieval and Renaissance Drama in England* 5 (1991): 195–209. p. 199.

78 McManus, "Women and English Renaissance Drama," p. 786.

79 *Tarltons Iests* (London, 1613), C2r-v.

80 Gayton, *Pleasant Notes upon Don Quixote* (London, 1654), pp. 271–2.

81 See expenses roll at E351/542 (1582), MS, The National Archives, Kew, London.

82 *Documents Relating to the Office of the Revels in the Time of Queen Elizabeth*, ed. Albert Feuillerat (Louvain, 1908), p. 349.

83 *English Professional Theatre*, p. 153.

84 *Records of Early English Drama: Cheshire*, pp. 202–3.

85 See C.18.e.2[74], MS, British Library, London; reproduced and discussed in John H. Astington, "Trade, Taverns, and Touring Players in Seventeenth-Century Bristol," *Theatre Notebook* 71.3 (2017): 161–8.

86 "Casting *The Roaring Girl*: Embodied Skill, History, and Lived Experience," *Gender on the Transnational Early Modern Stage, Then and Now: A Performance as Research Approach*, eds Peter Cockett and Melinda Gough (in progress). See also McManus, "Feats of Activity and the Tragic Stage," Shakespeare Association of America Conference (Panel Session: Rhetorics of Performance), 19 April 2019; and McManus's forthcoming work.

87 E.K. Chambers, *The Elizabethan Stage*, Vol. 2 (Oxford: Clarendon, 1923), p. 262.

88 Manley and MacLean, p. 32.

89 *English Professional Theatre*, pp. 446–7.

90 Philip Butterworth, *Magic on the Early English Stage* (Cambridge: Cambridge University Press, 2005), pp. 46–7.

91 Nandini Das, João Vicente Melo, Haig Z. Smith, and Lauren Working, *Keywords of Identity, Race, and Human Mobility in Early Modern England* (Amsterdam: Amsterdam University Press, 2021), p. 276.

92 Das et al., p. 278.

93 Butterworth, p. 47.

94 "Feats of Activity and the Tragic Stage," and forthcoming work.

95 Jean Williams, "The Curious Mystery of the Cotswold 'Olimpick' Games: Did Shakespeare Know Dover… and Does It Matter?", *Sport in History* 29.2 (2009): 150–70. p. 159.

96 Cotswold Games, *Annalia Dubrensia* (London, 1636), B2r.

97 Games, E2r; H4r.

98 *Records of Early English Drama: Cambridge*, Vol. 1, ed. Alan H. Nelson (Toronto: University of Toronto Press, 1989), pp. 571–2.

99 John Taylor, *Taylors revenge, or, The rymer William Fennor firkt, feritted, and finely fetcht ouer the coales* (London, 1615), A2r.

100 William Fennor, *Fennors defence: or, I am your first man* (London, 1615), A3v.

101 Taylor, A3r-v.

102 Preiss, p. 90.

103 Preiss, p. 92.

104 Anthony Munday, *A second and third blast of retrait from plaies and theaters* (London, 1580), D4r.

105 Quoted in Preiss, p. 92.

106 *REED Cumberland, Westmorland, Gloucestershire*, p. 314.

107 *REED Cumberland, Westmorland, Gloucestershire*, p. 314.

108 *REED Cheshire*, Vol. 1, pp. 250–2.

109 Ben Bechtel, "Improvisation in Early Music," *Music Educators Journal* 66.5 (1980): 109–112. p. 110.

110 *Tarltons Iests*, B2r-v.

111 *Tarltons Iests*, B4r.

112 *The Rare Triumphs of Love and Fortune* (London, 1589), F2r.

113 For more on stage directions, see Alan Dessen, *Elizabethan Stage Conventions and Modern Interpreters* (Cambridge: Cambridge University Press, 1984); Dessen and Leslie Thomson, eds, *A Dictionary of Stage Directions in English Drama, 1580–1642* (Cambridge: Cambridge University Press, 1999); Andrew Gurr and Mariko Ichikawa, *Staging in Shakespeare's Theatres* (Oxford: Oxford University Press, 2000).

114 Christopher Marlowe, *Doctor Faustus* (London, 1604), D3v.

115 Stephen Purcell, "Editing for Performance or Documenting Performance? Exploring the Relationship between Early Modern Text and Clowning," *Shakespeare Bulletin* 34.1 (2016): 5–27. p. 14.

116 "Textual Embodiment: The Case of Etcetera," *The Oxford Handbook on Shakespeare and Embodiment*, ed. Valerie Traub (Oxford: Oxford University Press, 2016): 527–49. p 528; p. 539; p. 548.

117 See Preiss and Purcell.

118 Purcell, p. 25.

119 Taylor, A3r.

120 *English Professional Theatre*, p. 543.

121 See Christopher Marsh, *Music and Society in Early Modern England* (Cambridge: Cambridge University Press, 2010), p. 131.

122 Lucy Munro, "Music and Sound," *The Oxford Handbook of Early Modern Theatre*, ed. Richard Dutton (Oxford: Oxford University Press, 2011), 543–59. p. 548; p. 550.

123 Simon Smith, *Musical Response in the Early Modern Playhouse, 1603–1625* (Cambridge: Cambridge University Press, 2017); see also Munro.

124 Lucy Munro, "Children's Companies and the Long 1580s," Forum, ed. Andy Kesson, *Shakespeare Studies* 45 (2017): 97–105. p. 104.

125 See Tiffany Stern, *Documents of Performance in Early Modern England* (Cambridge: Cambridge University Press, 2009), pp. 120–5.

126 *REED Kent*, Vol. 1, lxviii.

127 *REED Kent*, Vol. 1, p. 102.

128 *REED Kent*, Vol. 2, p. 304.

129 Marsh, p. 181.

130 T.F., *Newes from the North* (London, 1579), C3r.

131 *REED Cheshire*, Vol. 1, p. 391.

132 *REED Cheshire*, Vol. 2, p. 779; see also a constable at Darnhall, presented in 1602, pp. 663–4, and discussion in Vol. 1 at p. lx.

133 See Peter Watlyn indictment, among a list of others, at C/2/9/1/1/8 p. 92, MS, Suffolk Archives, Ipswich.

134 ZQSF 36/32, MS, Chester Record Office, Chester. Transcribed in *Intoxicants and Early Modernity, 1580–1740* database. Online. Accessed 7 Aug. 2021.

135 Joachim Frenk, "Games," *The Ashgate Research Companion to Popular Culture in Early Modern England*, eds Andrew Hadfield, Matthew Dimmock, and Abigail Shinn (Abingdon: Routledge, 2016): 221–34. p. 223.

136 Gina L. Bloom, *Gaming the Stage: Playable Media and the Rise of English Commercial Drama* (Chicago: University of Michigan Press, 2018), *escholarship.org*, p. 1.

137 John Stow, *Survey of London* (London, 1598), Aa1v.

138 Paul Hentzner, *Paul Hentzner's Travels in England*, trans. Horace Walpole (London: Jeffery, 1797).

139 For a summary, see Julian Bowsher, "Twenty Years on: The Archaeology of Shakespeare's London Playhouses," *Shakespeare* 7.4 (2011): 452–66.

140 See Duncan Salkeld, *Shakespeare among the Courtesans: Prostitution, Literature, and Drama, 1500–1650* (Abingdon: Routledge, 2012) and *Shakespeare and London* (Oxford: Oxford University Press, 2018). The records of the Bridewell Court (which punished behavioural and moral transgression) include numerous mentions of the playhouse in connection with work.

141 For an introduction to the history of puppetry in performance, see Tiffany Stern, "If I could see the Puppets Dallying': *Der Bestrafte Brudermord* and Hamlet's Encounters with the Puppets," *Shakespeare Bulletin* 31.3 (2013): 337–52. For a discussion of technology in performance, see Chapter 3, Callan Davies, *Strangeness in Jacobean Drama* (London: Routledge, 2020).

3

CROWD CAPACITIES

The "haunting of great multitudes" defined the early modern playhouse. London's corporation complained of the sheer numbers who went "to Plays, interludes, and shows," which resulted in unchaste thoughts, secret "inveigling and alluring," and "sundry slaughters and mayhemings."[1] Their apparent disdain for playhouse crowds was matched, however, by a pragmatic interest in regulating and even profiting from the playing industry.[2] Meanwhile, crowds only increased across the sixteenth and seventeenth centuries, as cities grew in size and the commercial leisure industry expanded. The government spy Maliverny Catlyn observed in 1586 that "the play houses are pestered, when the churches are naked/at the one, it is not possible to get A place, at the other, void seats are plenty."[3] Depending on who you asked, a packed crowd was a sign of commercial success, moral failure, or an urban planning headache. This chapter focuses on the movement, management, and consequences of crowds.

Crowds "pestered" playhouses not only to enjoy the activities set out in Chapter 2 but also because of the appeal of their wider environs. In 1593, the writer Henry Chettle ventriloquised the ghost of the late comic actor, clown, and fencer Richard Tarlton to offer comment on London's ever-expanding leisure scene. "While Plays are used," he wrote, "half the day is by most youths that have liberty spent upon them, or at least the greatest company drawn to the places where they frequent."[4] This is a knotty and difficult sentence—perhaps that's a consequence of speaking from beyond the grave—but at its essence is the fact that groups of young people flocked to the "places" where plays took place (quite separate, the "at least" implies, from play performances). Chettle also suggests that such company spent time both in and around the playhouse over the course of possibly many hours. Although young people were one demographic frequently associated with playhouses, discussed below, they were not the only people who formed the busy crowd. Guests ranged from mothers with their children to visiting European dignitaries. Rather

DOI: 10.4324/9781003231127-4

than thinking of "playgoers" in this period, perhaps we should more broadly talk about playhouse-goers.[5]

Chettle's company represents a substantial cross-section of urban traffic. In being "drawn" to playing locations, their repeated journeys carved out new routes and conferred recreational identities on specific locales. In other words, playhouses both physically and conceptually re-shaped their surroundings, sometimes quite literally redrawing the local map. At the same time, these playhouse-going crowds were seen by certain authorities and commentators as a potential threat to order and public health.[6] Officials across the country sought to regulate travel to and attendance at play events. This is often framed as "antitheatrical" sentiment—born from a fundamental hostility to play. Yet such crowd control was complex and sometimes contradictory, part of a wider debate over popular commercial leisure forms.

The two areas explored in depth in this chapter—Shoreditch in London and several towns across Cheshire and Lancashire—testify to the effect playhouses had on local infrastructure and help us appreciate how playhouse crowds fitted into both public policy and personal experience. Here, we meet some of the people who represent both. They take us on journeys like that of Chettle's "youths." In doing so, they demonstrate why people were "drawn to the places" where play took place and show us the impact of such regular play journeys.

Going to Play

In 1583, standings in the bear-baiting arena on Bankside known as Paris Garden collapsed. A pamphlet was published shortly afterwards that condemned the pastime and similar ungodly exercises. Its author, John Field, lists those who were killed in the disaster, memorialising them by reference to their name, place of residence, and sometimes occupation:

- Adam Spencer, a feltmonger, in Southwark
- William Cockram, a baker, from Shoreditch
- John Burton, clerk, from St Mary Wolmers in Lombard Street
- Mathew Mason, servant with Master Garland, dwelling in Southwark
- Thomas Peace, servant with Robert Tasher, dwelling in Clerkenwell
- Alice White, servant to a pursemaker without Cripplegate
- Marie Harrison, daughter of John Harrison, water bearer, dwelling in Lombard Street[7]

These seven lost lives are testament to the traffic and varied backgrounds of those attending early modern playing places. Two were resident in Southwark, in the vicinity of the Paris Garden arena, while many had come from elsewhere in the city—in central Lombard Street, or from the outer liberties of Shoreditch or the wall-side parish of Cripplegate. Some, like Alice White or Mathew Mason, were servants, perhaps young men and women starting out in life. Service was, particularly for women, a way to move towards independent adulthood before marriage. Others held occupations like baking or worked in literate professions as a clerk. The list sets out a spectrum among audience members from the young and precarious to the established. A similar tragedy four years later saw a woman and child killed at a performance of the Lord Admiral's men, after an actors' prop gun, "being charged with bullet, missed the fellow he aimed at and killed a child, and a woman great with child forthwith, and hurt another man in the head very sore."[8] It seems even young children were present for an afternoon of play at the Rose. These are awful and morbid occurrences—atypical, in the grand scheme of early modern entertainment—but they provide some rare clues of who precisely were playhouse-goers.

More lively records (in every sense) also give insight into the demographics attending playhouses and their role in social life. Arrest records and court depositions (in which individuals are posed set questions in a legal case) help furnish us with more detail about playhouse-going. A case in the Consistory Court of London (which managed moral and behavioural issues) in 1611 offers particularly rich evidence about the way Londoners folded play and recreation into their wider lives.[9] John Newton and Joan Waters were at loggerheads before the court authorities, because John insisted the two were legally married, while Joan argued they were never properly wedded. Such an argument was a common occurrence in consistory courts up and down the country. The depositions given in the case weave a web of social movement around early modern London that spanned taverns and domestic residences in Smithfield to the Curtain in Shoreditch to the Boar's Head playhouse in Aldgate.

Various questions were posed to witnesses about Newton's economic standing and the money he might bring to the marriage, which allegedly formed part of his promise to Waters. The haberdasher William Duke, the servant Thomas Hackleton, and a household maid all confirmed that

> Newton is a common player & so commonly accounted of & this deponent upon Whitsun Monday last was present at the Curtain in Holywell at a play there & there saw […] Newton publicly play a part in the same play upon the stage.[10]

Duke also observed that Newton played at the Boar's Head, too. The presence of such friends or associates at the playhouse was important for confirming Newton's claims about financial security. He alleged, as a sharer in his company, the Duke of York's men, that he could make a very healthy sum of up to 5 shillings a day and promised that he would bring in at least 20 shillings a week to the marriage.[11] Duke, Hackleton, and the maid would have had to travel from their houses in the city centre or in the north west in Smithfield across London to see the Duke of York's men perform. Hackleton would have made his way through the fields north of London, where (as we will see below) a range of other (licit and illicit) activity took place.[12] Here we have a sketch of daily life in London, in which residents moved as a matter of course from their homes or workplaces to the playhouse and then elsewhere.

All witnesses eventually found themselves in the same room at the Queen's Head tavern in Smithfield, where Newton and Waters caroused and were "very loving familiar & friendly together."[13] When Joan Waters departed home, she found the alleged marriage contract and asked her young male servant to read it aloud to her. Waters was surprised at the contents. She claimed that she did not realise what was written in the paper that she had signed at the tavern and did not consciously consent to signing a binding document of marriage. Newton insisted the contract was signed in "very good sense, reason, and temper."[14] This drama of personal life and public engagement unfolded at playing locations. Each deponent's testimony ranged between different leisure sites, at which important details arose—evidence of profession and proof of character at the playhouse, eyewitness accounts of oaths and conversations in the tavern. This spousal quarrel implicitly indicates the quotidian nature of playing traffic for ordinary Londoners. Such visits folded into the warp and weft of urban experience. Accordingly, they feature as a relevant but unexceptional articulation of that experience in court.

For the many thousands who came and went from playhouses on a regular basis, there was no cause for textual recording of visits: unremarkable events typically go unremarked upon. Yet some individuals did record daily matters in a diary-like format. The astrologer and sometime royal physician Simon Forman noted visits to the Curtain in his diary, during which he unsuccessfully attempted to court a woman called Sarah Archdel.[15] In Canterbury, Thomas Cocks recorded in his diary from 1606–7 numerous sums "spent going to the play," including one entry that factors in a pence worth of damsons.[16] These moments of life-writing suggest ways outside of legal institutions in which individuals recognised themselves as playhouse-goers and recorded their activities both within and around the play event and its location. Indeed, many recorded instances of playhouse-going centre on areas adjacent to as well as within performance venues—in fields, in areas retailing food and drink, in nearby businesses. The activities set out in Chapter 2 combine with these memoranda to remind us that play was multiple and (as emphasised in the following sections and Chapter 4) that playhouse peripheries were vibrant spaces.

Many different nationalities lived around and visited playhouses. When Newton was performing on the Curtain stage and his acquaintance Duke and household servant Hackleton were enjoying the spectacle, they might have rubbed shoulders with the Venetian Ambassador: Antonio Foscarini insisted on visiting the venue and refused to spectate from the pricier "boxes" reserved from the better-off. He "preferred to stand below in the middle, among the rabble of porters and carters, pretending that he needed to stay close because he was hard of hearing." An outrageously satirical letter from his compatriot, Antimo Galli, sent to Florence, detailed Foscarini's exploits and noted that he had "not given up visiting other theatres."[17] As well as visiting dignitaries, London was home to a diverse population of possibly more than 7,000 European immigrants by the later sixteenth century. "Newcomers in Elizabeth's reign were predominantly Huguenots displaced by Spanish persecution from France and the Low Countries," Duncan Salkeld explains, and "some of these were merchants, but others were artisans, textile workers, musicians, and painters."[18] So-called "stranger churches" were set up in the capital to cater to residents who wanted service in Italian or French tongues. The Canterbury resident Thomas Cocks would similarly have enjoyed his damsons amongst Huguenots, in a city that attracted many European immigrants and refugees and that had a Huguenot church from the late sixteenth century.[19] Plays and playhouses in locations across the country were often framed by their immediate cosmopolitan contexts.

The area around the Shoreditch playhouses provides a demographic snapshot of an immediate playhouse neighbourhood. The surrounding streets included numerous immigrant silkweavers, both men and women. It was home to the famed Lanyer/Bassano family of court musicians, including the writer and poet Amelia Lanyer. Nearby lived Thomasine Barny, who "useth shoemaking" and came from south-west France. Barny employed two (likely French) servants, John Morsonne and Jakery du Roye.[20] Round the corner lived Petruccio Ubaldino, an "Italian gentleman" of the court involved in acting, bookselling, government intelligence, and writing and translation.[21] By 1576, the year the Theatre was built, the area was home to another Italian called Francis Marquino. He established an international school there and was termed a "schoolmaster" by 1583, with 24 scholars, "strangers' sons," in his charge.[22] His wife's name is documented here as "Levina." When *Titus Andronicus* was performed a few years later, what might local audiences have made of the character name Lavinia? Marquino seemingly ran a sizeable "stranger" school for second-generation immigrants in the suburbs surrounding Finsbury and the Shoreditch playhouses, offering important contextualisation for the nature of the drama on stage.[23] The rich trade skills and cultural contributions of numerous European residents shaped the writing and reception of dramatic play, as well as other play forms (such as fencing and tumbling, as we have seen) across this period.

London was also characterised by a degree of racial diversity. Imtiaz Habib has importantly set out the range of Black people resident in early modern England who can be traced through the archive. Habib's research forms part of ongoing work by a range of scholars to "re-see" people marginalised by both historical and contemporary social structures as well as by the biases and limitations of the archive and of past scholarly research.[24] Farah Karim-Cooper observes that "it is not beyond the realm of possibility that Shakespeare and his contemporaries encountered non-white people in London during this period," and explains how research "might prompt us to question or re-evaluate the composition and demographic of the early modern theatre audiences." Not only were there numerous foreign travellers and immigrant communities, but there were Black residents in play-rich locations like Bankside, such as the silkweaver Reasonable Blakemore.[25] "It is possible that he attended shows in the playhouses in Southwark," Karim-Cooper explains, and "perhaps even supplied the acting companies with costume items. This kind of archival recovery is of use to a discussion of theatre technology and racial imper-sonation."[26] Habib's attention to provincial Black lives suggests we might extend these observations to locations elsewhere, especially in mercantile port cities (such as Bristol). Just as a range of European identities were represented on stage, so people of colour also feature in numerous forms of the period's play—from the tumbling discussed in Chapter 2 to staged drama, like Marlowe's *Tamburlaine*, Shakespeare's *Titus Andronicus*, or George Peele's *The Battle of Alcazar*. The black-face make-up or prosthetics used to represent racial otherness on the English stage must be contextualised within a multi-racial playhouse crowd as well as multi-racial play-makers.

We have already met the haberdasher William Duke, who testified in the did-they-didn't-they-marry court case of 1611. He acknowledged he had been part of that crowd, having witnessed Newton's playing company "play their parts on the stage at the Curtain & the boar's head." Duke was described by a fellow deponent in the case as "a black man."[27] The terminology can sometimes be used in the period to denote hair colour, but both Habib and Kim F. Hall warn against this blanket interpretation as potential historical whitewashing. Hall has shown how the descriptor "black" was always fraught with racial meaning in a period in which both the discourse of race-making and the lived experience of racial violence were developing.[28] Duke's presence in the playhouse and his important testimony in the marriage case should at the very least encourage us to resist any assumption that theatre audiences in this period were always white. As Karim-Cooper reminds us, "as we learn more about the growing population in London of people of color, it seems less and less likely that audiences were racially homogeneous. This new understanding of an early modern racially diverse audience then should force us to consider more deeply how the performance of race developed over time and how it was received."[29]

We have already witnessed the occupational diversity of those visiting playing venues, but issues of status extended to both the social and structural features of playhouse-going. Venues seemingly operated a hierarchy of entrance fees. William Lambarde hinted at a uniform pricing structure for all forms of early modern play, from fencing to bear-baiting to playing, in 1570s London (repeated in its second edition in the 1590s): "they first pay one penny at the gate, another at the entry of the Scaffold, and a third for quiet standing,"[30] and legal records relating to the Theatre show that individuals (including James Burbage and Margaret Brayne) collected money at such locations, having "to stand at the door that goeth up to the galleries of the […] Theatre to take and receive […] the money that should be given to come up unto the said Galleries at that door."[31] During a period of substantial price inflation, the cheapest entrance fee of one pence made these entertainments affordable even to the least well-off: one pence would also buy such staples as a printed ballad sheet, a quart of beer, a "penny" loaf, or a yard of ribbon.[32] Pricing points are difficult to ascertain for provincial playhouses outside of London, where surrounding printed commentary is less plentiful. Yet when Thomas Crosfield visited a bull-baiting arena in Oxfordshire, he marked the costs at "1d a piece for every person that goes in & 2d in a chamber."[33] Such a structure may mirror London's by then established commercial entertainment fees, but given such play was long accessible outside the capital, too, it is equally likely that this was the common bottom-line price, with room for social stratification via seating upgrades.

Indeed, playbills like the bear-baiting advert in Chapter 2 did not stipulate venue entry costs. There may therefore have been a universal assumption of one pence entry "for every person that goes in" to these more popular venues.

More elite locations, however, predictably charged higher rates. Smaller indoor theatres were active for children's performances at the likes of St Paul's or the First Blackfriars from at least the 1570s, but by 1609, the King's Men had established an indoor theatre (at another location in the Blackfriars), a move followed by other companies. There is little clue as to the earlier entry prices for these smaller indoor playhouses. St Paul's, one such small and ostensibly "elite" venue, may well have been open to a more democratic range of people from as little as two pence entry.[34] Yet smaller indoor places certainly drew a wealthier clientele by the early seventeenth century, when playhouses like the Second Blackfriars or the Cockpit began to develop a socially elite reputation.[35] These venues charged up to five times more than the one pence minimum for larger venues. Indeed, while outdoor playhouses catered for up to a thousand and beyond (audience capacities coming in at something like the Theatre, c. 800, the Curtain c. 1,400, the Globe around c. 2,000, and the Rose around 1,000),[36] smaller theatres hosted only around a couple of hundred or so spectators.

Questions of pricing were as much about visually displaying one's status as about what coins were in one's purse. Theatrical sightlines came with social connotations. In outdoor playhouses, the high-end boxes behind or either side of the stage were the most desirable seats for those wishing to see and be seen. Similarly, early modern fashionistas enjoyed paying extra pennies to sit on stools on the stage itself, forcing actors to perform (in Ben Jonson's words) "In compass of a cheese-trencher,"[37] as we saw in Dekker's satire of playgoing spangle-babies in Chapter 2. Sightlines and status were at issue in other playing spaces, too. When Captain Essex and his wife secured a "box in the playhouse at the Blackfriars," their sight was obscured by one Lord Thurles "coming upon the stage" and standing "before them":

> Captain Essex told his lordship they had paid for their places as well as he and therefore entreated him not to deprive them of the benefit of it. Whereupon the lord stood up yet higher and hindered more their sight. Then Captain Essex with his hand put him a little by. The lord then drew his sword and ran full butt at him, though he missed him, and might have slain the Countess as well as him.[38]

Playhouse stages showcased real social dramas as well as fictional ones—quarrels in which labels like "lord" or "captain" were self-consciously paraded through positioning, deportment, and inter-audience dynamics. Thurles and Essex remind us, for instance, how some but not all in the audience, like their theatrical counterparts, wielded swords: a display of masculine martial prowess and, in a period in which the right to carry a sword was based on worth and social standing, a mark of distinction. This potentially lethal skirmish indicates how the cost of play—and of one's rightful stage view—overlapped with questions of status, honour, and masculinity even in more well-heeled playhouses. Visual access to the play event was often not equal—indeed *is* not equal. Productions in recreated theatre spaces continue to draw "on the social stratification of its audience," Pascale Aebischer reminds us, where those in "privileged" seats are granted a different level of actorly interactivity than those in the cheapest high-up standing rows, whose view of the stage is always partially obscured.[39] The negotiation of these spaces was not simply about what one could see but about both one's social and physical relationship with others, reminding us that being in a playhouse audience was always an active and deeply embodied experience.

These questions of status had an impact on the way contemporaries figured mass audiences or crowds. Commentators often overlooked higher-paying, higher-status, older, or distinguished visitors to characterise playhouse-goers as homogenously youthful. The complaint about "mayhemings" by London's corporation that opened this chapter targeted its scoffing in particular at the "inordinate … haunting of great multitudes of people, especially youth, to Plays, interludes, and shows […]."[40] The authorities' framing of play as an "especially" youthful pursuit was connected to the broader position of young people in the early modern English imaginary. Their presence was particularly noticeable in bigger cities, to which they flocked in search of advancement and aesthetic and intellectual engagement. Susan Brigden suggests the upmooring of individuals from their provincial homes might have fostered a sense of solidarity based on age and occupational status and thus generated something of a shared youth connection.[41] Indeed, many migrants to cities like London, Canterbury, Chester, Bristol, or York went to pursue apprenticeships that would, or could, set them up in the world. But (as in any other period of history) potential exploitation in these roles, as well as resentment, loneliness, and boredom, meant that relationships between masters and apprentices were sometimes strained. Occasionally, cross-apprentice solidarity and discontent bubbled to the surface and erupted into public disorder in ways perceived to be aligned with the playhouse. In 1592, "great multitudes of people," the majority of whom were apprentice feltmakers, assembled on Bankside "by occasion, & pretence of their meeting at a play," resulting in a tumult and affray (including with officers of the nearby prison of the Marchelsea).[42] The Lord Mayor's combination of "occasion" and "pretence" here illustrates how playhouses were understood both to facilitate unruly gatherings and to provide excuses for "the greatest company" to be "drawn to the places where they frequent" (as Chettle phrased it the following year).[43] As with skirmishes between elite figures within the playhouse like Captain Essex and Lord Thurles above, apprentice unrest around and outside entertainment venues was bound up with what Ian Archer calls "status uncertainties."[44]

The combination of early modern adolescence and playhouses was therefore sometimes perceived to be a potential threat to order and stability. Apprenticeships in this period typically lasted for around seven years (with some differences), and young men and women would often have been single and in such roles until at least their early 20s. Around 40 percent of London's population were under the age of 15.[45] More than one in ten of the urban population were apprentices, with even more being young people in or searching for work.[46] As such, few people under the age of 23 or 24 had households to run, which afforded them greater leisure time. If you were to follow some of these young Elizabethans or Jacobeans back in time, you would "see them meeting at the close of the day in the early hours of the evening, on Sundays and other holidays," as well as "outside the household during the working day."[47] "Young lives were not solely structured by the physical boundaries of the household and the pressures of service," Paul Griffiths explains, so "many young people had freedom to organize leisure time, and thoughts quickly turned to play at the close of the working day."[48] Certain times of the year were particularly associated with play, with "special days on which youthful collective activities reigned, and great time spent in leisure activities and out of work—all this amounted to cultural forms typical of the young."[49] Shrovetide was especially known for apprentice disorder and riotousness, and accordingly London targeted its young population when proscribing "any shouting, whooping noises, sounding of drums or instruments, shooting of guns or using of cymbals or any demeanour other than shall be fit for quiet and sober persons […] using their time of honest recreation."[50] Elsewhere in the country, a boy as young as 14 named John Mort was apprehended in Cheshire in 1608 for travelling round different venues with his bear to ply his trade as a bearward.[51] England's youth were therefore often framed as its chief play-makers and playhouse-goers.

Yet much of this discussion comes from authorities invested in policing behaviour and maintaining order. In reality, we know that the activities enjoyed by the young were equally enjoyed by householders and, as we have seen, ambassadors, lords, and captains, or even by mothers with their children. The notion of a cohesive youth culture, as intimated by some of the repeated apprentice proclamations, "was undermined by other, no less powerful, forces, and such cultural forms were an integral part of broader patterns of recreation and culture shared by youths and adults."[52] While there may well have been a sense of community or joint imaginative engagement with specific play forms among the young, these forms took place in spaces shared with the rest of society—not least in the many different types of playhouses explored in this study.[53]

The playhouse crowd was therefore never an undifferentiated mass. It was made up of the full spectrum of early modern inhabitants—excluding, perhaps, those whose religious bent made them particularly hostile to mimetic representation or ludic abandon. The individuals and groups discussed in this section were drawn to the playhouse for the many activities offered there, such as those laid out in Chapter 2. They also represented a mass movement that redefined urban travel.[54] While a level of antipathy is often on display in the writings and orders of certain authority bodies, there were also positive engagements with and among the playhouse crowd. The remainder of this chapter explores in two case studies how Shoreditch outside London and north-west England viewed, policed, and understood these playhouse crowds.

Shoreditch and the Traffic of the Stage

Anne Thorne was 74 in 1602 and had known the site and precinct of Holywell in Shoreditch, where she lived, for over 60 years. Her account of the area and its history forms an important part of a court case concerning the rightful lease and alleged trespass of ground in the area—including land rented by the proprietors of the Theatre. She recalls in her deposition seeing swathes of "new buildings" develop on the site and explains that

> since the building of the Theatre there is a way made into the fields, and that [the landlord] and his Tenants have for a long time used another way out of the said Site of the Priory that the said [landlord] holdeth into the high street of Shoreditch.

Her testimony is echoed by another resident, who similarly deposes that "she doth not know any ancient way into the fields, but a way used after the building of the Theatre which leadeth into the fields."[55]

Anne Thorne attests that the development of playhouses in this area created new access routes from the site of the playhouses to Moorfields on their west. Moorfields was a vast swathe of land known for recreational pursuits and grand summer houses. It was marked on maps from the 1550s and 1560s by characters practising archery, washing clothes, or wandering. According to the two deponents, playhouse visitors would leave Moorgate and approach through the new "way" from the fields in the west. Thorne's testimony bears witness to the urbanisation of Shoreditch, where in the road northward "upon the streets' side many houses have been builded with alleys backward, of late time too much pestered with people."[56] Thorne gives voice to the urban creep, usually detectable only in maps or topographical descriptions, and provides a useful local example of the changing landscape of suburban London in the wake of the dissolution. Indeed, the roadways that predate the establishment of Shoreditch playhouses on this map were important incentives for theatrical prospectors, who targeted what Laurie Johnson calls "an existing and reliable flow of people."[57] Roadways came before theatres, he emphasises, and "the mobility of prospective audiences" was accordingly a key element of playhouse development.[58] Theatrical activity may have turned these areas into destinations, but they emerged from the traffic that had long moved by and beyond them.

Thorne's testimony also indicates something of the way playhouses and "Bowling Allies, and Dicing houses, which in all places are increased, and too much frequented" in the area north of Shoreditch[59] altered the environment of Moorfields. In doing so, they redefined the city's mass movement. The fields had long been associated with recreation, but the type of crowds occasioned by the two large playhouses instituted a new and particular leisure movement across London. One of the chief concerns of London's corporation in these years regarding leisure activities was the assembly of people; swathes of corporation material testify to decades

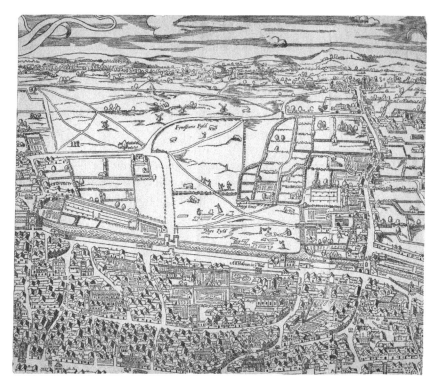

FIGURE 3.1 Map of London attributed to Ralph Agas (detail). MAP L85b no.3.

Used by permission of the Folger Shakespeare Library under a Creative Commons Attribution-ShareAlike 4.0 International License.

of concern about recreational crowd control and "all manner of Concourse and public meetings of the people at Plays, Bearbaitings, or Bowlings, and other assemblies for sports […] and Congregating of people together."[60] Visitors to the city like Louis de Grenade affirmed (in 1577) that the journey towards the playhouses took place "As one leaves the city through the gate of Moorgate, [and …] at the end of this meadow are two very fine theatres."[61] The close association of the fields with the new play precinct in Shoreditch materially reshaped the concourse and assembly of people. The link between Moorfields and the playhouses was described by Richard West in 1607:

> About Moorfield the grounds all levelled new
> The winds too high, the dust flies in your eyes,
> 'Tis paltry walking there, till th'elms be grown;
> A better place then that you can devise,
> Towards the Curtain then you must be gone […].[62]

West acknowledges the new landscaping that reshaped Moorfields itself in the years following the establishment of the Theatre and Curtain. Tree-lined walks were planted between 1605 and 1607[63] (hence the diminutive stature of the elms in West's verse). The poem implies a connection between this new development and the recent access routes from Holywell. While leisure walking is often regarded by historians as an eighteenth-century development,[64] much earlier London venues like the Theatre and Curtain generated an idea of walking *to* leisure, with concomitant reshaping of the routes such a journey took. These playhouses helped set down a new model for "urban leisure activities"—an early indication of a shift towards, in the context of the 1620s to the 1650s, what Julie Sanders calls the "predominance of pleasure gardens as a key aspect of urban experience and intra-urban mobility."[65] The bustle of activity clustering around the playhouses and spilling into the fields thereby inscribes the once "open" space of Moorfields with arborically defined routes that demarcated and portioned off "recreational" journeys.

Indeed, the development of Moorfields as a recreational destination explicitly overlapped with playhouses. The Theatre was identified as being "erected in the

FIGURE 3.2 City of London, 1658, by Faithorne and Newcourt.

Reproduced from Maps of Old London, ed. G.E. Mitton (London, 1908), via Project Gutenberg and in the public domain.

fields."[66] The Curtain is likewise seen as synonymous with this expansive area. In 1601, Margery Copeland met with a Mr Benedick "in the lower end of chapel side and not knowing her [he] took her by the hand and drew her into the field towards the Curtain in Holloway."[67] Simon Forman, the astrologer and physician, followed the Curtain equivalent of the path described by the two deponents by the Theatre when on the 19 April 1599 he courted a Sarah Archdel nearby:

> I was at the Curtain and there she came & with her uncle & friends and sat before me and after the play we went into the fields together and I had some parley with her but nothing of any thing touching the matter and she seemed very kind and courteous.[68]

The fields beside both the Curtain and the Theatre playhouses came to serve as an extension of commercial recreation—one that resulted, like Thorne's Holywell, in their physical reshaping.

Play journeys also influenced perceptions of the city. "The creation of spaces of 'resort,'" in Sanders's terms, "was dependent on new technologies of transport and movement."[69] Mark Jenner's and Andy Gordon's work has shown how, across these years, new and fashionable materials affected the urban imagination. The introduction of the hackney coach, for instance, in the late sixteenth century and its increasing accessibility across subsequent decades produced "a re-conceptualisation of the urban environment in terms of fares, a new form of mental map that reimagined spatial relations across the city."[70] Testimonies from Shoreditch suggest that playhouses and their environs effected a similar reconceptualization in terms of leisure. They drew a mental map that reimagined early modern leisure relations, of where and how an individual might spend their time and money and how to navigate the city to do so. The earls who owned the land of Holywell Priory and their tenants responded to the playhouse crowds by blocking off the access route from Shoreditch high street, "and so kept the same chained as a private footway not suffering any to pass but by their licence."[71] Although tourist Johanes de Witt in 1596 situates the Curtain and the Theatre north of Bishopsgate, leisure-seekers would (at least as long as the earls continued to "bar up" the route) have found it a tricky if not impossible route to take, making Moorfields not only a more leisurely approach than the main road north from Bishopsgate but perhaps the only viable one.

While across the country arguments about "private" real estate raged, as certain gentry sought to enclose land that had long been commonly held and farmed, private owners in London responded instead to commercially driven mass movement.[72] Such a response to playhouse crowds made mass leisure assemblies a material feature of streetlife. Other such features, like the hackney coach, proved to be "a profoundly disruptive element within the urban environment," which fundamentally altered the streetscape—including the removal of causeys and the jamming of traffic and businesses.[73] Evidently, playhouses had a similar effect. They emerged (like inns) from the "material opportunities of dissolution,"[74] which made attractive plots of land once held in perpetuity by the church available to anyone with sufficient capital or credit. Amid this proto-capitalist appetite for control of space, it is perhaps no surprise that the Shoreditch playhouses initiated a renewed restriction on private roads (with owners perhaps even charging for ingress and egress). New routes were created in response to these restrictions, to accommodate large crowds looking for a concentration of leisure and service industries. Here, then, we start to see the earliest signs of London's communal or public space being commercialised. As Anne Thorne's testimony tells us, those living in and around developing play precincts not only recognised their material impact on the city but also register its mental and social consequences.

Indeed, where Shoreditch was once defined by enclosed walls and residential sleepiness, new forms of community, traffic, and "dwelling" became possible.[75] We have already seen how young people flocked to playhouse locations quite apart from the plays taking place—to enjoy the broader leisure packages on offer. The Theatre was adjoined to a former brewhouse perhaps serving in some victualling capacity. The Curtain was built on the same plot of land that had once hosted a victualling house, whose operations may have overlapped with the playhouse.[76] Surrounding these playhouses were bowling alleys, dicing houses, and (as elsewhere in London and its liberties) numerous inns, including the Sugar Loaf and the King's Head, which was owned by the family of a major playing figure and later playhouse owner and builder, Christopher Beeston. This corner of north London began to call to London residents, thanks to an array of commercial leisure ventures.

The playhouses themselves were intersections for this wider leisure market and sit within a history of service, shopping, and victualling. In the centre of the city, locations like St Paul's had long modelled the benefits of bringing multiple types of recreation together. Around England's chief cathedral, one could dally in "Sempsters' shops, the new Tobacco-office, or amongst the Book-sellers": "there you may spend your legs [...] a whole after-noon: converse, plot, laugh, and talk any thing."[77] Such hotspots brought together recreational pastimes such as browsing, gossiping, shopping, and playing within a delimited, and commercialised, urban locale—a phenomenon explored in detail in Chapter 4.[78] The increasing development of such leisure precincts adds a new angle on the longer history of shopping laid out in Bruno Blondè, Peter Stabel, Jon Stobart, and Ilja Van Damme's edited collection, *Buyers and Sellers*. They acknowledge the complex social history of retail spaces and the growth of what they call "specialist retail areas."[79] Playhouses and related play enterprises shaped their own surroundings as specialist commercial leisure areas. Indeed, one clue as to why playhouse environs were attractive might be found in Karen Newman's reading of the goldsmiths' shop. For Newman, these outlets offered more than commodities. They were places where material, sexual, cultural, and economic exchange combined.[80] Simon Forman's field romance and the sexual trysts spilling out of the Curtain playhouse suggest a similar pattern of cultural vibrancy and opportunity. In turn, these broader areas created both new ways of socialising and, simply, "new ways" (in Thorne's formulation)—fresh physical and social journeys.

These field journeys and their leisure opportunities found their way onto the playhouse stages, enacting before contemporary audiences many of the observations made here. One of the earliest surviving plays from commercial playhouses, the *Three Ladies of London* (1581), likely performed at the Theatre, begins with four people coinciding on their journeys towards London. They all meet at a location just outside the city, to which they are headed to find "preferment" or "entertainment": "To London to get entertainment there."[81] This phrase invokes a crucial double sense, meaning both to find maintenance or employment via a patron, master, or mistress as well as to search out hospitality and enjoyment. The drama itself depicts an extraordinary and theatrically vibrant picture of a city teeming with merchants, tradespeople, moneylenders, and landlords and landladies from across the globe. It is also characterised by a succession of such journeys in search of recreational or economic preferment, which form the basis for its balance of realism and moralism. Two of the three titular characters (Love and Conscience) finish the opening scene declaring their intention to travel in the fashion that those in the playhouse audience would just have done (and were shortly to do again): "Is't your pleasure to walk abroad a while, / And recreate yourselves"?[82] In essence, *The Three Ladies of London* opens one of the earliest surviving dramatic artefacts from the commercial London playhouses with a recreational stroll into the heart of "entertainment." Meanwhile, those seeking such entertainment meet at the start of the play in a place that sounds, from the perspective of a performance at the Theatre, suspiciously like Moorfields.

Outside the playhouse walls, crowds made journeys both to and across London for preferment and entertainment. In their wake, they transformed the landscape north of London, permanently changing the traffic routes of Anne Thorne's home and the recreational fields over the road. After some 20 years of operation, the Shoreditch playhouses had redefined their surrounding environments. By the 1590s, crowds were "drawn to the places where [plays] frequent,"[83] spending their legs both within and around what was now a go-to leisure area.

Travel and Control in the Northwest

The play traffic of Shoreditch not only reshaped the city's mental and physical geographies but raised tricky questions about crowd control. In June 1584, the recorder of London, William Fleetwood (responsible for judicial duties in the city), wrote a detailed letter to the Lord High Treasurer William Cecil, Lord Burghley, about antics around the Theatre. Fleetwood implied the city's bustle depended upon playing traffic; accordingly, all began well on Whitsunday: "by reason no plays were the same day, all the City was quiet." Yet by Monday evening the atmosphere of London was quite different, with watchmen all over the city trying to keep order. The

> cause thereof was for that very near the Theatre or Curtain at the time of
> the plays there lay an apprentice sleeping upon the Grass, and one Challes

(alias Grostock) did turn upon the Toe[84] upon the belly of the same prentice, whereupon the apprentice started up and after words they fell to plain blows.

Challes's provocative choreography on the stomach of a dozing apprentice drew a crowd of "at least" 500 people. Fleetwood finds it difficult to distinguish between the Theatre and the Curtain, and his phrasing makes them almost a metonym for playhouses generally. This small toe-turning incident burgeoned into "mutinies and assemblies" in which apprentices "did conspire to have broken the prisons and to have taken forth the prentices that were imprisoned."[85]

On the Wednesday of Fleetwood's busy week, a serving man in a blue coat by the name of Brown ("a shifting fellow" with a "perilous wit") "did at the Theatre door quarrel with certain poor boys, handicraft prentices, and struck some of them, and lastly he with his sword wounded and maimed one of the boys upon the left hand." Brown's aggression indicates the type of violence that many associated with playing in the period, though the relatively infrequent nature of such incidents (at least in surviving records) suggests that extremes of violence were hardly commonplace at playhouses—all the more remarkable, considering the large crowds that frequented places like the Theatre. Nonetheless, Brown's actions drew a gathering similar to spectators visiting a play, attracting what Fleetwood counts as 1,000 people. On the Sunday, playing was suppressed and the city succeeded in gaining the assent from the Privy Council for the "pulling down of the Theatre and Curtain" (with agreement by all except for the Lord Chamberlain and Vice-Chamberlain, who must eventually have acquiesced). The owner of the Theatre, James Burbage, refused to show up when summoned, and eventually acted with consummate rudeness to Fleetwood, claiming his "Lord" (ie the Lord Chamberlain, Hunsdon, who patronised his company at the Theatre) would back him all the way.

The "puritan zealot"[86] Fleetwood was never easy-going when it came to entertainment gatherings, but his recollections about this riotous episode, which clearly prompted a theatrical chain reaction across the city, confirm the notion that London's youth were drawn to the places of plays during leisure time. He noted, after all, that it occurred *near* the Theatre or Curtain, during the period in which plays were being performed. The sparring apprentices, professionals, and lesser gentry involved in the skirmish were part of a wider playhouse-going crowd, even if they were not at the time stood watching the stage. The Theatre door, where Brown first met the handicraftsmen, was a locus for all sorts of assemblies. At this location, crowds could become either audiences or rioters;[87] they might enter inside the playhouse circumference or find other recreation nearby. The "sundry broils" of 1584 point to one way authorities might react to such crowd disturbance: demanding the "pulling down" of playhouses. Such acts of suppression were periodically ordered throughout the sixteenth and seventeenth centuries.[88] Yet never was a serving playhouse actually demolished at the orders of authorities. Most typically, objections to play—both from the national Privy Council and from London's own corporation—quite understandably centred on the dangers of spreading plague through mass assemblies. Plays were duly restricted during bad outbreaks, seemingly with cooperation from playhouse owners: surviving records indicate only infrequent breaches of plague restrictions. Indeed, playhouse crowds and business owners may have occasionally erupted into public discontent but for the most part were characterised by orderly leisure-seeking.[89] The playhouse crowd might sometimes need managing, but it was never liable to disappear in a gust of regulatory fiat.

Unsurprisingly, it was not just London that had playhouse crowds like these to police. Although a great deal of detailed evidence, like that of Fleetwood's letter, comes from the capital, vast crowds elsewhere also made their way to playhouses. In north-west England, at some distance from London, similarly regular playhouse traffic either attracted or demanded the intervention of various local authorities. The counties of Lancashire and Cheshire both saw a concerted effort from the late sixteenth century onwards to regulate and proscribe undesirable forms of play. Jurisdictional and gentry overlaps aligned the two counties. While local government attempted to crack down on the likes of bear-baiting, for instance, the paperwork generated by these attempts suggests the game was vibrant, popular, and widespread well into the mid-seventeenth century. It is an irony of such attitudes that official hostility towards a given play form generates a vast quantity of evidence about it taking place: Quarter Sessions and other jurisdictional bodies were officious in punishing those undertaking illicit play, meaning their surviving records furnish us with a great deal of evidence about such play. Lancashire and Cheshire are among the richest for recreational reprimands.

Crowds in the sparsely populated region's playing venues were sometimes so packed that by 1637 one could not stoop to pick up a beer off the floor: Thomas Fyney described one alehouse he visited as having such "abundance of people on both sides of the house, and so great a throng that he had no room to drink in," despite the fact it was not near a high way. Those gathered there were keen to watch the bear-baiting.[90] Fyney and his fellow merry-makers had travelled some way off the beaten track to get to the alehouse in question, and his mention of this detail emphasises the planned and deliberate bee-line—or, more appropriately, bear-line—locals made to get to defined playing locations. Around the same time, the butcher Thomas Gleave exemplified the privately run commercial entertainment venues that spanned Cheshire, especially those associated with animal sport. He was cited for a disordered house after

> Entertaining of an unlicensed bearward with bears and Causing him to bait his said bears within his backside whereby a multitude of people, men's servants, and Children and others were gathered together to the great offence of several householders of the said town [...].[91]

Even though many of the locations in question were far removed from urban centres, people travelled sometimes substantial distances on journeys just like those headed to Shoreditch's Theatre. Similarly, numerous individuals appear repeatedly across the two counties' citations for unlicensed play, suggesting a recognisable "scene" and a defined set of play-makers at work. For instance, crowd numbers were explicitly emphasised in one of several complaints about the bearward Peter Brome. In 1616, his repeated commercial play activities were seen to "Draw many disordered people together; in which assemblies diverse fearful accidents have happened," including (allegedly) two people being "worried" or even "devoured" by his bears.[92] On one such occasion, in Middlewich, the boisterousness of Brome's bears in the market-place resulted in the overthrowing of numerous stalls and standings.

Brome's drawing of "disordered" crowds to Middlewich's marketplace represented a perception from certain quarters of disorder among Cheshire towns and villages, in which assemblies at play were sometimes viewed as a threat to economic as well as social order. The overthrowing of market stalls can be seen as a metaphor for the wider worries about the play crowd and both its physical and abstract dangers. Cockfights, in particular, drew large crowds in this neck of the woods. As early as 1515 in Winwick in Lancashire, the householder Thomas Butler complained of the riotous assembly of over 80 people in the highway outside of the "Cockfight place" near to his house. He warned that "great mischief and murder" might have ensued had not the company eventually been dispersed by a local gentleman partly responsible for the gathering.[93] This early play assembly represents a similar associ-ation between commercial playing place and riotous leisure-seekers to Fleetwood's Theatre "broils" some 70 years later.

While recreational assemblies like these were clearly commonplace across the north-west, attitudes towards crowd control were divided. Although known for certain Catholic enclaves and (particularly in Lancashire) widespread recusancy, the region was also influenced by growing puritanism within religious, civic, and municipal institutions.[94] In the late 1560s and early 1570s, the city of Chester came under pressure to reform its attitude towards festivity. Annual play performances were viewed by some as hangovers from the pre-Reformation world. The city's Whitsun plays, which included a variety of pageants over several days, sponsored by local craft companies, were suspended in 1572. They were controversially revived by the mayor Sir John Savage for the year 1575, in the face of objections by local puritan and preacher Christopher Goodman, who busied himself writing letters to near and far ecclesiastical authorities about the mayor's audacity. Yet Savage insisted his revival of play traditions were "set forward as well by the Council of the City as for the Commonwealth of the same."[95] Indeed, many argued for the benefit of these performances. One sixteenth-century writer recognised that they profited the city economically, "for all both far and near came to see them,"[96] and contemporary testimony seems to confirm as much. Nearby resident Blanche Webb travelled to the city to see them in the early 1570s, explaining to the ecclesiastical court that she had come from Backford (some four miles north) "in company with her sister […] by reason of the plays of Chester."[97] Yet individuals like Goodman had a different understanding of playing crowds. He disagreed with the doctrinal qualities of the drama, but his objections about text and content were bolstered by a wider concern about ludic and mimetic play. Goodman thought mass recreational gatherings espe-cially threatening and irresponsible in the midst of economic turmoil and repeat plague visitations. He accordingly supported his opposition with appeals to a wide array of "religious, economic, social, and legal fields."[98]

In Lancashire, similar puritanical pressure affected the commercial playing industry. From the late 1580s onwards, a strict "Sabbatarian campaign" sought to restrict activities outside of churchgoing on Sundays, largely led by Edward Fleetwood (rector of Wigan). The observance of the Sabbath was a persistent and recurring bugbear for religious authorities in post-Reformation England, with commercial leisure at the forefront of complaints.[99] Lancashire was subject to an especially concerted attempt to crack down on so-called "Sunday sports." From 1587, Fleetwood and fellow preachers, along with 16 Justices of the Peace (local law-enforcement officials) wrote a series of advisory documents intended to influence county policy. Several Justices of the Peace suggested, for instance, "that the quarter sessions be used as the principal means of dealing with sabbath breakers, but that the chief authors of Sunday sports be arrested immediately and taken before a JP for punishment."[100] Although the success of the thrust against Sunday sports dwindled in the immediate years following, the campaign did not disappear. Fleetwood targeted one of the county's Assize judges in a letter to Lord Burghley in 1590, pointing out that "our Churches even in this short time [...] are exceedingly emptied of our people, and the streets and alehouses filled with all dissolute and Riotous Concourse, the Sabbath, and the holy exercises profaned with lewd games & pastimes," and that the judge in question had "given to the heady multitude no small Encouragement."[101] Fleetwood's language, like Goodman's in Chester, emphasised the traffic and assemblies attendant on play—the "Riotous Concourse" it occasioned and its opposition to appropriate Sunday church-going. These Sunday games drew crowds into the public realm, according to their opponents, swelling the streets and supporting local commercial playing spots like alehouses—the type of location, as we have seen, where drinkers went to watch bear-baiting. These Sabbatarian concerns received renewed spirit in 1616 "when Justice Edward Bromley signed orders at Lancaster assizes on 8 August suppressing Sunday sports and pastimes."[102] However, the energy of Sabbatarian reform was perhaps curtailed a little after King James defended certain Sunday sports while at Lancashire's Hoghton Tower in 1617. James's well-known "Declaration of Sports," or "Book of Sports," was extended from Lancashire to apply nationally the following year. The Book defended people's right to recreation on Sundays, pushing back against the more censorious end of Protestant attitudes. Despite some opposition, then, James encouraged various Sunday exercises, from piping and dancing to archery, leaping, vaulting, ales, and may games (but not animal baiting, interludes, or bowling).[103] Nonetheless, the local justice systems continued to prosecute those engaging in commercial leisure on Sundays, fining playhouse proprietors or play facilitators at exorbitant rates.[104]

The policing of playing crowds in the north-west accordingly centred on several overlapping political, social, and religious factors, not all of which were consistent. Local puritanism came up against conflicting ideas about what benefitted a town or city and the economic consequences of commercial leisure.[105] The preacher Goodman objected not only on doctrinal issues but because he thought play gatherings were "vain" when there was much charitable and health work to be done in the city following plague outbreaks and losses of ships at sea.[106] Others argued for the profitability of recreational enterprise. Indeed, as the Bishop of Chester observed of both the counties of Lancashire and Cheshire, the campaign to restrict Sunday sports was undermined by many middling and gentry individuals.[107] Certainly, some of those who were supposed to police illicit commercial play had their own dogs in the game, so to speak. The local gentry leader Lord Strange sat on the Quarter Sessions commissions in Lancashire. In 1587, he was present in Manchester while several members of the Radcliffe family and other names were cited "For Causing a bear to be baited upon Sunday."[108] Strange and his family famously patronised bearwards during this period, including John Seckerston in nearby Nantwich.[109] Bears were synonymous with the Stranges and the Derbies (also known as the Stanley family) in local culture. Strange's affinity for the animals was well-established enough to be part of an impromptu protest song by the 1620s: "The Constable ere next Assises shall loose both his ears / For serving a warrant upon my lord Strange his bears."[110] The song may well have been a known and recycled verse, like an early modern oral meme (not least given the prevalence of other folk songs about bears based on early modern events in Cheshire that are still sung today[111]). The ballad of Strange's bears was sung in this recorded instance as a libel[112] during an argument in Northwich, when ale-seller John Venables ignored the local constable's commands by baiting bears at his venue. It accordingly reveals the muddiness of play regulations at local levels, and the opening couplet neatly sums up the paradoxes and conflicts involved in policing play: sometimes those charged with prosecuting such transgressions were themselves strong supporters of the animal entertainment industry and its purveyors. On the other hand, while patronised bearwards ostensibly had some protection and support, zealous prosecutors either overlooked or were sceptical about entertainers' licences and credentials. Even the King's official servants, sent into Hampshire in 1611, were accused by a magistrate of falsifying documents and roughly and rudely imprisoned.[113]

It was not only the region's elite who held conflicted attitudes towards play and its crowds. In the 1620s, an imprisoned bearward was broken out of the stocks by an anonymous local in Nether Peover, and the freed man went onto bait his animals in express contempt of local justices of the peace.[114] A little north, in Manchester, the town's court ordered restrictions on all forms of celebratory ales or "drinking in assembly" in 1568 with attendant fines, "provided always that this order shall not extend to ales for highways, bridges, or churches."[115] Evidently, play (encompassing a variety of performance types or sports, such as bear-baiting) was happily licensed when it had wider community benefits through fundraising. Similarly, the puritanical impulses of some vocal churchmen and aldermen divided a city like Chester, as demonstrated by arguments over the 1575 Whitsun pageants. While more explicitly pre-Reformation-style pageants were proscribed, Chester instituted other forms of formalised play—in set-ups that parallel many of the playhouse structures described in Chapter 1 of this book. 1610 saw the launch of an annual St George's Day horse racing event on the Roodee—the plot of marshland outside Chester's walls—which still takes place today. The races were marked by a "people-pleasing spectacle" of all manner of visual intrigue, from climbing the top of church steeples to speeches and dramas.[116] A published pamphlet capturing the inaugural event and its celebratory shows pointed out the character Joy, mounted on horseback, was seen to be "rejoicing at so great a concourse of people, never there before seen, and praising the good meaning of what there was undertaken and performed."[117] Such performances channel both earlier forms of street performance, like the Whitsun plays that had proved so controversial by the 1570s, and the wider pageantry that typified urban politics across early modern England, transmuting it into a new framework—one that championed classical and British mythology and that sought to emphasise the even greater crowds drawn to the event. In line with the "secularisation of civic ritual" Tracey Hill detects in London,[118] the shows initiated a movement away from religious performance and towards competitive sport, game, and physical feats sponsored by the city itself (a conjunction of play and urban policy discussed in Chapter 4). The author describes the races as "a memorable and worthy *project*," a term whose practical connotations are tellingly linked to new empirical methods of invention, commerce, and planning.[119] Accordingly, many spectators watched the first ever Roodee race and continued to do so over the subsequent decades and centuries. The city's approach to "concourse" had shifted within 40 years, towards a celebration of mass spectatorship within the approved institution of an official horse race, regardless of periodic puritanical opposition. Races had been run on the "perfect natural amphitheatre" of the Roodee since the mid-sixteenth century,[120] but the St George's day races from 1610 represents a crystallisation of early modern England's ever-commercialising sport industry—with city-sponsored prizes for the winners, to boot.

Many of the city's population formed a play traffic of their own. Where visitors like Blanche Webb travelled to Chester to see its dramatic outputs, so in the wake of their suppression the city's middling and elite made their way to recreational centres like Congleton—with its fixed places of play, including the cockpit described in Chapter 1 and discussed at length in Chapter 4. Congleton paid regular concessions for wine for visiting gentleman from nearby locations. In 1601, for example, visiting gentle-folk were named in the city accounts in a rare instance of specificity. The distinguished visitors included John Brereton and a kinsman in his company, while further money was paid out for "wine bestowed upon Sir John Savage knight & the gentlewomen."[121] Brereton was later to be an alderman and mayor of Chester, while we have already met John Savage, who pushed through the Whitsun plays in the city in 1575 despite some local outrage. Congleton is over 40 miles east, as the crow flies, of Chester, yet these gentlemen formed part of its leisure traffic—quite likely on repeat occasions, given the numerous expenses for unnamed gentlemen and the cultural cross-traffic between Congleton and Chester. In London, recreational journeys were repeated over a short distance, but here in the more sparsely populated county of Cheshire they formed expansive distances. Such travels were not exclusive to men and women of substance. Numerous records testify to the lengths travelled by ordinary individuals in the name of sport and leisure. A group of Chester butchers made their way to Barnhill in 1612, for instance, to set their dogs on a bear at a baiting over ten miles from their home.[122]

These playing journeys occasioned a different kind of working traffic—that of the humans and animals who made play possible. Dogs like those of Chester's butchers are a case in point. They travelled with their owners to baitings—and, if lucky, back again. The journey of one such dog is mapped out in detail in a deposition from 1609. Roger Thropp (often before the courts for his questionable behaviour) explained that he and one Richard Browne had recently met at Chester's Northgate, from where they planned to travel to Norley, over ten miles east. On their way out of Chester, they opened the back gate of a tanner called William Lynyall and whistled for his dog. When it came running from the back garden, Thropp and Browne dognapped the animal and took it to Browne's father's in Boughton, just outside Chester. From there, they eventually travelled up to Norley and "did there bait him with a bear that was then in the same town & was there wounded & hurt by the same bear, and that the [next] day the said Browne returned towards Boughton and brought the said dog with him" to Tarvin—another small town east of Chester—"and left him there at an alehouse, for that the said dog was not able to go any farther."[123] After about four days in the alehouse, Browne eventually brought the dog with him back to Chester and dropped him at the city bars. The poor animal promptly ran back to his master's house. This cruel and descriptive tale vividly recreates a playing journey for one of its many unwilling participants. It enigmatically leaves out a few details we might like to hear about—why did they go to Lynyall's gate? Did they want his dog in particular, and if so why? Why did they want to go to such trouble to participate in animal blood sport some distance from their home? Nonetheless, the dog's journey is one of the few instances in which archival documents focus on an animal's itinerary.[124] It strikingly mirrors human recreational journeys, down to a stay at an alehouse, and indicates how the leisure industry in Cheshire both demanded and created more-than-human traffic, too.

Over the border in Lancashire, one angry resident got so cross with bearwards who "refuse the broad way" (or high way) and "Cometh with their bears" via "the foot way which lieth by the Cheek of [his] house door" that he took a petition to the court. The unwelcome traffic was compounded by the fact that the bears in question were "very Cursed bears, for fear of his wife, Children, and Family in putting them in a fright as they have been heretofore." The petitioner pleaded for the judges to issue an order that all bear traffic must use the high roadway and not the footway.[125] These traffic concerns seem distinct from Londoners' journeys over fields to playhouses, but they represent a similar concern about access and land use to Holywell's new "ways." Each discrete playing journey had an impact on individual lives. Here, one man's concern was for his family's wellbeing as numbers of bears trooped up and down the walkway of his house. From the bearwards' perspective, however, such journeys were part of a necessary playing network that spanned the sparser settlements of Cheshire and Lancashire. As we have seen with Peter

Brome, many of the same bearwards can be found ranging between the towns and villages of these counties.

For play purveyors like these, the very idea of *journeying* was fraught with meaning; it formed a central focus of regulations aimed at bearwards, who were associated with vagrancy and criminality.[126] In Bunbury, John Boland was presented before the court as "a wandering rogue travelling with his bears from place to place contrary to the statute in that case provided."[127] National restrictions on who could make their living through performance or sports (limiting "masterless men" who made a living through illicit play) made it difficult for "wandering" entertainers to escape such legal sanctions. The very idea of "travelling" therefore had an uneasy relationship with play and the ability to draw crowds. Yet repeated arrests of the same bearwards over many years, including John Boland, suggest it did not dissuade everyone. Indeed, Mark Brayshay has noted the importance of a huge upsurge in travelling entertainers during Elizabeth's reign and beyond. "Their passage along the highways of the realm would certainly not have gone unnoticed," he observes, and "in addition to numerous carriers, drovers, traders, peddlers, postboys, pursuivants, messengers and soldiers likely to be encountered with increased regularity on the highways of England by the later sixteenth century, there was a sizeable corps of touring entertainers."The wandering play-purveyor therefore formed part of England's "growing volume of road traffic."[128] This recreational traffic in turn played an important role in shaping conceptual understandings of both place and nation. Not only did many of England's bearwards represent local power brokers (like the Stanley family or the monarch) but their routes linked communities across the country. Bears, for instance, "formed part of a complex flow of bodies and cultural practices around the nation," Julie Sanders explains, "acting as a bridge between metropolis and region, and between those smaller 'circuits of knowledge' constituted by those regions themselves."[129]

The examples here have sought to look beyond anti-play sentiments to gain a more textured picture of recreational crowds in the northwest. Yet authorities' vocabulary still dominates. How do we recover other contemporary notions of the crowd? Looking towards depositional evidence, like that touched on above, can help expand our accounts of the playing industry beyond regulatory frameworks, which typically dominate theatre history.[130] Indeed, a wider account of leisure in early modern Chester helps contextualise and individualise the playing crowd. Numerous depositions from sites of play indicate who attended these events and what their motivations were for doing so.

In 1585, for instance, the shoemaker John Sale indicates a typical play routine for a skilled, middling artisan in early modern Chester. At 9 o'clock, after dinner with his wife, he visited his brother and fellow shoemaker James for half an hour, before they both went to Robert Bushell's alehouse. There, they drank a pot of ale in an impressively quick half an hour. They then went together to Richard Weeks' (a cooper) and spent an hour with two men—John Tompson and Edward Chorleton—who were playing at tables, a game like backgammon very popular in early modern playing places and alehouses. John himself "did take on parts to play at the tables and there spent a penny and from thence came home again after evening prayer about four of the clock and sat by the fire till supper." After supper, he returned to Darwall's alehouse where he, a carter called Phillip, and a Manx clerk or servant played at cards. He was home by nine, after twelve hours of leisure spent in between prayers and supper. Others who observed John's routine claimed he was overcome with drink at points throughout the day, and that he was out much later than asserted (hence his appearance before the court).[131] Nonetheless, this play schedule indicates some of the impulses involved in play traffic in a regional city like Chester: visiting family and making bonds with fellow tradespeople (both in one's craft and in adjacent ones); gambling and competition; and drink. John Sale's detailed routine, as with others elsewhere in such records, suggests a regularity in visits to certain Chester establishments: here, Darwall's; elsewhere, venues like Thropp's tavern or Aldersey's (for the better-off), Duddon's, Foxall's, the Crow, the Saracen's Head. Although many such playhouse-goers do not leave behind "diaries" or other forms of life-writing like those mentioned above, these depositions help us piece together, with indicative time-frames, the leisure journeys of early modern England and the kinds of social networks that undergirded them.

We can take a visit back in time to Chester in order to bring into concentrated focus the play experiences of those in the city. Let us return, then, to two months at the end of 1612. In November that year, we find ourselves observing more shoemakers' companionship. We call in at Widow Duddon's alehouse, where we drink with five journeymen shoemakers until four in the morning, helping them see off their nine or ten cans of ale.[132] We then return the following month, as it seems Duddon's was a regular haunt for our new friends the shoemakers. We find seven of them there in December, drinking with a soldier who was so drunk he could not properly object when they steal his sword.[133] The craft solidarity that underpinned apprentice riots in London could also, it seems, occasion more companionable sociability in alehouses and similar venues (if with similar hostility to outsiders). When a visiting shoemaker from York came to Chester, he was able to find several others of his trade drinking at Randall Ince's and join them for several hours.[134] Back on our travels in 1612, however, we decide to sample some of the wider entertainment hosted by play venues. The same week we meet the shoemakers at Duddon's, we call in at the vintner William Moores. Here we find Elizabeth Craddock, who is visiting Chester to see her mother. Another lodger, John Peacock, is also staying the night, and he happens to be a professional piper. We hang around long enough to hear Peacock playing late into the night in the company of other revellers and even join him and a maid in dancing the night away. Thankfully for our reputations, Moores assures us in the morning that "not any of the watch came to this examinate's house this night last past, to command him to shut his doors or go to bed."[135] In other words, despite orders restricting the hours and nature of play, this establishment fell under the radar of the watchmen responsible for regulation. A whistlestop leisure tour like this of Chester in late 1612 indicates how crowds visiting sites of play were not homogenous "assemblies," as many authority documents imply. We can get a small glimpse through such depositional journeys into the motivations, personalities, and itineraries of the playing crowd—and imagine ourselves among them.

Those playing journeys were an important and increasingly central part of early modern Chester's socio-economic landscape. In 1577, a visitor from York and his wife "came to this City […] chiefly to see the pastimes here."[136] The notion of leisured walking was as prevalent in Cheshire as it was in Moorfields. Across the mid-Elizabethan period, the idea of journeying towards defined sites of commercial play was increasingly commonplace. By 1623, visitors were even more frank. When asked why he was visiting Chester after an alleged horse theft, Thomas Parker explained that "he came to this City in company with one Mr Bagnall where [they] met with Mr Harcott and they all three had promised to meet one Mr John Cottingham here at Chester, having no other business here but to be merry."[137] This honest admission frames journeys into the only city in Cheshire through play. Just as London's traffic was reshaped by playhouses, so Chester became defined as a recreational destination, its racing course, alehouses, musical performances, and nearby animal sports drawing people whose motivations encompassed the many early modern meanings of "entertainment," in the language of the *Three Ladies of London*. At the same time, Chester individuals of all social stations departed out of the city on longer journeys of play of their own, visiting the likes of Congleton, Barnhill, or Norley to defined sites and events of play like animal baiting or cockfighting.

Northwest England was therefore characterised by a multitude of different playing journeys, from the trip to the local alehouse to tens of miles to a known gathering or a play hub like Congleton. Not all these journeys were made by humans. Dogs and bears populated the landscapes and streetscapes of Lancashire and Cheshire, causing a perhaps unwilling traffic generated by local recreational proprietors and purveyors. As elsewhere in England, attitudes towards such playing traffic were ambivalent. There are plenty of examples of concerted campaigns to restrict illicit, illegal, or broadly undesirable forms of play, underscored by religious sentiment and economic conviction. Yet despite a notable legal crackdown on such activities from the late sixteenth century onwards, the many records from the area testify to the frequency with which individuals and communities disregarded official orders. The crowds drawn by playing events in an inner-city alehouse, a well-fitted town-sponsored cockpit, or a rural marketplace were not just mass "assemblies," as so much anti-ludic sentiment would suggest. Depositions from the period help us understand the rationale of those willing to journey miles for recreation. Sometimes, as with all historical sources, they might also add further mystery and intrigue by avoiding many of the questions we would like to ask ourselves from 400 years in the future. Yet even among those who do not typically leave written paper trails in dairies, memorandum books, or letters, we can discover historic play itineraries: visits to Widow Duddon's alehouse, plans to make merry, pipers keeping guests up all hours, and visits to see relatives. These are the stories that make up the playhouse crowd.

Playhouses and playing locations transformed both their physical and social environments. Visitors to venues of all stripes made journeys that shaped early modern cities and towns, generating human and more-than-human traffic that resulted in new built infrastructure. It also produced fresh conceptions of what it meant to travel for leisure and where one would go. As play commercialised across England from the sixteenth century onwards, and especially in the wake of the dissolution of the monasteries, land was available for new recreational purposes. Anne Thorne's testimony about Shoreditch in London relates the changes made by new landlords with an eye on the leisure market. In Cheshire, new play forms replaced older traditions even as political and religious figures objected—gambling and competitive racing and an expansion in travelling bearwards and their game. We often think of historical theatres as fixed places, where individuals were transformed into audiences by the price of admission.[138] Yet the field of modern performance studies has long stressed the importance of journeys: "An audience not only goes to the theatre; it goes to the particular part of the city where the theatre is located."[139] This chapter has explored the nature of that *going* and its effects—not on the reception of drama but on the wider physical and mental infrastructures of the early modern town or city. The shaping of such infrastructures was crucial to early modern playhouseness. Chapter 4 continues to explore the relationship between venues and their immediate environments by thinking about the types of community catalysed or generated by playhouses.

Notes

1 JORS 20 fo. 187 (6 Dec. 1574), COL/CC/01/01/020-21, MS, London Metropolitan Archives, London.
2 William Ingram's *The Business of Playing* (Ithaca: Cornell University Press, 1992), pp. 131–46. See also discussion in this book's introduction.
3 Harleian 286 fo. 102, MS, British Library, London.
4 Henry Chettle, *Kind-Harts Dream* (London, 1593), C3r.
5 Michael West has queried the idea of there being "playgoers" at all in the 1580s and earlier, suggesting there was little sense of the idea of attending a play as a distinct activity: "Were There Playgoers During the 1580s?", Forum, ed. Andy Kesson, *Shakespeare Studies* 45 (2017): 68–76.
6 For a discussion of the crowd and its association with political discontent, see John Walter, *Crowds and Popular Politics in Early Modern England* (Manchester: Manchester University Press, 2006). This chapter takes a different approach, considering the idea of "concourse" in the context of commercial leisure rather than popular political sentiment (though, as we shall see, the two do overlap).
7 John Field, *A Godly Exhortation* (London, 1583), C2r-v.
8 *English Professional Theatre, 1530–1660*, eds Glynne Wickham, Herbert Berry, and William Ingram (Cambridge: Cambridge University Press, 2000), p. 277.
9 For discussion of this and other playhouse consistory court cases, see Loreen L. Giese, "Theatrical Citings and Bitings: Some References to Playhouses and Players in London Consistory Court Depositions, 1586–1611," *Early Theatre* 1 (1998): 113–28.
10 DL/C/0220 (also at microfilm X079/041) fo. 529v, MS, London Metropolitan Archives, London.
11 DL/C/0220 420v; 530r.

12 In particular, see records in the Bethlem Bridewell Hospital, which policed London's moral misdemeanours. For discussion of these records in relation to play, see Duncan Salkeld, "Literary Traces in Bridewell and Bethlem, 1602–1624," *Review of English Studies* 56.225 (2005): 379–85; *Shakespeare among the Courtesans: Prostitution, Literature, and Drama, 1500–1650* (Farnham: Ashgate, 2012)

13 DL/C/019, fo. 409v.

14 DL/C/019 fo. 440r.

15 Ashmole 219, MS, Bodleian Library, Oxford.

16 Canterbury Cathedral Archives, Literary MS E31 f 2; f. 4, f. 7, f. 7v, MS, Canterbury Cathedral Archives, Canterbury, Kent.

17 *English Professional Theatre*, p. 416.

18 Duncan Salkeld, *Shakespeare and London* (Oxford: Oxford University Press, 2018), pp. 130–1.

19 See Avril Leech's doctoral thesis, which includes mention of the economic and civic accomplishments achieved by second-generation immigrants in Canterbury (see, ie, p. 115): "Being One Body: Everyday Institutional Culture in Canterbury and Maidstone Corporations, 1600–1660," PhD Thesis, University of Kent (2019), unpub.

20 *Returns of Aliens Dwelling in the City and Suburbs of London*, Vol. 2, eds R.E.G. Kirk and Ernest F. Kirk (Aberdeen: Aberdeen University Press, 1902), p. 369.

21 *Returns*, p. 367. See also SP 9/102, MS, The National Archives, Kew, London; Add. MS 48082 fos. 87–121, MS, British Library, London.

22 *Returns*, p. 370.

23 For discussion of terms like "stranger" (and related economic terms to these long-term residents, like "denizen") see Nandini Das, João Vicente Melo, Haig Z. Smith, and Lauren Working, *Keywords of Identity, Race, and Human Mobility in Early Modern England* (Amsterdam: Amsterdam University Press, 2021).

24 Imtiaz Habib, *Black Lives in the English Archives, 1500–1677*, 2008 (Routledge: Abingdon, 2020).

25 Imtiaz Habib, "The Resonables of Boroughside, Southwark: An Elizabethan Black Family Near the Rose Theatre," *Shakespeare* 11.2 (2015): 1–13. See also Salkeld's discussion in *Shakespeare and London* of Black residents and the stage, pp. 142–8.

26 Farah Karim-Cooper, "The Materials of Race," *The Cambridge Companion to Shakespeare and Race* (Cambridge: Cambridge University Press, 2021): 17–29. pp. 22–3.

27 DL/C/0220 (14 June 1611) (also at microfilm X079/041); DL/C/0219 f. 411r (also at microfilm X079/040), MSS, London Metropolitan Archives, London.

28 Kim F. Hall, *Things of Darkness: Economies of Race and Gender in Early Modern England* (Ithaca: Cornell University Press, 1996), p. 71. See also Habib, p. 157; p. 180.

29 Karim-Cooper, p. 27.

30 William Lambarde, *Perambulation of Kent* (London, 1576), Aa2v.

31 C24/228/10, MS, The National Archives, Kew, London.

32 See Angela McShane, "Drink, Song, and Politics in Early Modern England," *Popular Music* 35.2 (2016): 166–90; for questions of cash, see Craig Muldrew, "'Hard Food for Midas': Cash and Its Social Value in Early Modern England," *Past and Present* 170 (2001): 78–120; for foodstuffs, see Joan Thirsk, *Food in Early Modern England: Phases, Fads, Fashions, 1500–1760* (London: Bloomsbury, 2006).

33 *Records of Early English Drama: Oxford*, Vol. 1, eds John R. Elliott Jr, Alan H. Nelson, Alexandra F. Johnston, and Diana Wyatt (Toronto: University of Toronto Press, 2004), p. 535.

34 Reavley Gair, *The Children of Paul's: The Story of a Theatre Company, 1553–1608* (Cambridge: Cambridge University Press, 1982), p. 10.

35 For distinctions between indoor and outdoor theatres and their demographics and cultural meanings, see Sarah Dustagheer, *Shakespeare's Two Playhouses: Repertory and Theatre Space at the Globe and the Blackfriars, 1599–1613* (Cambridge: Cambridge University Press, 2017) and Eoin Price, *'Public' and 'Private' Playhouses in Renaissance England: The Politics of Publication* (Basingstoke: Palgrave, 2015).

36 Thanks to Heather Knight's personal correspondence for these estimated figures, based on crowd modelling software and archaeological plans.

37 Ben Jonson, *The Devil Is an Asse* (printed with *Bartholomew fayre*) (London, 1631), N2r.

38 *English Professional Theatre*, p. 527.

39 See Pascale Aebischer's discussion of *The Changeling*, dir. Dominic Dromgoole (Sam Wanamaker Playhouse, Shakespeare's Globe, 2015) in *Shakespeare, Spectatorship, and the Technologies of Performance* (Cambridge: Cambridge University Press, 2020), pp. 53–4.

40 JORS 20 fo. 187.

41 Susan Brigden, "Youth and the English Reformation," *Past and Present* 95.1 (1982): 37–67.

42 Lansdowne 71 fo. 28, MS, British Library, London.

43 Chettle, C3r.

44 Ian Archer, *The Pursuit of Stability: Social Relations in Elizabethan London* (Cambridge: Cambridge University Press, 1991), p. 4. See also John Walter, "A Foolish Commotion of Youth? Crowds and the 'Crisis of the 1590s' in London," *The London Journal* 44.1 (2019): 17–36.

45 A.L. Beier, "Social Problems in Elizabethan London," *The Journal of Interdisciplinary History* 9.2 (1978): 203–21. p. 213.

46 Ilana Krausman Ben-Amos, *Adolescence and Youth in Early Modern England* (New Haven: Yale University Press, 1994), p. 84; Steve Rappaport, *Worlds Within Worlds: Structures of Life in Sixteenth-Century London* (Cambridge: Cambridge University Press, 1989), noting that there were "approximately 15,000 apprentices […] and another 12,000 young men working as journeymen" by the end of the sixteenth century, p. 11; p 232.

47 Paul Griffiths, *Youth and Authority: Formative Experiences in England, 1560–1640* (Oxford: Clarendon, 1996), p. 134.

48 Griffiths, p. 134.

49 Ben-Amos, p. 194.

50 JORS 20 fo. 388.

51 *Records of Early English Drama: Cheshire (including Chester)*, Vol. 2, ed. Elizabeth Baldwin, Laurence M. Clopper, and David Mills (Toronto: University of Toronto Press, 2007), pp. 780–1, trans. pp. 985–6.

52 Ben-Amos, p. 194.

53 For more on debates surrounding cohesiveness of "youth culture," see Edel Lamb, "Youth Culture," *Ashgate Research Companion to Popular Culture in Early Modern England* (Farnham: Ashgate, 2014): 31–42.

54 For discussion of the significance of roads to early modern drama and literature, see *Reading the Road, from Shakespeare's Crossways to Bunyan's Highways*, eds Lisa Hopkins and Bill Angus (Edinburgh: Edinburgh University Press, 2020).

55 E134/44and45Eliz/Mich18, MS, The National Archives, London.

56 John Stowe, *Survey of London* (London, 1598), I8r.

57 Laurie Johnson, "Not So Tedious Ways to Think about the Locations of the Early Playhouses," *Reading the Road, from Shakespeare's Crossways to Bunyan's Highways*, eds Lisa Hopkins and Bill Angus (Edinburgh: Edinburgh University Press, 2020): 107–26. p. 122.

58 Johnson, p. 107.

59 Stowe, Aa1v.

60 REPS 17, fo. 168r, COL/CA/01/01/019, MS, London Metropolitan Archives, London.

61 *The Singularities of London*, eds Derek Keene and Ian Archer (London: London Topographical Society, 2014).

62 Richard West, *Court of Conscience* (London, 1607), D3v.

63 Laura Williams, "Green Space and the Growth of the City," *Imagining Early Modern London*, ed. J.F. Merritt (Cambridge: Cambridge University Press, 2001): 185–215. p. 191.

64 For a nuanced account of walking and theatre from the 1620s onwards, see Julie Sanders, *The Cultural Geography of Early Modern Theatre, 1620–1650* (Cambridge: Cambridge University Press, 2011), especially chapter 4. More widely, for leisure walking as part of new middle-class conceptions of politeness and fashionableness, see Peter Borsay, *English Urban Renaissance: Culture and Society in the Provincial Town, 1660–1770* (Oxford: Oxford University Press, 1991); Peter McNeill and Giorgio Riello, "The Art and Science of Walking: Gender, Space and the Fashionable Body in the Late Eighteenth Century," *Fashion Theory* 9.2 (2005): 175–204; Miles Ogborn, *Spaces of Modernity: London's Geographies 1680–1780* (London: Guildford P, 1998).

65 Sanders, p. 134.

66 John Stockwood. *A Sermon Preached at Paul's Cross* (London, 1578), I7v.

67 Bethlem Museum of the Mind, CLC/275/33011/4, fo. 291r.

68 Ashmole 219 fo. 56r, MS, Bodleian Library, Oxford.

69 *The Cultural Geography of Early Modern Drama*, p. 135. This exploration of Shoreditch and Moorfields looks some fifty or so years earlier than Sanders's case studies, to suggest that playhouses shaped travel and infrastructure in the area from as early as the 1570s.

70 Gordon paraphrasing Mark Jenner, see: Andy Gordon, "Materiality and the Streetlife of the Early Modern City," *The Routledge Handbook of Early Modern Material Culture in Europe*, eds Catherine Richardson, Tara Hamling, and David Gaimster (Abingdon: Routledge, 2015): 130–40. p. 136; Mark Jenner, "Luxury, Circulation and Disorder: London Streets and Hackney Coaches c. 1640–c.1740," *Streets of London: From the Great Fire to the Great Stink*, eds Tim Hitchcock and Heather Shore (London: Rivers Oram, 2003): 40–53.

71 E134/44and45Eliz/Mich18 (Thorne). Three other deponents also confirm this detail, implying it was a longstanding arrangement ("the same lane then was not used as a common high way"), but how long they "barred up" the route is not clear.

72 For more on enclosure, right, and resistance, see Andy Wood, *The Memory of the People: Custom and Popular Senses of the Past in Early Modern England* (Cambridge: Cambridge University Press, 2013).

73 Gordon, pp. 136–7.

74 Phil Withington, "Intoxicants and the Early Modern City," *Remaking English Society: Social Relations and Social Change in Early Modern England*, eds Steve Hindle, Alexander Shepard, and John Walter (Cambridge: Cambridge University Press, 2013), p. 253.

75 See Tim Ingold on the patterns of repetition and practice that mean a world "continually comes into being around the inhabitant"; *The Perception of the Environment* 2000 (Abingdon: Routledge, 2011), p. 153.

76 The National Archives MS C24/170.

77 Thomas Dekker, *Guls Horn Booke* (London, 1609), D2r.

78 See Roze Hentschell's study, *St Paul's Cathedral Precinct in Early Modern Literature and Culture: Spatial Practices* (Oxford: Oxford University Press, 2020) and *Old St Paul's and Culture*, eds Shanyn Altman and Jonathan Buckner (Basingstoke: Palgrave, 2021).

79 Bruno Blondè, Peter Stabel, Jon Stobart, and Ilja Van Damme, "Retail Circuits and Practices in Medieval and Early Modern Europe: An Introduction," *Buyers and Sellers: Retail Circuits and Practices in Medieval and Early Modern Europe* (Turnhout, Belgium: Brepols, 2006): p. 17.

80 Karen Newman, "'Goldsmith's Ware': Equivalence in *A Chaste Maid in Cheapside*," *Huntington Library Quarterly* 71.1 (2008): 97–113. p. 106.

81 Robert Wilson, *The Three Ladies of London* (London, 1583), A3r.

82 Wilson, A3v.

83 Chettle, C3r.

84 A confusing phrase, perhaps meaning to kick or stamp on.

85 Lansdowne 41 fos 31v-37r, MS, British Library, London.

86 John Twyning, *London Dispossessed: Literature and Social Space in the Early Modern City* (Basingstoke: Palgrave MacMillan, 1998), p. 216.

87 For a discussion of the crowd and its association with political discontent, see Walter, *Crowds*.

88 See, ie, Privy Council orders in 1597, PC 2/22 pp. 325–7, and 1597-8, PC 2/23 p. 181, MSS, The National Archives, Kew, London.

89 This is what Ian Archer describes as the status quo in early modern London's social fabric in *The Pursuit of Stability*.

90 *Records of Early English Drama: Cheshire (including Chester)*, Vol. 2, eds Elizabeth Baldwin, Laurence M. Clopper, and David Mills (Toronto: University of Toronto Press, 2007), p. 684.

91 pp. 693–4.

92 CHES 24/113/3, MS, The National Archives, Kew, London.

93 DL 3/7 f. 50, MS, The National Archives, Kew, London.

94 For background to religion in Cheshire, see R.C. Richardson, *Puritanism in North-West England; A Regional Study of the Diocese of Chester to 1642* (Manchester: Manchester University Press, 1972).

95 Harley 2173 fo. 107v, MS, British Library, London.

96 *REED Cheshire*, Vol. 1, p. 580.

97 *REED Cheshire*, Vol. 1, p. 137.

98 *REED Cheshire*, Vol. 1, p. xxxviii.

99 For background to the social significance of the Sabbath and its relationship to revelry, see Kenneth Parker, *The English Sabbath: A Study of Doctrine and Discipline from the Reformation to the Civil War* (Cambridge: Cambridge University Press, 1988); David Underdown, *Revel, Riot, and Rebellion* (Oxford: Clarendon, 1985).

100 *Records of Early English Drama: Lancashire*, "Historical Background," ed. David George (Toronto: University of Toronto Press, 1991), p. xxv.

101 Quoted at *REED Lancashire*, p. xxv.

102 *REED Lancashire*, p. xxv.

103 *REED Lancashire*, p. 230; "Historical Background" xxv-i.

104 Keith Wrightson argues that the courts of Lancashire were concerned with adjudicating local arguments rather than implementing a religious or political reform: "Two Concepts of Order; Justices, Constables, and Jurymen in Seventeenth-Century England," *An Ungovernable People: The English and Their Law in the Seventeenth and Eighteenth Centuries*, eds John Brewer and John Styles (New Brunswick: Rutgers University Press, 1980): 21–46.

105 Ethan Shagan sees the exchange of religious ideology and local pragmatism as key to the English Reformation more generally: "With fiscal considerations so intertwined with spiritual ones, [...] many communities divided over appropriate responses to the government's policies, and local factions often used the dissolutions [of monasteries and religious lands] as pretexts for financial manoeuvres and power plays," *Popular Politics and the English Reformation* (Cambridge: Cambridge University Press, 2002), p. 237.

106 *REED Cheshire*, p. 169.

107 *REED Lancashire*, xxv.

108 *REED Lancashire*, p. 58.

109 Elizabeth Baldwin, "John Seckerston: The Earl of Derby's Bearward," *Medieval English Theatre* 20 (1998): 95–103.

110 *REED Cheshire*, Vol. 2, pp. 752–3.

111 In 2020, Jackie Oates and John Spiers released a single, "Congleton Bear/Whittlesey Straw Bear," partly based on the folk song still sung in Cheshire that memorialises an alleged incident in which Congleton (or "Beartown") spent money needed to replace the parish bible on a new bear for baiting.

112 Clare Egan defines the early modern libel as "the public dissemination of information that was damaging to a person's reputation," involving "personal scandals creatively couched in verses, elaborate visual symbols, or mock ceremonies, and read, sung, posted, and published in local communities." Egan reads this as part of the wider performance culture of the period. "Performing Early Modern Libel: Expanding the Boundaries of Performance," *Early Theatre* 23.2 (2020): 155–68. p. 155.

113 MSS 002, Article 015, MS, Dulwich College Archive, Dulwich, London.

114 *REED Cheshire*, Vol. 2, pp. 744–6.

115 *A Volume of Court Leet Records of the Manor of Manchester in the Sixteenth Century*, ed. John Harland (Manchester: Chetham Society, 1864), p. 121.

116 Richard Davies, *Chesters Triumph in Honor of Her Prince* (London, 1610), A2r–A3r.

117 Davies, A4v.

118 Tracey Hill, *Pageantry and Power: A Cultural History of the Early Modern Lord Mayor's Show, 1585–1639* (Manchester: Manchester University Press, 2010), pp. 27–8.

119 Davies, A3r. For context on the term "project" as part of new approaches to government and financial organisations, see Henry S. Turner, *The Corporate Commonwealth: Pluralism and Political Fictions in England, 1516–1651* (Chicago: University of Chicago Press, 2016), pp. 45–7.

120 R.M. Bevan quoted in J.S. Barrow, J.D. Herson, A.H. Lawes, P.J. Riden, and M.V.J. Seaborne, "Leisure and Culture: Chester Races," *A History of the County of Chester: Volume 5 Part 2, the City of Chester; Culture, Buildings, Institutions*, eds A.T. Thacker and C.P. Lewis (London: Victoria County History, 2005): 255–60. p. 255.

121 *REED Cheshire*, Vol. 2, p. 627.

122 *REED Cheshire*, Vol. 1, pp. 18–9.

123 *REED Cheshire*, Vol. 2, pp. 749–50.

124 For more detailed such journeys, and their significance for human–animal relations and "human-ness," see Erica Fudge, *Perceiving Animals: Humans and Beasts in Early Modern English Culture* (Basingstoke: MacMillan, 2000), and for livestock animals, *Quick Cattle and Dying Wishes: People and Their Animals in Early modern England* (Ithaca: Cornell University Press, 2018).

125 QSB 1/130/35 (1635), MS, Lancashire Archives, Preston, Lancashire.

126 See the association of bearwards with vagrants and rogues following the 1547 Vagrancy Act and numerous subsequent legislation, which identified classes of vagabonds, ruffians, rogues, and "masterless men" as well as common players, the terms of which technically pertained to all commercial entertainers with no official patron. For more on vagrancy and social venues like alehouses, see Patricia Fumerton, "Not Home: Alehouses, Ballads, and the Vagrant Husband in Early Modern England," *Journal of Medieval and Early Modern Studies* 32.2 (2002): 493–518.

127 *REED Cheshire*, Vol. 1, p. 30 (1618).

128 Mark Brayshay, "Waits, musicians, bearwards and players: the inter-urban road travel and performances of itinerant entertainers in sixteenth and seventeenth century England," *Journal of Historical Geography* 31.3 (2005): 430–58. p. 451. Brayshay also speculates on how bear-baiting's commercial arrangements influenced the traffic and movement of animals: "bearwards were permitted to collect entrance charges from other spectators who came along to the bear-garden to see the show," he notes, and "as the creatures would have to be transported well-tethered or inside a cage loaded onto a wagon drawn by carthorses or mules, and costs of feed and other items must be kept, the relatively high income yielded by each performance was clearly necessary," p. 443.

129 Sanders, p. 8.

130 *English Professional Theatre, 1530–1660* devotes a third of its contents to "documents of control." *English Professional Theatre* (Cambridge: Cambridge University Press, 2000).

131 See ZQSF 36/?? [sic], MS, Chester Record Office, Chester. Transcribed in *Intoxicants and Early Modernity, 1580–1740* database. Online. Accessed 7 Aug. 2021.

132 ZQSF 61/37, MS, Chester Record Office, Chester. Transcribed in *Intoxicants and Early Modernity, 1580–1740* database. Online. Accessed 7 Aug. 2021.

133 ZQSF 61/46, MS, Chester Record Office, Chester. Transcribed in *Intoxicants and Early Modernity, 1580–1740* database. Online. Accessed 7 Aug. 2021.

134 ZQSF 49/32 (1600), MS, Chester Record Office, Chester. Transcribed in *Intoxicants and Early Modernity, 1580–1740* database. Online. Accessed 7 Aug. 2021.

135 ZQSF 61/47, MS, Chester Record Office, Chester. Transcribed in *Intoxicants and Early Modernity, 1580–1740* database. Online. Accessed 7 Aug. 2021.

136 ZQSF 30/72, MS, Chester Record Office, Chester. Transcribed in *Intoxicants and Early Modernity, 1580–1740* database. Online. Accessed 7 Aug. 2021.

137 ZQSF 69/79, MS, Chester Record Office, Chester. Transcribed in *Intoxicants and Early Modernity, 1580–1740* database. Online. Accessed 7 Aug. 2021.

138 Andrew Gurr's *Playgoing in Shakespeare's London* offers a thorough take on what happens from the admission fee onwards (Cambridge: Cambridge University Press, 1987).

139 Marvin Carlson, *The Haunted Stage: The Theatre as Memory Machine* (Ann Arbor: University of Michigan Press, 2003), p. 140.

4
COMMUNITY HUBS

The playing traffic mapped in Chapter 3 produced concentrated sites defined by play: commercial leisure destinations. These destinations were not only attractive to visiting travellers but facilitated a sense of neighbourhood. Indeed, early modern English ideas of community were not limited to the parish or the ward. Playhouses occupied important roles as community-facing and community-transforming institutions.[1] We have already seen how they altered their environments through human and animal concourse. This chapter follows that lead by thinking about the individuals surrounding the playhouse and the social identities it helped shape. In a period of heightened urbanisation, playhouses and their surrounding complexes represented alternative ways of community-making centred on consumption, cultural and economic capital, and recreation.

There were inevitable regional differences in the social, cultural, and political possibilities afforded by play. This chapter therefore focuses on three locations in different areas of the country: a council-run sports complex in Congleton in Cheshire; the playhouse in Wine Street in central Bristol with close ties to the city's elite; and London's Blackfriars playhouse, operating in a bustling cosmopolitan enclave from 1576 until the mid-1580s. Each was part of a network of nearby leisure enterprises, from high-end shops to sports facilities. Accordingly, this chapter thinks of playhouses as one part of a local concentration of recreational offerings. It brings together different examples of the playhouse's social benefits and its imbrication with neighbouring institutions, crafts, and individuals. It also points to the beginnings of a fan culture in which local identity and association were promoted through sports and leisure—not unlike, for example, football clubs today. Playhouses were never singular or discrete entities; they were part of the fabric of the early modern parish, liberty, street, or town.

DOI: 10.4324/9781003231127-5

Cockpit, Congleton

Congleton in Cheshire was and still is a small market town. In the early modern period, it was an incorporated borough, meaning it had its own municipal administrative bodies, was governed by a corporation made of freemen, and boasted privileges granted by the crown (in distinction from, for example, a manor whose judicial and administrative functions were dictated by the lord). The town had "between 1,500 and 2,000 inhabitants" by the 1660s, although it had suffered particularly badly from plague in the 1640s.[2] Its population from the late sixteenth century to this date is difficult to establish but is unlikely to have been much shy of these late numbers.[3] While the town itself was, therefore, small to medium sized, it was larger than many other Cheshire market towns. It also benefited from busy traffic, which was reflected in its service industry. In 1585 alone, there were three licensed innkeepers and 42 people running alehouses.[4] This is an extraordinary number for such a small community,[5] suggesting that Congleton was a regional centre for both travel and leisure and that there was "a very active intercourse kept up between this and other towns."[6] Their businesses were situated on one of the larger towns in the west of Cheshire, and while Congleton may not have sat directly on a major road, it was one of the few settlements in the area that might accommodate those travelling into or out of Cheshire on their way to Lancashire or London. This small Cheshire town accordingly had an outsize local presence. It paralleled much larger strategically and politically important places such as York—a city whose "economy of intoxication" represented its "role as a centre of consumption [...] in a rapidly expanding market economy."[7] The inn and alehouse licences of Congleton also stipulated they must host no unlawful games, a common requirement that sought to regulate the types of play, from animal baiting to dicing, frequently on offer at such venues. The sheer number of such places in Congleton and their capacity for—and, as we shall see, connection with—various leisure forms suggest that visitors came not only on their way elsewhere but purposefully to play—part of the leisure traffic explored in Chapter 3.

Substantial elements of Congleton's leisure and service industry were managed and funded by its corporation—the group of freemen who ran the town. Restrictions on unlawful play in alehouse licences were accordingly balanced by forms of lawful, municipally sanctioned and controlled play. Like other towns across the country, Congleton made regular payments to visiting bearwards, in particular, (but not exclusively) during wakes or ales (discussed in Chapters 1 and 3), as noted by Elizabeth Baldwin.[8] Less usual, however, is the extent of its expenditure on playing locations and structures. From 1582–3 (the earliest extant records from the town borough), substantial sums were lavished on its cockpit, which benefitted from expensive repairs or adaptations almost every year. Similar attention was paid to surrounding leisure infrastructure. In 1613, the town constructed (either from scratch or adapting an older site) a bull ring, which included paving around the site—indicative of importance and endurance.[9] In 1617, the town's archery butts were repaired and perhaps expanded.[10] Archery had always been encouraged by the crown and local authorities across early modern England as a virtuous pastime—one that set up martial skills and possessed admirable historical credentials. Here, its close relationship with other forms of town play perhaps confers some of archery's legitimacy on activities less universally praised across the country. The cockpit lay at the centre of Congleton's leisure facilities and formed the focal point for regular entertainment. 1614, for example, saw over five days' worth of work on the venue ahead of a "great Cockfight" at which visiting gentlemen enjoyed plenty of wine.[11] The event was part of a number of regular entertainments that characterised Congleton's social calendar and its corporate affairs.

The precise location and structure of the cockpit is difficult to ascertain from records, but it is very possible that it was in or on the grounds of an existing or former schoolhouse. Records refer occasionally to the site of the cockfight by a different name, as when John Wagge was paid in 1601 for "dressing the schoolhouse at the great cockfight."[12] There is precedent for such uses of school buildings: a teacher in Somerset was accused of keeping a grammar school only "under pre-tence and colour to keep school and teach and instruct youth" but in truth "did keep a school of defence commonly called a fence school […] And did likewise […] keep in the same a Cockpit game, and fighting Cocks."[13] It is possible that Congleton's schoolmaster was similarly involved in running its "cockings," as he claimed "all runaway cocks as his perquisite."[14] The possible cockpit-schoolhouse would be an impressively adaptable playhouse and was available for a variety of entertainment forms. It was regularly built up, modified, and re-lain with straw—suggesting regular wear and tear from its activity and perhaps a gradual expansion or improvement of the venue (part of a wider move in civic buildings discussed below). The work of thatchers, for instance, was central to yearly expenses on the site. It was also surrounded or set out with physical structures of uncertain form, and it featured timber piles, perhaps for tying up the fighting birds or perhaps foun-dation work to support other building or adornment. Robert Wilkinson was paid numerous times for work across the late sixteenth and early seventeenth centuries, including "for mending the Cockpit Rings and floor & for a board thereunto," the sizeable sum of 4 shillings and 3 pence, with wood used to make the piles for the cockpit rings.[15] The accumulation of work over 30 to 40 years indicates a sizeable structure with multiple such rings, which the town regularly refreshed and adapted. Indeed, in 1600, Wilkinson set about the task of "transposing the Cockpit from the lower part to the sills," suggesting a multiple level playing space for cockfights and audiences.[16]

Congleton's cockpit and surrounding leisure facilities—a kind of early modern municipal sports complex—clearly drew distinguished visitors like the "gentlemen" at the great cockfight in 1614, as well as a wide popular audience. Indeed, we saw in Chapter 3 how Chester's elite journeyed to Congleton for entertainment—individuals like sometime mayors of the city, John Brereton or Sir John Savage (who, as prominent local gentry, were influential across the county). Both men had close connections with the town itself, Savage being its high steward (and

Brereton's half-uncle).[17] The town's wakes or ales were, as elsewhere in the county, vibrant and democratic affairs that attracted crowds from all walks of local life. In Congleton, these events seemingly centred on bear-baitings. Bearwards were paid up to 15 shillings for bringing their game—nearly three times higher than common payments elsewhere in the country.[18] Three in particular—locals Raphe Shelmerdyne, William Kelsall, and John Boland—brought their bears to the town regularly in the 1610s. Given the crowds typically occasioned in the county by animal baitings, these events would have left Congleton's streets and playing venues packed with people and make sense of the numerous alehouses in the town, which would have been in great demand (and stood to make great profit) at such occasions.

Visitors came to Congleton not only to be wined and dined (as expenses tell us) but presumably to bet upon the cockfighting and other "sports" and perhaps to take in other entertainment, too. In 1623, Brereton enjoyed the corporation's hospitality "when the piper was here."[19] Music was closely bound up with sport and game. Elsewhere in Cheshire, in Wybunbury in 1605, a piper, Oliver Lacebie, was paid to

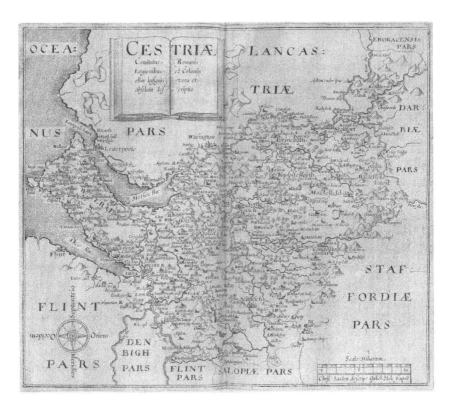

FIGURE 4.1 Map of Cheshire, from William Camden's *Britain, or A chorographicall description.* STC 4509 copy 1.

Used by permission of the Folger Shakespeare Library under a Creative Commons Attribution-ShareAlike 4.0 International License.

perform during a cockfight held by Jacob Bromsoe.[20] Cockfighting may well have been typically accompanied by music and perhaps other forms of entertainment. In 1620, Congleton paid the Cally brothers of Chester, musicians, to support a play taking place in the town, for which a scaffold was set up at the school-cum-cockpit: "Given to Cally the musician with Consent of the four overseers for his pains in coming from Chester [...]."[21] The payment suggests not only a multiplicity of play like that described in Chapter 2—characteristic of playhouses across England—but also testifies to the interactivity between Chester's urban leisure scene and the recreational hub of Congleton. The facilities offered by the town clearly earned it a reputation as a destination for play and sport.

The expenses discussed here testify to the town corporation's determination to strengthen and expand this element of its social identity and, in turn, reveal a defined economy of play. Garthine Walker has recognised the dominance of the leather industry in Congleton, as in other nearby market towns in Cheshire;[22] yet the corporation's investment in play seemingly generated another diffuse but discernible sub-industry. We have already seen how Robert Wilkinson was repeatedly paid for work on the cockpit. He was responsible for a variety of tasks from 1588 to the mid-1620s, including cleaning the venue, transporting earth and stone to shore it up, as well as "dressing the cockpit" or "making the Cockpit"—vague phrases that suggest a specialised practice perhaps difficult to recover today from patchy accounting entries.[23] Similarly, the venue depended on straw-drawing—a labour often undertaken by women—a subject explored at length in Chapter 5's exploration of Margaret Swayne, one such straw-drawer. Regular payments were awarded to women for carrying, watering, and drawing thraves of rye straw and sometimes this extended to arranging them in the cockpit, a job that fell to a man and his wife in 1600.[24] These cockpit dressers and makers drew on a range of skills and specialised knowledge in order to build and maintain Congleton's important recreational institutions. Their repeated acts of labour, stretching across nearly half a century, offered reliable income in exchange for physically shaping community amenities. Indeed, the town's cockpit was in many ways an early modern expression of *placemaking*—the collective reinvention or shaping of place for and by a particular community.[25]

These institutions correspondingly became symbols of Congleton's identity—both at home and abroad. In a period when traditional festive celebrations like Whitsun plays or Midsummer shows were contentious and largely in decline, the town substituted church-run and -orientated holidays with secular forms of leisure. Its built infrastructure provided new institutional outlets for play that helpfully shored up Congleton's political identity: not only were they able to draw in powerful figures through their hospitality, they made play and playing venues a point of pride. Indeed, the corporation's investment in its cockpit, archery butts, and bull ring occupied a parallel social and political position to the town hall. Such buildings "came more than ever to represent a strategic doorway to the urban community and to the values which came to prevail in that milieu," according to Robert Tittler: "Here more than anywhere else therein were located those facilities for representing and inculcating the values of the town and of its bourgeois leadership, both in regard to outsiders and to townsmen themselves."[26] Congleton's playing infrastructure suggests that conviviality, festivity, and drawing and hosting visitors (from local gentry to Cheshire works to passers-by) were values prized by the town and perpetuated via venues like the cockpit. During the later sixteenth and early seventeenth centuries, town halls increased in size and ornament—a Protestant shift away from the physical and institutional domination of the church towards a newly expanded secular power. Tittler's work has emphasised the importance of town halls to medium-sized locations like Congleton. "In addition to its role in facilitating economic interchange between the town and country," he observes, "the hall served as a doorway between two sets of values: that of greater licence, potential disorder, and subversion on the one hand, and that of order and authority on the other."[27] Tittler accordingly notes the decline in playing across most towns by the end of the sixteenth century. He identifies a reluctance to allow ludic activity in what were increasingly well-decorated and expensively constructed buildings.

Yet Congleton does not fit this mould. Rather, the energies invested in the town hall in so many of Tittler's case studies were spent in this Cheshire settlement on playing venues. They came to fulfil many of the same functions as the civic or municipal building, not least in offering "opportunity for civic authorities to regulate" play and in turn granting them the ability to "place their own stamp upon them as a means of shaping the cultural tenor of urban society."[28] Accordingly, the urban attitudes that shaped commercial leisure and consumption in metropolitan centres like London could be found, also, in this small market town. Congleton's playing venues, like town halls, offered an opportunity to fashion an institution for the benefit of the community and to shape and adopt an urban commercial mindset—one rooted in the organisations, practices, and systems of the English city.[29] The scale and population that underpinned such systems might not have been present in Congleton, but investment in its playing infrastructure guaranteed a fashionable and potentially lucrative source of entertainment that proved attractive enough to rival Chester, the largest urban centre of the area.

At the same time, the municipal playing venues reflected and shaped town pride and heritage and formed part of its inhabitants' sense of place. Robert Wilkinson, chief "maker" or "dresser" of the cockpit for nearly 40 years, held a respectable position in the town similar to the "mayor" of the bullring in Exeter (discussed in Chapter 1)— a form of officeholding and civic influence predicated on play. It is perhaps unsurprising, then, that we find the same Robert Wilkinson loudly intervening in a debate about blood sports in Newbold Astbury, a few miles south, in 1605. An eyewitness reported that,

> being at Astbury [...] where [there] was a Wakes & a Bearbait, [he saw one [...] Wylkenson of Congleton aforesaid draw his dagger & lift] up his staff[.] He saw the Bearward lift up his staff & Lay his hand on his dagger, to whom he heard [...] Robert Wilkenson of Congleton aforesaid say, 'take heed what you [...] do for if you offer any blows to any Congleton man it were better for you, you did not,' or [words] to that effect.[30]

The exchange indicates the effect of the town's playing culture on its citizens. Wilkinson was at Astbury in company with numerous other men and women of Congleton, there to "beat the bear."[31] The bearward in question had allegedly refused Wilkinson's fellow Congletonian, Hugh Whitacre, a course against the bear with his dog. Those from Congleton seemingly saw this as an affront against the town, leading to Wilkinson's warning not to lay a hand on "any Congleton man" and resulting in an affray between the bearward, Astbury locals, and Congletonians.

The skirmish lays bare the politics of early modern play and game, in which the particularities of a given sport (how many courses a bear should fight or what dogs should be set upon it and how) combined with local allegiances. Congleton's reputation as a place of play in the period and its enduring soubriquet "Bear Town" (still advertised in visitor materials today) were on full display in Astbury, where the "maker" of the town's playing venues felt compelled to defend its honour and reputation when questions of sport were (quite literally) at stake. Indeed, an entry in Congleton's court leet in 1590 indicates something of the town's sporting culture. The corporation ordered that "every person or persons that now do or hereafter shall keep any mastiff Dog or bitch unmuzzled during the space of one day & a night except the same be tied, shall for every such time forfeit & lose 3s 4d."[32] This fine for keeping unmuzzled mastiff dogs perhaps testifies to the centrality of bear-baiting in the town; ordinarily, such orders were prompted by multiple and repeated occurrence of the practice in question.[33] The community investment in animal sport was apparently matched, then, by individual residents who kept fighting dogs on their own property, ready to put them into game when possible. This telling entry gives insight into the society of Congleton and helps us understand occasions like the dispute at Astbury: these were men and women invested in blood sports on both a personal and a collective level.

Wilkinson's defence of Congleton men indicates a developing regional fan culture. The late sixteenth and early seventeenth centuries saw local rivalries increasingly expressed through sport, in particular, cockfighting. Indeed, Cheshire has form for such geographical competitiveness. In Shrewsbury in 1597, a

> match was made between the Cocks of Cheshire and Lancashire against the cocks of Shropshire and Wales; thither came Londoners with their cocks, which held with Shropshiremen, but in the end the Cheshiremen and Lancashire had the victory and went away with the gayness of great sums of Money.[34]

Not only was money at stake here, but the contest, like at Astbury, was predicated upon regional identity. Elsewhere, butchers from Chester were restricted from direct participation in the running of the game in 1612. One of them explained to the court that at a bear-baiting in Barnhill, which resulted in a fatal quarrel, "no Chester men should Carry any staves but put A Countryman indifferent from them to stave off their dogs."[35] In fact, this participant, Richard James, handed his stave (the stick used in the game to control or separate the animals) to a local woman. Although animal sport is often framed in this period in masculine terms, clearly women were also directly and actively involved in its running. The woman's role as an "indifferent" party suggests that geographical or civic identity conferred some bias on the travellers and would accordingly interfere with fair and proper play. These examples reveal how Cheshire's playing infrastructures extended beyond their phys- ical footprints into the minds, actions, and identities of its inhabitants. More specif- ically, Congleton's play complex paralleled the town hall, bringing together many of its symbolic associations—of pride, town history, and "civic authority, power, and legitimacy"[36]—as well as its practical functions, such as regulating play, entertaining powerful dignitaries, attracting visitors, and generating income. These qualities also exerted power abroad, undergirding residents' sense of identity and belonging. For Congletonians, whenever questions of play were at issue, questions of home and community were, too.

Wine Street, Bristol

Playhouses run by individuals also played important community roles. Bristol's Wine Street offers a focused example of community-building-by-play. The street was home to one of the longest-running documented playhouses outside of London (c.1605–c.1625), the tenement "commonly called the playhouse,"[37] run in its early years by Nicholas and Margaret Woolfe—an "inn" style property, with multiple rooms let out for different uses. The playhouse sat on a major road in central Bristol lined largely with two- to three-storey tenements occupied by middling trades- people, craftspeople, and widows with varying degrees of local political agency. Rather than generating antitheatrical resistance, the playhouse, like Congleton's cockpit, reflected and shaped this milieu. It seemingly supported Bristol's official entertainment offerings and had a mutually sustaining relationship with the city's corporation and members of the civic elite. Its proprietors also went out of their way to connect the playhouse to the surrounding neighbourhood by tying its legacy and profits to local causes, charities, and companies.

By the early seventeenth century, Bristol was a busily expanding port on its way to replacing Norwich as England's second city.[38] It had a population of roughly 12,000—considerably less than London's 200,000 but equal with York's and only 3,000 shy of Norwich. Bristol was also notable in having a substantial number of freemen—those who had completed an apprenticeship (or bought their freedom with money) and were able to trade or pursue their craft under the protections of the civic charter. Jonathan Barry estimates this number at about 20% of the population, equal to half of all adult men.[39] Therefore, although Bristol was an oli- garchical city ruled by elite men—often defined by their "merchant capital"[40]—it had a "large middle ground of masters, apprentices, and journeymen" who, despite occupying lower offices, were a substantial and politically important demographic.[41] Such individuals were central to the city's leisure offerings across every social status. For instance, Barry explains, "the merchant elite of 1600 were investing heavily in rich furnishings and plate, and they were more likely than others to possess pictures and musical instruments"; however, "many of these cultural items were produced by local craftsmen, and reflected local tastes and methods."[42]

Wine Street, the home of the playhouse, sat at the heart of this busy city and represented in miniature Bristol's changing physical and social world. The city centre was divided into small tenancies and had undergone significant structural shifts in the sixteenth century (in line with the "Great Rebuilding" discussed in Chapter 1). By around 1600, "investment had […] been made in the building of houses of three storeys across the city."[43] Inner areas saw a process of what we might now call "gentrification," with larger two- or three-storey shops inhabited largely by those who "were not poor, but nor were they members of the ruling or merchant elite"; in broader terms, "overseas merchants, rich retailers such as grocers, mercers, and drapers, and small shopkeepers such as shoemakers and tailors dominated" the area encompassing Wine Street.[44] It was here that Nicholas and his wife Margaret Woolfe had their playhouse—likely at Number 7, part of a trio of houses backing onto the parish church of Christ Church.[45] In 1589, Nicholas requested permission to enlarge this tenement, and by 1605, the property began to host players performing for a paying public. He and his wife were described at the time as putting up "certain Comedians whom he suffered to act and play within the said Rooms" for which both he and Margaret "took money"—all in the tenement identified by a complainant in a legal quarrel, Richard Cooke, as a "Common Inn."[46] The inn in question contained multiple rooms with only one exit. Like Richard Farrant's Blackfriars playhouse, discussed in the final section of this chapter, the playing part of the venue apparently occupied a part of a larger building, with a main entrance off Wine Street itself. Nicholas Woolfe explained how the property said to host the comedians had "very many Rooms," with only one "outer street door […] which is but one and the only way into all the whole house" and used "in Common between" occupants "for their several entries into their several and respective parts of the said whole house."[47]

The Woolfes' Playhouse therefore sat at the intersection between domestic interior and commercial streetlife that characterised central Bristol. This Wine Street business was essentially a house of multiple occupancy, described by contemporaries as both a playhouse and inn, in which commercial performance sat alongside residents who used it for other purposes. Such arrangements were typical of the street and of much of wider early modern England. Inventories from the playhouse's neighbours demonstrate that they too lived and worked, as was usual for the period, in the same building.[48] Life on early seventeenth-century Wine Street meant living in "multifunctional houses and spaces" characterised by the "penetration of work and leisure, domestic and commercial production."[49]

The broader neighbourhood of Wine Street indicates how it brought together those interested in various forms of cultural "play" and positions its environs as a particularly defined destination: a place to shop for medium-to-high-end goods, engage in varied forms of play and music, and socialise with the political elite. The playhouse itself sat at the entrance to Wine Street alongside several other commercial institutions. Its immediate neighbours either side (nos 6 and 8) were the prominent goldsmiths Humphrey Clovell and Richard and Edward Harsell, whose goods characterised south-west metalwork of the period. Round the corner lived Isacke Bryan, an instrument-maker whose family was resident in the vicinity of Wine Street's local parish church, Christ Church. The playhouse was also a few doors up from an important local inn, the White Hart, which was also owned by the Woolfes and that (as we shall see) played an important role in community cohesion. At the other end of the street was a recently built meal market (for selling grains and corn), which also provided standings or stalls for goldsmiths from all over the country at regular annual intervals.[50] The close concentration of such businesses on Wine Street mark it out as a commercial leisure district—one that delimited and shaped acts of consumption and recreation in the city. Indeed, the wider seventeenth century was a period in which luxury consumption and the theatre and service industries were exponentially expanding.[51] Wine Street's attractiveness to visitors interested in such non-essential spending therefore aligns it with the "specialist retail areas" that grew across the period and that form part of the long European history of shopping.[52] Here, the sale of high-end or luxury items overlapped with a burgeoning commercialised "play" industry selling services, and the two were closely connected. Inns and playhouses were, as Phil Withington observes of drinking venues, "inextricable from modern rituals of consumption and company among the wider populace," while Karen Newman has shown how goldsmiths' shops, like theatres or drinking holes, acted as centres of material social interaction.[53] These sites, where company and consumption overlapped, unite with the playhouse as institutions where commercialised leisure helped form and re-perform one's social identity.

Indeed, the playhouse sat at the intersection of local politics and play. When Nicholas Woolfe died, he entrusted two overseers with his estate and his son's upbringing: his "good friends" the Wine Street soapmaker and alderman Henry Yate and Joseph Rattle.[54] Woolfe's seemingly pre-existing relationship with Yate links this playhouse-owning cutler with an alderman who would go onto become mayor of Bristol in 1631, after two spells as churchwarden of the local parish, Christ Church. Yate links the playhouse's operations with the political elites of the city and hints at some of the personal networks that play facilitated in and around Wine Street. Not only was Yate himself the overseer of Nicholas's will, he also ran the playhouse, or at least administered its profits, in the years after Woolfe's death.[55]

Yate's investment in this commercial playhouse likely went beyond the duties of an overseer. The venue offered plenty to an alderman with eyes on the mayoralty. It seems likely it was used as a regular location for civic entertainment by the mayor and aldermen of the city. Performances were recorded in Bristol at the Guildhall for most decades of the sixteenth century, but after 1598 there is no explicit mention of the location where visiting players performed, prompting speculation that Woolfe's playhouse acted as an alternative venue.[56] These civic-sponsored performances are similar to Congleton's cockpit, which hosted a range of visitors and acted as a political meeting point for the region. Sally-Beth MacLean identifies a gradual decline in payments to players across the period, with the south-west moving from the most profitable of English touring circuits in the sixteenth centuries profitable to "one of the least rewarding in the seventeenth century."[57] The opening of Wine Street's commercial venue may well have made redundant the civic-sponsored performances at the Guildhall. Where Congleton used a municipal playing complex to host its official leisure activities, Bristol shifted to a privately run playhouse— one that could work alongside civic performance but equally be independent of city authority. Bristol's official payments to players may have declined steeply in the early seventeenth century, but the Wine Street playhouse generated revenue enough to operate until at least 1625.[58] The playhouse represented a new civic institution in Bristol, one that had a semi-autonomous relationship with the corporation and presented a commercial alternative to the city's Guildhall.

The Woolfes' venture offered social connections for more than just the city elite. Civic audit entries give clues as to who might have been spectating: a fee in 1587 notes that the visiting Lord of Leicester's players "played in the guild hall before them [the mayor and alderman] and others of the Common Council with diverse Citizens"[59]; the wording suggests both an elite and a middling or artisanal audience, and this may well have been the demographic of the Wine Street playhouse. These were the same individuals, then, who would have been involved in recreation at the parish level, linking play at the major level of city authorities with smaller-scale community structures. Wine Street was also home to prominent inns, the Rose and the White Hart, which hosted both parish and civic meetings. The White Hart was in fact owned by Margaret Woolfe, who inherited it from her previous husband, Thomas Thomas. Although the playhouse on Wine Street may already have been in operation by the time Margaret brought this property into her marriage to Nicholas in 1605, the conjunction of personal and business collaboration between them represents part of a concentrated play network formed from neighbouring, sometimes shared, enterprises.

Indeed, the White Hart occupied a similar social space to the playhouse. Margaret's late husband recorded 10 shillings spent during his tenure as churchwarden at the White Hart "after the parishioners had walked the bounds of the parish."[60] Walking the bounds of the parish (or beating the bounds) was an important act of parochial identity confirmation, both in the literal sense of marking parish territory and in bringing together parishioners as part of a ritualised expression of community.[61] Nicholas found in his wife's inn an existing model for community cohesion through commercial enterprise. Together, the two of them ran both businesses (discussed further in Chapter 5). Perhaps unsurprisingly, then, both commercial recreational spaces had ties to local governance and community organisation. Accordingly, like prominent parish inns, the playhouse offered an opportunity both to shape the community and to profit from it. It was an institution that channelled some elements of the corporation: a town or city's political body, which demanded both money and labour from members but rewarded office-holding with power, prestige, and an enviable social network. Neither Nicholas nor Margaret Woolfe belonged to Bristol's corporation, but the playhouse afforded them presence and participation both in the immediate community and the wider city.

The playhouse's community value is perhaps most forcefully articulated in Nicholas Woolfe's will. He left numerous charitable bequests, but all such benefaction was dependent upon the theatrical continuance of the playhouse:

> Provided always […] so long only as the same house shall continue a play house at that such players as do resort to the said City or inhabit within the same do usually play there and may be permitted and suffered quietly to play there […]."[62]

This remarkable document shows Woolfe attaching multiple values to his theatrical legacy that go beyond mere financial motivation. He was not the only playhouse proprietor to ensure his ludic legacy was perpetuated. When Edward Alleyn rebuilt the Fortune playhouse in north London in 1623 after it was destroyed by fire, he ensured the group of 12 owners who financed it were bound by lease not to alter or convert the playhouse "to any other use or uses than as a Playhouse for recreation of his Majesty's subjects."[63] The profits from the playhouse were a central part of Alleyn's bequest to the poor scholars of Dulwich College, which he had founded in 1619. Woolfe, however, is especially specific in his bequests and their relationship to "recreation." He left money aside for the company of Cutlers (of whom he was a practising member), but also recognised his role as a community figure by providing requests for other organisations, such as the poor of St Peter's parish and the poor parishioners of Newgate jail, the children of the city hospital, and almshouses in other Bristol parishes. By doing so, he affirmed his commitment to play as the enabler of these charitable acts, leaving the playhouse's commercial profits permanently intertwined with its community benefits. It accordingly continued to generate revenue to fund these requests for some 11 years after his death.[64]

The Woolfes' playhouse demonstrates a complex relationship between commercial venues and governmental institutions. The venue served not only as a social centre within the concentrated recreational zone of Wine Street, it had formal connections with civic government—through Nicholas's overseer Henry Yate and through likely civic performances at the venue. Nicholas's will suggests that he himself thought of the playhouse as central to the local community, as its continuance was essential to his posthumous charitable bequests. Often, individuals such as James Burbage and Philip Henslowe (Alleyn's father-in-law) are characterised (partly as a result of contemporary accounts and depositions) as nascent capitalists or entrepreneurs, but better understanding their Bristolian peers Nicholas and Margaret Woolfe suggests there are more complex factors involved in running a playhouse than profit—a point elaborated upon in Chapter 5's exploration of playhouse economics and personal motivation.

Blackfriars, London

We do not know what plays took place at the Wine Street playhouse, nor exactly what entertainment was on offer. Siobhan Keenan has argued there is "a strong possibility" the children's company founded under John Daniel's authority in 1615 might have performed there.[65] As we have seen, there is also a high likelihood that travelling players appeared at the playhouse, while later playbills for another venue in Wine Street—the Rose—suggest the kind of gymnastic tumbling discussed in Chapter 2.[66] Yet we cannot say for certain what went on in the rooms of Number 7 Wine Street or what plays "comedians" were performing. The Blackfriars in London offers a different case study that can help sharpen the relationship between the "community hub" of the playhouse environs and the precise nature of the play on offer.

In 1596, James Burbage had designs on a new playhouse to be built in the Blackfriars liberty of London. Certain residents found the idea distasteful, and they came together in a petition against the plans. This petition has long been read as a demonstration of community antitheatricalism, spurred by well-to-do residents and the godly reputation of the area. Yet Christopher Highley has questioned this assumption, pointing out that the petition's complaints "eschew religious and biblically inspired objections to playing for pragmatic arguments based on concerns about social order and public health." Moreover,

> the petitioners' anxiety about the disorder that a playhouse might bring to their neighbourhood was compounded by their recognition that, in the event of trouble, they could not rely on the City authorities for help. Blackfriars residents were themselves responsible for the upkeep and policing of their precinct, an arrangement that had its advantages as well as its drawbacks.[67]

The Blackfriars was known as a "liberty"—an area outside of the jurisdictional control of the city. Whereas Wine Street depended on a collection of retail and service businesses to mark it out as a defined locale, London's Blackfriars benefited from defined legal, material, and ideological forces, which, Mary Bly explains, "shaped each liberty into a unique space in the early modern imagination."[68] The petition drew on this sense of self-government to present the Blackfriars as a community who thoughtfully, and by necessity, regulated commercial play in their environs.

Yet the Blackfriars had hosted such commercial play for as long as it had been a liberty. The 1596 petition discussed by Highley was part of a much longer debate in the area about circumscribing or regulating the growing leisure services in its vicinity. Like Wine Street and Congleton, the Blackfriars was from the 1550s a fast-developing recreational complex. The former friary was sold into private hands in the 1540s and was early on populated with "an house 2 tennis plays with certain other void grounds late in the occupying of the Warrens" at the sizeable sum of £30 for the year, present until at least the early 1560s.[69] David Kathman's research has shown that those records that describe a "house" alongside tennis courts often indicate commercial recreation, with legal wording about these set-ups aimed at those who ran tennis courts for paying customers.[70] In a separate part of the vicinity, in the west half of the chamber that would become the first playhouse there, one Richard Frith—described as a schoolmaster—was listed as being "the proprietor of a 'dancing School'."[71] Frith's dancing school likely sat alongside the Warrens' tennis plays as a site of spectatorship and recreation, as well as a serious space to study the humanistically approved pursuit of graceful dance. Close by, a fencing school run by William Joiner and then by the Italian Rocco Bonetti drew both tutees and spectators. The very inception of the secular Blackfriars, then, was characterised as a destination for leisure, gain, and gambling.

By the 1570s, this reputation was enhanced further by the series of bowling alleys established in the former cloisters of the friary by Henry Naylor. These set a precedent for the anti-playhouse tenor of the petition in the 1590s. The overarching landlord of the Blackfriars liberty, William More, consolidated residents' complaints[72]:

> One Harrie Nayler of London Clothworker hath of late set up within the said precinct three common bowling Alleys: an alley for a play Commonly called nine holes & a place as it is reported provided for a game called black and white or else for a Dicing house To which plays there resort in great number as well prentices and servants as others being for the most part very poor men, who there spend and consume their time & very much money to their undoing, using there also detestable swearing, Noise and Crying to the great offence & annoyance & disturbance of all the Neighbours and diverse other honest persons, which unlawful games and assemblies the said Harrye Nailer maintaineth Contrary to the Queen Majesty's laws and Statutes of this Realm.[73]

Naylor's alleys in the "Inner Cloister" and garden were clearly successful, and his enterprise was also timely, chiming with the apparent popularity of such spaces in this period. Yet partly because of that popularity, More objected to the venture as a "place of Corrupt gain" and in an earlier draft observed that "the said Nayler only for lucre & gain there maintaineth."[74] These objections rest on the practical inconveniences afforded by public thoroughfare through the ostensibly private liberty, while also suggesting a distaste about open commercial gain from questionable pastimes—a distaste made clear by contrasting Naylor's activities with the liberty's proper character as "a place of good order Civil and quiet dwelling" that aimed to suppress "disorders and annoyances."[75] Again, prominent voices in the community, led by landlord More, sought to demarcate appropriate forms of play and regulate commercial activity.

Yet the Blackfriars nonetheless accommodated and perhaps even profited from its new concentration of leisure spaces. Highley observes that the petition of 1596 was eventually subject to a change of opinion (some years later) and that the economic benefits of theatrical traffic would have doubtless been attractive to the many artisans living in the neighbourhood.[76] Similar observations apply to the earliest years, too. While petitions like the one against Naylor disapproved of recreational resort, they equally served to negotiate and influence the identity of the local area. They were not necessarily outright bans on, for instance, gambling activities.[77] The Blackfriars community, it seems, had a complex and sometimes contradictory relationship with commercial play—which both characterised the area but could occasionally galvanise individuals into concerted opposition.

It was at the core of this incredibly dense recreational complex that William Farrant, choir master of the Chapel Royal, decided to build a playhouse in 1576. While More may have felt uncharitable towards Naylor's bowling alleys, he nonetheless leased several rooms to Farrant, in at least partial knowledge of his plans. More later protested that he issued the lease under false pretences, because Farrant "pretended […] to use the house only for the teaching of the Children of the Chapel, but made it a continual house for plays, to the offense of the precinct."[78] Yet there is no such promise or caveat in the correspondence or lease. Indeed, More's objection came after the playhouse had been operating for nearly a decade, with no other signs of trouble, and at a point when it was expedient for More to annul an agreement that had undergone a chaotic series of subleases. In the 1570s, then, Farrant added to the Blackfriars's play-scape of tennis courts, dancing school, fencing school, and bowling alleys with a "continual house for plays."

This new space hosted the Chapel's children's company, who proceeded to play for profit for several years at the venue. Their repertory can be partially recovered, thanks to surviving plays (which acknowledge performance at the Blackfriars) and court performances that record the name of plays performed there: *The Wars of Cyrus* (late 1570s/early 1580s?),[79] Anthony Munday's *Fedele and Fortunio* (c.1579–84), John Lyly's *Campaspe* (1583) and *Sapho and Phao* (1584), and George Peele's *The Arraignment of Paris* (1581–4). This list constitutes the earliest known repertory for any professional company in a commercial playing space. Children's performance of this period is often seen as a courtly affair, removed from plebeian day-to-day business,[80] yet these plays express a broad urban consciousness that complements the playhouse's own imbrication in the wider industries of the Blackfriars. Although the plays of the First Blackfriars Playhouse are ostensibly set in distant climes and/or distant times, they often signify (as arguments go for Shakespeare's *Comedy of Errors* or *Measure for Measure*)[81] topographical markers of the English city and the Blackfriars neighbourhood itself. Indeed, plays of the First Blackfriars can be seen as early examples of city comedy—plays that "took familiar London places as their setting."[82] In particular, Lyly's, Peele's, and Munday's plays demonstrate how "the places of wit in English comedy" are, long before the seventeenth century, "increasingly urban and increasingly familiar to its audiences."[83] The Blackfriars therefore allows us to understand the relationship between playhouse and community by reading these plays as belonging equally to both.

Attending to a dramatic play at the Blackfriars reveals what play petitions do not: that there was a symbiotic relationship between recreational enterprise and the local community. The repertory demonstrates how "the affordances of the local environment […] would inform the ways in which that play made meaning in the world."[84] Indeed, I follow Julie Sanders in "thinking from the playhouse outwards"—considering "what is proximate to the playhouse and how in turn that influences both what is staged and how what is staged at specific venues in turn has agency in the surrounding parish."[85] The Blackfriars is especially informative in this regard, because it offers an unusual wealth of surviving documentation—both about the operation of play institutions in the liberty and surrounding contexts as well as surviving play texts. Such connections are hard to establish when it comes to Congleton or Wine Street, where play content is now largely lost. The First Blackfriars therefore helps us understand the place of the playhouse in the community by taking us back to a neighbourhood in which the stage represented and reflected the local community.

Peele's *Arraignment of Paris*, Munday's *Fedele and Fortunio*, and Lyly's *Campaspe* explicitly draw on developments in the labour market, shifting immigration patterns, and technological and craft innovations brought in from abroad to speak to the world surrounding the playhouse. Highley has recognised the national diversity of inhabitants and craftspeople in the Blackfriars—a space that took in a range of churches and accommodated a plurality of tongues (at the very least English, French, Dutch, and Italian):

> the area was far from being an exclusive gated-community as some have claimed, and dwelling alongside the well-off were artisans and skilled alien craftsmen […] as well as the city's ubiquitous poor who huddled in the Blackfriars' alleys and tenements.[86]

The concentration of such artisans added to a sense that the liberty was not only religiously and socially eclectic but also positioned as a hub for foreign fashions, new technologies, and luxury manufactured goods—also forms of high-end recreation. The Blackfriars attracted alien hatband makers, button makers, gilders, perfume makers, and feather dressers, a confit maker (for luxury sweets), several jewellers, and a "goldbeater," coppersmiths, and cutlers. Blackfriars also included two clockmakers in 1583, Francis Noway and Francis Roian, who combine with the presence of two cross bowmakers, Glode Benvoys, (in 1571, 1582, and 1583) and Francis Vassal (1583) as further proof that the Blackfriars offered not only high-end goods but also technological products of practical use.[87]

Beyond the economic benefits of these trades, such crafts had cultural value, particularly when it came to technology. Clocks were associated with craft and design—especially more elaborate and visually spectacular clock-jacks—and functioned as ostentatious displays of innovative engineering. In the following century, Henry Peacham aligned clockwork and related mechanics with *sprezzatura*—the humanist ideal of manners and courtly behaviour taken from Castiglione's Italian *Il Cortegiano*—and the elite nature of clockmaking is particularly closely associated with pocket-watches.[88] The Italian Rocco Bonetti ran the elaborately decorated fencing school downstairs from the playhouse. It boasted a carpeted "fringe of gold" and a "Clock, with a very fair large Dial,"[89] representing not only continental fencing fashion but channelling more widely the international style elements of the Blackfriars. Bonetti carried his new and fashionable continental fencing artistry into the principles of his interior design. Perhaps the clock was even made or repaired by local clockmakers Noway or Roian, whose shops would have been heard and/or passed on the way to both fencing school and playhouse.

Early in Peele's *Arraignment of Paris*, an "artificial charm" rings out, a sound that would have echoed such inventions and trades in the vicinity and called to mind for certain audience members the continental clockwork on offer both in print and in the craft shops or leisure venues of the Blackfriars. In the play, Pomona calls for Pan and Flora to hearken to an offstage noise: "here is melody, / A charm of birds and more than ordinary," included in the quarto with the stage direction, "An artificial charm of birds being heard within."[90] While such sounds could be made with a bird whistle, they also recall the artificial song or organ-sounds that were associated with innovative machinery; indeed, in 1589 William Bourne compared artificial birdsong with "clocks, that do keep time."[91] The association of artificial sound effects with surrounding technology suggests that delicate or elaborate special effects were not confined to court sensation but had their place in the urban playhouse, too. Peele's *Arraignment* is filled with trees rising from the stage, thunder and lightning, and rolling golden balls; while many of these elaborate effects might be court-specific, they would certainly not be out of place in a liberty filled with strange crafts—even on the tiny Blackfriars stage.

Fedele and Fortunio and *Campaspe* are more clearly signalled to audiences as Blackfriars plays. Both are preoccupied with the spaces of the street and stall—spaces that form much of the Blackfriars precinct and that are figured onstage in these plays. The majority of *Fedele*'s action takes place in public spaces: Attilia finds the conjuror Medusa when "walking through the street alone"; she seeks to find Fortunio "By the piazza" where he walks and talks (and she is told, "Him at his house, or walking in the street you shall not miss"); and Victoria is found "here so early in the street."[92] The alleys and streets characteristic of central London and its liberties are absorbed into the play world in *Fedele and Fortunio*.[93] *Campaspe*, too, is rooted in the painter's shop and its surroundings. The play creates a fluid relationship on stage between the shop and the street, marked by the "outside" status of the boys and servants and by Apelles, Campaspe, and Alexander moving in and out of the shop. Psyllus, Apelles's boy, observes, "It is always my master's fashion, when any fair gentlewoman is to be drawn within, to make me stay without."[94]

More pointedly, *Fedele*'s preoccupation with strange languages reflects the multi-lingual character of London as a whole and the Blackfriars specifically. The character of Pedante the schoolmaster is especially metatheatrical, reflecting back on the figures of Farrant (and/or William Hunnis, depending on the date of its first performance) and of other masters running children's playing companies such as Sebastian Westcote at St Paul's. A send-up of the pompous and self-important teacher, a stock-figure of early modern stage, full of Latinate verbosity, the scheming Pedante was no doubt an in-joke enjoyed by the boy actors and acknowledged equally by audiences. Yet Pedante's vocabulary extends beyond ludicrously overegged Latin mottos to flirtations with Italian. The play's self-consciousness about language is made clear in one particularly playful moment of translation: in the middle of the play, Fedele receives mail from Victoria, who "comes to the window, and throws out a letter, which Fedele taketh up, and reads it at the lamp, which burneth in the Temple."[95] While the play is largely adapted from an Italian source, Luigi Pasqualigo's *Il Fidele* (printed 1576 and 1579), and marked as a "pleasant Comedy of two Italian Gentlemen" in the running title of the quarto, it is markedly in colloquial English and peppered with idiomatic speech. Yet Victoria's letter plays with the notion of its Italian setting and characters, shifting without explanation from the English in which all characters speak to Italian for the written letter. Pedante enquires, "What news in your letter Sir, tell mee?", and Fedele requests that Pedante read it himself (aloud); after several lines of Italian, Pedante acknowledges "This is strange upon strange."[96] The play's ostensible setting and its "correct" language becomes a joke for the audience, and Pedante is forced (as the quarto puts it in a marginal note) to "interpret the Letter" and translate for non-Italian speakers in the audience into English.

The metatheatrical joke in *Fedele* that references its Italianate source material and translation similarly points to thriving multilingual trades—and the trade of language learning—present in the Blackfriars neighbourhood.[97] The play is written some time after 1579 in the wake of a swell in popularity of language study and of language texts, including John Florio's *First Fruits* (1578). The joke in Munday's play draws on the structure of language books such as Florio's in offering Italian and English phrases as parallel translations: as *First Fruits* lays it out, "Scriueteli vna lettera. / Write a letter unto her."[98] The thriving language trade also extends to the printing industry, and the neighbourhood was home to one of the most significant European stationers, Ascanius Renialme, from the 1570s onward—a member of the Stationers' Company with important links to the Plantin printing firm of Antwerp.[99] He can be situated alongside local schoolmasters and international printers as part of a wider multilingual book trade in London partly based within the Blackfriars. Pedante speaks to and tutors audience members in foreign tongues, and he provides the most explicit indication of how the Blackfriars' linguistic trade formed a fundamental part of the play's wider performance of language learning, text translation, and cultural exchange.

While the languages of strangers infuse *Fedele and Fortunio*, surrounding alien crafts inflect the central subject matter of Lyly's *Campaspe*. A significant part of the play's action happens outside or inside the painter Apelles's "shop." Marguerite Tassi and Chloe Porter have both explored the significance of Apelles in relation to Lyly's play and to his wider reception in Elizabethan England.[100] Tassi also explores the personal dimension to Lyly's representation of Apelles, suggesting the "likely candidate" of Nicholas Hilliard, the miniaturist.[101] Yet beyond a personal connection with a court miniaturist such as Nicholas Hilliard, Lyly's interest in practical craft—with Apelles's "shop," its materials, and the processes of his trade—root the play in its playhouse locality. In 1583, the Blackfriars was home to numerous creative practitioners who have not to date been recognised as constitutive of the playhouse environment. They included two alien artists: William Vosher and Jacques le Moyne de Morgues. The Normandy-born Vosher was a non-denizen resident in England for 30 years, though little can be traced of him or his work beyond his description as a "painter of painted papers."[102] Jacques le Moyne de Morgues, however, has recently become appreciated as a significant sixteenth-century painter, one of the earliest European artists to visit and document America and a fine detailer of plants and animals. After travelling to Florida and fulfilling royal commissions in France, Le Moyne appeared in England in 1581 in the Blackfriars for religious reasons, where he attracted powerful patrons including Sir Walter Raleigh. He featured in travel writing, including a personalised mention in Richard Hakluyt's translation of Laudonnière's Florida travel narrative emphasising Le Moyne's residence in the Blackfriars.[103]

Le Moyne's works are also marked, in a similar way to Bonetti's fencing school, as Blackfriars products. He published a collection of images of birds and flowers

> which might serve those who love and wish to learn good and seemly things; among whom are the young, both nobles and artisans, these to prepare themselves for the arts of painting or engraving, those to be goldsmiths or sculptors, and others for embroidery, tapestry and also for all kinds of needlework.[104]

The collection, *La clef des champs* (1586), is tellingly, is printed "aux Blackefriers." The likely printer of the collection is a Blackfriars resident, one Thomas Vautrollier.[105] Vautrollier was himself a Huguenot exile and a scholar, and he had been publishing various texts for over a decade (including Blackfriars residents John Baildon and John de Beauchesne's writing manual, the latter of whom wrote a prefatory sonnet for *La clef*). While the surviving fruits of Le Moyne's labours date largely from after the closure of the Blackfriars playhouse in 1584 and after the first performance of *Campaspe*, Le Moyne's longer residence in the liberty is testament to a community of stranger artists, patronage, and printing—one that continued in the neighbourhood for another century, including the residence of the great court painter Anthony Van Dyck in the 1620s and 30s.

Apelles's "shop" in Lyly's play therefore speaks not only to the likes of Nicholas Hilliard but to the comings and goings outside the playhouse and its environment, rooting the play in city-cum-liberty life. The realistic portrayal of painting and painters is emphasised by the play's interest in demonstrating the processes of painting, not least in the scene where Alexander attempts himself to master the art with advice from Apelles: "If you will paint as you are, a king, your Majesty may begin where you please; but as you would be a painter you must begin with the face."[106] Building on Porter's observation of how the scene "hints at the weakness of the king," it also points to the practicalities of the painter's shop and the technicalities of the art: the strokes and pressure used on the pencil, instructions as to where to begin, the appropriate colours.[107] While Apelles represented for Elizabethans the ideal painter, uninterested in wantonness, he is also in Lyly's play a figure of the working world of the city: Apelles's shop features cracking charcoal, half-finished portraits, and demanding patrons. Artistically inclined audience members would also be aware, amid Lyly's attention to the painter's pencil, that one of Le Moyne's neighbours, fellow Frenchman John de Horse, was a member of the Stationers' Company who "used 'selling of pictures and making of brushes'", placing *Campaspe*'s performance within the centre of a commercial artistic network.[108] Indeed, Le Moyne's craft, unlike Hilliard's description of limning as a "a kind of gentle painting,"[109], is described as fit for both "nobles and artisans"[110] and is designed to appeal to a wide demographic (that perhaps maps onto audience members) from professional goldsmiths to women pursuing needlework. Given Le Moyne's growing status and patronage network, his likely public commercial offerings, and the attraction to the Blackfriars of shoppers in search of other fashionable craft goods and services, aspects of Apelles's workshop onstage in the playhouse are imbricated in Le Moyne's practice. Alexander pointedly remarks of the classical painter, "were you as cunning as report saith you are, you may paint flowers as well with sweet smells as fresh colours, observing in your mixture such things as should draw near to their savours" (3.4.74–7)— precisely the endeavour Le Moyne attempted in his collected plant images, the influence and reach of which are indicated by at least two embroidery examples at Hardwick Hall.[111]

Such practical, worldly realisations of the studio clash with Apelles's struggle to capture Campaspe's beauty. Apelles is presented throughout the play with the difficulties of negotiating both his sitter and lover, Campaspe, but also—more threateningly—his patron, Alexander, the client for whom he is painting the portrait. Navigating that hierarchical relationship prompts Apelles to play further the system of patronage and work stratagems into his craft, plotting "by device [to] give it a blemish that by that means she may come again to my shop."[112] The practical aspects of Apelles's wooing boil down to a necessity to keep Campaspe in the site of his craft, in order that he may continue to be with her and paint her image. The high-flown abstractness of his love is matched with a realistic approach to labour, elite clients, and site-specificity that would be a daily reality in the shops of Le Moyne, Vosher, and de Horse in the playhouse neighbourhood.

Commercial recreational enterprises in the Blackfriars precinct were thereby inseparable from their wider commercial environments, which were tellingly characterised by immigration and pioneering craft and technology. Bowling-alley-proprietor Henry Naylor, fencing school owners William Joiner and Rocco Bonetti, and the master of the playhouse, Richard Farrant, all modelled innovative money-making "play" spaces. Their respective institutions reflected and responded to the imported skills, innovations, and people of their cosmopolitan neighbourhood. Indeed, the plays produced in the early 1580s at the First Blackfriars Playhouse were built from a self-conscious awareness of the languages and crafts practised by strangers in the "removed" vicinity of the Blackfriars. This was a destination where leisure of all kinds was available. Like Wine Street, it offered visitors high-end shopping and luxury goods as well as new and fashionable play services. The Blackfriars was a liberty with no obvious central administrative town hall or other shared secular symbolic institution. The playhouse and neighbouring play venues—with their ability to shape and represent identity through theatrical or sporting performance, aesthetic display, technological innovation, and commercial strategy—perhaps offered an alternative way of embodying local identity and community values.

Congleton, Wine Street, and the Blackfriars demonstrate how certain early modern English locales, from the early sixteenth century onwards, became synonymous with play. While this inevitably attracted visitors from surrounding areas and even across the country, it also transformed the immediate neighbourhood. These playing destinations both reflected and shaped their communities, inculcating local pride and identity—such as the early examples of regional fan cultures emerging from Congleton—and adapting political and legislative structures. Indeed, the leisure operations at Congleton and Wine Street served as quasi-governmental institutions. Farrant's playhouse, however, had a more fraught relationship with the local community, which was itself already estranged from London's civic government—as a "liberty" with its own partial independence. Yet the institution clearly reflected the concerns, identities, and characteristics of its environs. Each of these playhouses, and the wider play complexes within which they sat, modelled fresh attitudes towards community in a period where secular civic authority came to supplant vanished ecclesiastical powers and during which the commercial service industry grew exponentially. In this world, play promised community influence as well as cultural and economic capital—subjects explored in Chapter 5.

Notes

1 William West sees them as "communities of production," with theatres generating different but important forms of community across early modern Europe; "Communities of Production: Lives in and out of Theatre," *A Cultural History of Theatre in the Early Modern Age*, ed. Robert Henke (London: Bloomsbury, 2019): 127–46. This wider collection thinks about the relationship between cultural history and theatre.

2 Figure quoted in Garthine Walker, *Crime, Gender and Social Order in Early Modern England* (Cambridge: Cambridge University Press, 2003), p. 18.

3 W.B. Stephens and Norah Fuidge, "Tudor and Stuart Congleton," *A History of Congleton* (Manchester: Manchester University Press, 1970): 45–81, p. 48.

4 Samuel Yates, *A History of the Ancient Town and Borough of Congleton* (Congleton, 1820), pp. 25–6.

5 Up the road, similarly sized Manchester limited their numbers to 30 alehouses and inns in 1573, *A Volume of Court Leet Records of the Manor of Manchester in the Sixteenth Century*, ed. John Harland (Manchester: Chetham Society, 1864), p. 130.

6 Yates, p. 26.

7 Phil Withington, "Intoxicants and the Early Modern City," *Remaking English Society: Social Relations and Social Change in Early Modern England*, eds Steve Hindle, Alexandra Shepard, and John Walter (Woodbridge: Boydell & Brewer, 2013): 135–63. pp. 157–8.

8 See Baldwin's recognition of bear-baiting sitting alongside other sports in Congleton and examination of bear travel and trade, in "'Selling the Bible to Pay for the Bear': The Value Placed on Entertainment in Congleton, 1584–1637," *The Middle Ages in the North-West*, eds Pat Starkey and Tom Scott (Liverpool: Centre for Medieval Studies, 1995): 257–67.

9   *Records of Early English Drama: Cheshire (including Chester)*, Vol. 2, eds Elizabeth Baldwin, Laurence M. Clopper, and David Mills (Toronto: University of Toronto Press, 2007), p. 638.

10 *REED Chester*, Vol. 2, p. 644.

11 *REED Chester*, Vol. 2, p. 639.

12 *REED Chester*, Vol. 2, p. 625.

13 STAC 8/49/8 item 10, MS, The National Archives, Kew, London. See also, the Grammar School at Crewkerne, who paid Thomas Fisher "for keeping the boys in order Cockfighting day," *Records of Early English Drama: Somerset*, Vol. 1, ed. James Stokes (Toronto: University of Toronto Press, 1996), p. 65.

14 Stephens and Fuidge, p. 64.

15 *REED Cheshire*, Vol. 2, p. 623.

16 *REED Cheshire*, Vol. 2, p. 623.

17 Stephens and Fuidge, pp. 65–8.

18 *REED Cheshire*, Vol. 2, p. 639.

19 *REED Cheshire*, Vol. 2, p. 654.

20 *REED Cheshire*, Vol. 2, p. 803.

21 *REED Cheshire*, Vol. 2, p. 647.

22 Walker, p. 19.

23 *REED Cheshire*, Vol. 2, p. 635; p. 637.

24 *REED Cheshire*, Vol. 2, p. 624.

25 While its origins stem from urban design approaches of the 1960s and 1970s, *placemaking* has gained employment more widely as a means of enabling "collective vision" to "re-imagine everyday spaces"—with application across architecture and anthropology to arts policy, heritage, and planning. See the foundational Project for Public Spaces at pps.org with acknowledgement of the term's history; recent studies have explored the creative elements of placemaking and its uses in contemporary arts initiatives, in particular, in *Creative Placemaking: Research, Theory, and Practice*, eds Cara Courage and Anita McKeown (Abingdon: Routledge, 2019), while the UK cultural sector has adopted the term for its approach to everything from parks to theatres; see, in particular, "Making Good—Shaping Places for People," eds Richard Brown, Kat Hannah, and Rachel Holdsworth (London: Centre for London, 2017), which brings together planners, academics, developers, and practitioners.

26 Robert Tittler, *Architecture and Power: The Town Hall and the English Urban Community* (Oxford: Clarendon, 1991), p. 133.

27 Tittler, p. 130.

28 Tittler, p. 139.

29 See Phil Withington, "Urbanisation," *A Social History of England 1500–1750*, ed. Keith Wrightson (Cambridge: Cambridge University Press, 2017): 174–98.

30 *REED Cheshire*, Vol. 2, p. 747.

31 *REED Cheshire*, Vol. 2, p. 748.

32 Robert Head, *Congleton Past and Present* (Congleton, 1887), p. 59.

33 A parallel example can be seen in Manchester, which also issued repeated orders against the "disorder and unquietness" committed by mastiffs, bandogs, and bitches and ask for them to be muzzled. *A Volume of Court Leet Records of the Manor of Manchester in the Sixteenth Century*, ed. John Harland (Manchester: Chetham Society, 1864), p. 94 (1562); p. 158 (1584). These are repeated over the course of decades, with emphasis on the wide ownership—such as a smith, John Cowpes, whose unmuzzled dog attacked the foreman of the jury on the 1 October 1590, *The Court Leet Records of the Manor of Manchester*, Vol. 2, ed. J.P. Earwaker (Manchester: Henry Blacklock and Co, 1885), p. 50.

34 *Records of Early English Drama: Shropshire*, Vol. 1, ed. J. Alan B. Somerset (Toronto: University of Toronto Press, 1994), p. 284.

35 *REED Cheshire*, Vol. 1, p. 20.

36 Tittler, p. 97.

37 C2/328/28, MS, The National Archives, Kew, London. This section draws on my article "The Woolfes of Wine Street: Middling Culture and Community, 1600–1620," *English Historical Review*, 137.585 (2022). Other than that, the playhouse has received only a few discussions; the key studies are: Mark C. Pilkington, ed. *Records of Early English Drama: Bristol* (Toronto: University of Toronto Press, 1997); Siobhan Keenan, *Travelling Players in Shakespeare's England* (Basingstoke: Palgrave Macmillan, 2002); Sarah Elizabeth Lowe, "Players and Performances in Early Modern Gloucester, Tewkesbury, and Bristol," unpub. thesis, University of Gloucestershire, Feb. 2008.

38 Jonathan Barry, "Bristol Pride: Civic Identity in Bristol, c. 1640–1775," *The Making of Modern Bristol*, ed Madge Dresser and Philip Ollerenshaw (Tiverton, 1996), p. 25.

39 Jonathan Barry, "Popular Culture in Seventeenth-Century Bristol," *Popular Culture in Seventeenth-Century England*, ed. Barry Reay (Beckenham: Crook Helm, 1985): 59–90. p. 59.

40 David Harris Sacks, *The Widening Gate: Bristol and the Atlantic Economy, 1450–1700* (Oxford: University of California Press, 1991): p. xvi; p. 84.

41 Barry, "Popular," p. 61.

42 Barry, "Popular," p. 77.

43 Roger Leech, *The Town House in Medieval and Early Modern Bristol* (Swindon: English Heritage, 2014), p. 28.

44 Leech, p. 126; Sacks, p. 149. See also Roger Leech, *The Topography of Medieval and Early Modern Bristol: Part I* (Bristol: Bristol Record Society, 1997).

45 The precise location of this property remains up for debate. Margaret testified that her husband held only his dwelling place and "one house with the appurtenances in Wine Street within the same city commonly called the playhouse" (C2/328/28). Her testimony distinguishes the playhouse from the known, named inns of the area, and she also does not "name" the place by a sign or any other distinguishing title or feature beyond "playhouse"; her phrasing indicates that the venue was popularly known by this word—something in keeping with Laurie Johnson's speculation about the Newington Butts theatre in Southwark in *Shakespeare's Lost Playhouse: Eleven Days at Newington Butts* (London: Routledge, 2017). I follow Keenan, Leech (*Topography*), and Lowe in cautiously concluding that the likeliest spot is the tenement recorded in Woolfe's hands at number 7 Christ Church-Wine Street, the lease of which permitted him to "'to New build the said Tenement and every part thereof with the appurtenances within four years next ensuing the date hereof,' and included permission for 'the rearing up higher' of the tenement" (Keenan, p. 148).

46 REQ 2/296/80, MS, The National Archives, Kew, London. Cooke complained about a break in the terms of his tenancy and argued that, having moved out, Woolfe rented out and used his rooms and neglected to return Cooke's money.
   C2/328/28.

47 REQ 2/296/80.

48 *Bristol Probate Inventories I: 1542–1650*, eds Edwin and Stella George (with assistance from Peter Fleming) (Bristol: Bristol Record Society, 2002): 62–4.

49 Tara Hamling and Catherine Richardson, *A Day at Home in Early Modern England: Material Culture and Domestic Life, 1500–1700* (New Haven and London: Yale University Press, 2017), p. 266.

50 F/AU/1/11, p.200; F/AU/1/13, p.34, MSS, Bristol Archives, Bristol.

51 For more on these patterns of leisure and consumption, see: Peter Earle, *The Making of the English Middle Class: Business, Society and Family Life in London, 1660–1730* (London: Methuen, 1989); Henry French, *The Middle Sort of People in Provincial England* (Oxford: Oxford University Press, 2007); Tara Hamling and Catherine Richardson, *A Day at Home*; Margaret Hunt, *The Middling Sort: Commerce, Gender, and the Family in England, 1680–1780* (London: University of California Press, 1996); Mark Overton, Jane Whittle, Darron Dean, and Andrew Hann, *Production and Consumption in English Households, 1600–1750* (London: Routledge, 2004); Carol Shammas, *The Pre-Industrial Consumer in England and America* (Oxford: Clarendon, 1990); Lorna Weatherill, *Consumer Behaviour and Material Culture in Britain, 1660–1760* (London: Routledge, 1998); Keith Wrightson and David Levine, *Poverty and Piety in an English Village: Terling, 1525–1700* (New York: Academic Press, 1979).

52 Bruno Blondè, Peter Stabel, Jon Stobart, and Ilja Van Damme, "Retail Circuits and Practices in Medieval and Early Modern Europe: An Introduction," *Buyers and Sellers: Retail Circuits and Practices in Medieval and Early Modern Europe* (Turnhout, Belgium: Brepols, 2006): 7–30. p. 17.

53 Withington, p. 181. Karen Newman, "'Goldsmith's Ware': Equivalence in *A Chaste Maid in Cheapside*," *Huntington Library Quarterly* 71.1 (2008): 97–113. p. 106.

54 PROB/11/124, MS, The National Archives, Kew, London.

55 C3/328/28.

56 *REED Bristol*, p. xxxvii.

57 Sally-Beth MacLean, "At the End of the Road: An Overview of South West Touring Circuits," *Early Theatre* 6.2 (2003): 17–32. p. 25.

58 *REED Bristol*, p. xxxix; Keenan, p. 147.

59 F/AU/1/13, p. 29.

60 P.Xch.ChW.1.a, fos 315r; 319r; 316v, MS, Bristol Archives, Bristol.

61 See Andy Wood, *The Memory of the People* (Cambridge: Cambridge University Press, 2013), pp. 205–45.

62 MS PROB/11/124.

63 Muniments 1, 063, MS, Dulwich College Archive, Dulwich, London.

64 *REED Bristol*, p. 224.

65 p. 150.

66 "Trade, Taverns, and Touring Players in Seventeenth-Century Bristol," *Theatre Notebook* 71.3 (2017): 161–8.

67 Christopher Highley, "Theatre, Church, and Neighbourhood in the Early Modern Blackfriars," *The Oxford Handbook of the Age of Shakespeare*, ed. Malcolm Smuts (Oxford: Oxford University Press, 2016): 616–32. p. 621.

68 Mary Bly, "Playing the Tourist in Early Modern London: Selling the Liberties Onstage," *PMLA* 122.1 (2007): 61–71. p. 65.

69 L.b.393. c.1550s and L.b.414 (c.1560s), MSS, Folger Shakespeare Library, Washington DC.

70 David Kathman, "'The Madnes of Tenys' and the Commercialization of Pastimes in Early Tudor London," *Games and Theatre in Early Modern England*, eds Tom Bishop, Gina Bloom, and Erika T. Lin (Amsterdam: Amsterdam University Press, 2021): 69–88.

71 Irwin Smith, *Shakespeare's Blackfriars Playhouse: Its History and Its Design*, (New York: New York University Press, 1964), p. 124. In 1556, Frith is also listed by Cawarden as renting a house "with that the Printer dwells in," likely referring to one of the European printers resident in the area: L.b.410 (c.1550s), MS, Folger Shakespeare Library, Washington DC.

72 The petitions are addressed to Nicholas Bacon, Lord Keeper, who died in 1579; the earliest reference to Naylor's presence comes in the Chief Justice's award to Naylor of 20 feet of ground in around 1570—ground that is likely connected to the land discussed in the petitions (see L.b.436, MS, Folger Shakespeare Library, Washington DC). More remained at litigation with Naylor until 1580.

73 LM 413/1. c.1570s, MS, Surrey Historical Centre, Woking, UK.

74 LM 413–4. c.1570s, MS, Surrey Historical Centre, Woking, UK.

75 LM 414.

76 Highley, pp. 627–8.

77 For more on the nature of petitions, see the Power of Petitioning project: www.petitioning.history.ac.uk.

78 Quoted in Smith, p. 467.

79 The play is undated and its provenance is contested. Martin Wiggins errs on the side of a later date and separates the play from Richard Farrant (d.1580), who is credited with a song for two of the characters from the play (435). Yet Michael Hirrel argues for a possible date range between 1577 and 1580 (193). It seems likely that *Cyrus* was a 1570s Farrant play that was revised in the following decade and found its way into print, thereby connecting the earlier and later years of the First Playhouse. Martin Wiggins, ed. *British Drama, 1533–1642: A Catalogue*, in assoc. with Catherine Richardson. Vol. 2: 1567–89 (Oxford: Oxford University Press, 2012), p. 435. Michael Hirrel, "Thomas Watson, Playwright: Origins of Modern English Drama," *Lost Plays in Shakespeare's England*, eds David McInnis and Matthew Steggle. (Basingstoke: Palgrave Macmillan, 2014), 197–207.

80 Lucy Munro defines this as a "critical tradition that has associated children's performance with comedy and ironic distance, and . . . often cast it as an alien presence within the early modern theatrical landscape," in "Children's Companies and the Long 1580s," Forum, ed. Andy Kesson, *Shakespeare Studies* 45 (2017): 97–105. p. 104.

81 See, for instance, Sarah Dustagheer's discussion of how "in early modern drama foreign settings are often merely a veiled or disguised version of early modern London," with regard to Shakespeare's *Measure for Measure* and Roman plays, in *Shakespeare's Two Playhouses: Repertory and Theatre Space at the Globe and the Blackfriars, 1599–1613* (Cambridge: Cambridge University Press, 2017), pp. 80–1.

82 Jean Howard, *Theater of a City: The Places of London Comedy, 1598–1642*. (Pennsylvania: University of Pennsylvania Press, 2007), p. 2.

83 Adam Zucker, *Places of Wit in Early Modern English Comedy* (Cambridge: Cambridge University Press, 2011), p. 55.

84 Julie Sanders, "Under the Skin: A Neighbourhood Ethnography of Leather and Early Modern Drama," *Staged Normality in Shakespeare's England*, eds Rory Loughnane and Edel Semple (Basingstoke: Palgrave Macmillan, 2019): 108–28. p. 117.

85 Sanders, p. 110.

86 Highley, "Theatre," p. 617.

87 These names are taken from periodic lists, or "returns," of individuals born abroad but resident in London. See the Returns of Strangers, see Richard E.G. Kirk and Ernest F. Kirk, eds, *Returns of Aliens Dwelling in the City and Suburbs of London from the Reign of Henry VIII to that of James I*, Vols. 1–4 (London: Huguenot Society, 1900–8).

88 Laura Wolfe, *Humanism, Machinery, and Renaissance Literature*. (Cambridge: Cambridge University Press, 2004), p. 28; Tiffany Stern, "Time for Shakespeare: Hourglasses, Sundials, Clocks, and Early Modern Theatre," *Journal of the British Academy* 3 (2015): 1–33. p. 21.

89 George Silver, *Paradoxes of Defence* (London, 1599), K1r.

90 Peele, *Arraignment* (London, 1584), A4r.

91 Bourne, *Inventions or devises* (London, 1590), O1v. Agostino Ramelli's popular *Diverse e Artificiose Machine* (N.p., 1588), also represents bird song and movement through clockwork machinations (Cc1v).

92 Anthony Munday, *Fedele* (London, 1585), C1v, D1v, C1r, D1v, D2v.

93 Confirming the street-centricity of the *Fedele and Fortunio*, one anonymous respondent to a *Before Shakespeare* questionnaire at Deirdre Mullins's Read Not Dead staged reading at Shakespeare's Globe (18 June 2017) felt the play reminded them of "how the little lanes and streets of Soho were in the '60s and '70s." Andy Kesson's discussion of the play at the Rarely Played seminar of that event pointed to the importance of characters meeting on the street. *Fedele and Fortunio*, dir. Deirdre Mullins, Read Not Dead, Shakespeare's Globe, London, 18 June 2017.

94 Lyly, *Campaspe. Campaspe and Sappho and Phao*, eds G. K. Hunter and David Bevington (Manchester: Manchester University Press, 2007): 45–139. 3.2.1–2.

95 C3r-v.

96 C3v.

97 For more on language learning, see John Gallagher, *Language Learning in Early Modern England* (Oxford: Oxford University Press, 2019).

98 John Florio, *Florio His First Fruits* (London, 1578), D1r.

99 Irene Scouloudi, *Returns of Strangers in the Metropolis 1593, 1627, 1635, 1639: A Study of an Active Minority* (London: Huguenot Society of London, 1985), p. 43.

100 Chloe Porter, *Making and Unmaking in Early Modern English Drama: Spectators, Aesthetics, and Incompletion* (Manchester: Manchester University Press, 2013); Marguerite Tassi, *The Scandal of Images: Iconoclasm, Eroticism, and Painting in Early Modern English Drama* (Selingsgrove: Susquehanna University Press, 2004), pp. 75–81.

101 Tassi, p. 80.

102 *Returns of Aliens*, Vol. 2, p. 357; see also his brief biography in Edward Town, *A Biographical Dictionary of London Painters* (London: Walpole Society, 2014).

103 René Goulaine Laudonnière, *A notable historie containing foure voyages made by certayne French captaynes unto Florida*, trans. Richard Hakluyt (London, 1587), ¶1v.

104 Le Moyne qtd. in Paul Hulton, *The Work of Jacques Le Moyne de Morgue: A Huguenot Artist in France, Florida, and England*. 2 vols. (London: Trustees of the British Museum, 1977), p. 187.

105 *Returns*, Vol. 2, pp. 179, 252, 355.

106 3.4.85–7.

107 Porter, *Making*, p. 114.

108 Scouloudi, *Returns*, p. 43; Kirk and Kirk, *Returns*, Vol. 2, pp. 308–9.

109 Katherine Coombs, "'A Kind of Gentle Painting': Limning in 16th-Century-England," *European Visions: American Voices* (London: Trustees of the British Museum, 2009): 77–84. p. 77.

110 Le Moyne quoted in Hulton, *Work*, p. 187.

111 William T. Stearn, "The Plant Portraitist and the Herbalist," *The Work of Jacques Le Moyne de Morgue: A Huguenot Artist in France, Florida, and England*, Vol. 1, ed. Paul Hulton (London: Trustees of the British Museum, 1977), p. 81.

112 3.5.67–8.

5

BUSINESSES

Early modern playhouses were commercial operations typically managed by one or a number of individuals. Perhaps the most familiar is the builder of the Rose, Philip Henslowe, a London dyer who invested widely, acted as a pawnbroker, and became an established urban landlord. Scholarly interpretations—some hostile and some kind—have characterised him variously as "the courtier, the capitalist, the leather-apron-man, the city squire."[1] Yet most tend to concur that Henslowe was, in a word, "a businessman," and sometimes "more than a businessman."[2] Being both indicates the range of motives and daily concerns of playhouse proprietors and, more widely, those who worked in the theatre industry, for whom playing enterprises were seen "indifferently as an art, a craft, and a means of producing wealth."[3] As previous chapters have shown, running or supporting a playhouse could entail anything from community investment and civic office to aesthetic innovation.

This chapter considers spaces other than the Rose to establish the wider array of business people and more-than-business-people who were involved in the early modern playing industry. Rather than focusing on the solo, male entrepreneur—a story that has been well told in theatre-historical studies[4]—I follow Chapter 4 in thinking about the collective and collaborative (if not always frictionless) business models that typified many playhouses across England and the many different types of people who owned and ran play venues. Theatrical enterprise was not limited to proprietorship; playhouses were built from and continually shaped by a fascinating range of skills, from straw-drawing to community organisation—forms of playing management in which women were particularly instrumental. Accordingly, this chapter asks: how and why might you build a playhouse? Who should we consider to be playhouse builders? And what forms of expertise and collaboration sustained the growing playing industry across the sixteenth and seventeenth centuries?

DOI: 10.4324/9781003231127-6

Why Build a Playhouse?

Motivations for building a playhouse varied widely, and in the reasonably few instances in which builders and proprietors are known to us, it is often difficult to identify the rationale behind the project. Yet loud and often disapproving voices furnish us with a logical starting point. Many of those who were hostile to the developing playing industry centred their invective on the earthly incentives of playhouse builders. Wordplay around terms like "profit" dominated public discourse about playhouse openings during the busy period of the 1570s. Sebastian Westcote's venture at London's St Paul's was deemed by London's corporation in 1575 to be a sinful enterprise, born of non-conformist tendencies and designed for "resort of the people to great gain and peril of the Corrupting of the Children with papistry."[5] In Shoreditch the following year, James Burbage and John Brayne's plan to build a playhouse was said to have arisen from "promises and speech […] passed from the said James Burbage to the said Brayne" about "the great wealth and profit that should rise unto them by building A Theatre or playhouse and other buildings."[6] In the Blackfriars, also in 1576, Richard Farrant adapted the upper rooms of a building into a playhouse. His landlord, William More, later pointed to the regular commercial traffic occasioned by this move in his objection to the building being "made" a "continual house for plays, to the offense of the precinct."[7] His language matches earlier complaints about nearby bowling alleys, which More deemed to have been built "only for lucre and gains."[8] These phrases, from irascible landowners to playhouse builders themselves, indicate a growing recognition of theatrical structures' relationship to profit. Certainly, potential profit, such as that imagined by Burbage and Brayne in their planning conversation, seems a likely incentive amid the turbulent economic environment of Elizabethan England. William Ingram's biography of Francis Langley, builder of the Swan playhouse, frames the mid-1590s project as a supplementary construction, designed to diversify income from a suite of tenements.[9] Whether as a pragmatic add-on or a central project, playhouse building promised (even if it did not always deliver) extra income.

The association between playhouses and profit is most pointedly expressed across so-called "antitheatrical" discourse, which contrasted the drives of the play industry with more acceptable motives, such as spiritual or educational edification: "woe is me," lamented Maliverny Catlyn in 1587, "the play houses are pestered, when the churches are naked/ at the one, it is not possible to get a place; at the other, void seats are plenty […]." He turns the language of profit into a pointed visual contrast: "It is a woeful sight to see two hundred proud players jet in their silks, where five hundred poor people starve in the Streets."[10] Accordingly, profit became symbolic of play's economic and moral place in early modern England, at least by the 1570s. Around this time, London's corporation began to tax, specifically, play-hosting landlords, skimming the top off playing profits to supplement public charitable institutions and poor relief.[11] In 1573, the corporation sought to appoint a regulator of the playing industry who would "have the appointment of places for plays and interludes within this city."[12] There is no surviving evidence to suggest this role went ahead, but these plans show London's inclination for an office to regulate the *places* of play some eight years before the well-known patent granted to Edmund Tilney. This early move to regulate the industry reflects, at least in part, the sheer numbers of playhouses operating in London by the early 1570s. John Stockwood identifies at least eight profit-making "ordinary places" of play in his sermon of 1578:

> For reckoning with the least, the gain that is reaped of eight ordinary places in the City which I know, by playing but once a week (whereas many times they place twice and sometimes thrice) it amounteth to .2000. pounds by the year, the suffering of which waste must one day be answered before God, by such as suffer it, and the unprofitable expense by such as give it.[13]

His eye-rolling disapproval of the leisure industry contrasts spiritual with commercial profit, a common move among those who saw play as a disreputable way to make a living.

The profit that might be gained from the playing industry emerged from a raft of commercial changes across the country. Commercialism was central to the social and economic developments that swept through England from the 1550s onwards.[14] The expanding market economy meant individual or collective enterprise was an increasingly common way to generate income; accordingly, playhouses represented a viable business choice—especially as former ecclesiastical land became increasingly available and affordable for purchase or rent following the dissolution. The year before Stockwood delivered his fulminating sermon, fellow preacher John Northbrooke bemoaned the "gain and profit" that "by play is gotten."[15] The comment is often read, like Stockwood's, as a gloss on London's leisure scene. Yet Northbrooke was a preacher in Gloucester, Wells, and Bristol during the 1570s.[16] This book has already demonstrated the vibrancy of the commercial leisure scene in the area, from Bristol's Wine Street to playing in Gloucester (discussed in Chapter 1). There is no reason to suggest that Northbrooke did not also have his eye on the south-west when observing the gains and profits of the playing industry. These contemporary accounts of the mid-Elizabethan playing scene—some hostile and some friendly to the industry—confirm that money was, at the very least, an important motive for playhouse builders and associates.

Yet proprietors often had more than economic impetus, and a broader set of incentives come into view when we look beyond the sceptical voices of the 1570s. The career of the mercer Henry Walton demonstrates how profit overlapped with questions of godliness, community work, and social mobility. Walton, as we saw in Chapter 1, began to build semi-commercial structures in London in the 1520s that were open for play for months at a time. There seems little doubt that he acted out of a commercial spirit, capitalising on a vibrant playing scene in the capital to construct stages for various churches. Yet churches had a long history of using the profits of play to fundraise for repairs or community ends—especially through wakes or ales, mentioned variously throughout this study, which were increasingly imbricated with commercial play. "People went to ales for the drink, food, games, plays, dances and conversations that kept them entertained," Judith M. Bennett explains, "but they also often went to contribute money to worthy causes."[17] Walton's "plays" for London churches therefore suggest ways in which proto-playhouse structures "worked within contemporary notions of charity,"[18] offering both spiritual profit and financial profit (for both the parish and, potentially, for Walton and his "fellows"). In their wider community functions and fundraising, Walton's stages for All Hallows and St Botolph's without Aldersgate suggest similarities to the corporation of Congleton, whose cockpit complex, discussed in Chapter 4, clearly served more than simply commercial ends.

Walton worked not only out of charity but towards the establishment of play as a viable and worthy way to earn a living. He appears in the King's accounts around the same time he was setting up summer-long stages at All Hallows and St Botolph's without Aldersgate. Henry VIII paid him for sourcing buckram (a fabric used in court performances and masques) as well as for several days of construction work on a pageant.[19] While this work evidently helped to pay the bills, it nonetheless offers opportunity and influence that went beyond the wallet. Access to court gave creative practitioners and makers of all sorts the chance to shape the aesthetic culture of the country—even of Europe—and to be at the forefront of innovation in building and designing structures, costumes, and surrounding elements of performance. A parallel career may be found in Nicholas Hilliard, a goldsmith from Exeter whose portrait miniatures were the products of a man who similarly moved between court commissions at home and abroad and sitters in his commercial workshop in Fetter Lane, London.[20] The combination of court patronage and city commerce had benefits for personal prestige and the advancement of one's creative practice, for both a goldsmith-artist like Hilliard and for the mercer-builder-player Walton.[21]

Walton's craft as mercer therefore sat alongside his occupation as player and playhouse-builder. These roles did not fit squarely into existing company structures, nor can they be neatly boxed into either service at court or charity work for the parish. It seems that Walton was motivated in part to establish a stage of his own. In 1529, St Botolph's recorded permission for him and his "fellows" to play in the yard where he had constructed a venue.[22] His motives for building his stage may therefore in part have been underscored by a wider interest in establishing a playing identity and making room for creative practice. Although Ingram identifies the 1570s as a "new economy" for playing proprietors, with fresh taxes on play-hosting landlords in 1574 prompting players to build and run their own venues,[23] Walton displayed a similar impetus earlier in the century. In the London of the 1520s, with pageantry controlled by the corporation and ludic activity largely defined by ecclesiastical production, Walton's London stages offered an early chance for personal if temporary control of a plot of land on which to start drawing regular audiences over the course of a season of playing—the prospect of a stable place to play.

Commercial play therefore presented myriad opportunities to advance one's personal interests outside of existing institutional structures like guild companies or parish bodies. These enabling social possibilities were central to the Bristol play-house in Wine Street from the early 1600s to the 1620s. We saw in Chapter 4 how the venue defined its local area and acted as a political centre for the city. The lives and deaths of its owners offer further insight into personal investment in playing venues, suggesting they were instrumental to the Woolfe family's fashioning of social identity. Among the few listed belongings inherited by proprietor Nicholas Woolfe's son, Miles, in 1614 were "two pairs of virginals," which he used while being taught for two years "in the Art of science of music."[24] The Woolfe play-house can perhaps be retrospectively understood, in part, by recognising the social significance of this bequest. Musical tuition was a key marker of upper middling status, especially as it offered proficiency in this small piano-like instrument typic-ally coded as an "elite" possession in the period. Indeed, the virginal's "restrained tones (and high cost) suited them perfectly to aristocratic interiors, and their pri-mary associations were therefore with sophistication and refinement."[25] Wine Street happened to be home to the virginal-maker Isacke Bryan, who may have been responsible for making the instruments, as well as a host of high-end cultural pro-ducers: jewellers and goldsmiths, soapmakers, and innkeepers. The playhouse there-fore sat at the heart of Bristol's changing fashions and seemingly helped shape them. Indeed, those who lived and worked in this area were key authors of its consumer culture. As the owner of the city's most important playing venue—host to aldermen and mayors, as we have seen in Chapter 4—at the same time as he was a practising cutler,[26] Nicholas Woolfe was placed some way between these two positions. He was a taste-maker, shaping the leisure world of the elite via the playhouse. Virginals may well have been a feature of that playhouse itself, as "there were numerous instances in which the instruments of the 'better sort' were heard at theatres, inns, alehouses, marketplaces, churches, cathedrals and other places not associated exclu-sively with the gentry."[27] The provision he made for Miles is further evidence that play could be a badge of social standing in the community. The playhouse offered the Woolfes the opportunity both to bring this desirable instrument to a wider audience and to instil in Miles a sophisticated musical facility—a way to adver-tise the family's cultural refinement. While commercial artistic performance could make social mobility possible, the cultivation of elite artistic skills demonstrated its achievement.

Woolfe accordingly sits alongside similar figures from earlier in our period who instrumentalised commercial play in the service of both self- and community-fashioning. Jennifer Bishop, for instance, has shown how the London haberdasher George Tadlowe was central to the various "institutions of civic government" in the 1540s while he hosted plays connected to his dwelling house and tavern, the White Horse, which David Kathman recognises as an early example of commercial playing in the capital.[28] We might think of Tadlowe as a "Haberdasher at Play," to adapt Jessica Winston's phrase—a soubriquet ideally suited to a man who used per-formance to further his political and social beliefs and to catalyse his professional and social advancement.[29] The cutler Nicholas Woolfe may be less prominent in records and based outside of London, but he and his wife also help us appreciate what personal and political reasons might motivate a couple of moderate means to invest in dramatic playing. Indeed, they sit alongside the cockpit at Congleton (Chapter 4) or the bullring in Canterbury (Chapter 1) in demonstrating the many different impetuses behind playhouses and play complexes, which often simultan- eously encompassed economic profit and political power, self- and community- fashioning, and pragmatic solutions to legal requirements (such as having to bait bulls before selling meat).

The career of the actor and proprietor Edward Alleyn united many of these various strands. By the late 1580s, Alleyn had established himself as a performer in London and had even joined his brother in taking out shares in materials, from playbooks to costumes, for the Admiral's Men. Just a few years later, he "had begun to form a business partnership with Henslowe," proprietor of the Rose, who shortly became his father-in-law.[30] Alleyn and Henslowe went on to form a formidable partnership, leasing and managing the Bear Garden in the 1590s and building the Fortune in partnership in 1600. Alleyn inherited the totality of Henslowe's theat- rical empire—including his share of the Hope, built in 1613 with Jacob Meade— upon the older man's death in 1616 (albeit subject to contentious lawsuits over the estate). Alleyn's theatrical career pivoted on crucial kinship connections, suggesting a dynastic element to the playing industry that matches the Woolfes in Bristol. Not only did Alleyn benefit from his elder brother's advancement in London's commercial performance scene at the outset of his career, but his close relation- ship with his father-in-law characterised their business arrangements. Alleyn's wife and Henslowe's daughter, Joan Alleyn (previously Joan Woodward), affectionately known to Alleyn as "Mouse," was fundamental to their ventures up to her death in 1623. Letters exchanged between the three of them indicate a broad overlap of fond conversation, domestic organisation, and business, and they suggest that Joan conducted some of Alleyn's financial dealings when he was away.[31]

In 1604, having established a successful suite of business interests and risen to celebrity status as an actor,[32] Alleyn secured with his father-in-law the office of Master of the Bears, Bulls, and Mastiff Dogs. The role meant that their proprietor- ship of the Bankside bear garden paired popular entertainment with royal office—a similar joining of public commerce and monarchical patronage to Walton's building career. "The Henslowe-Alleyn management was a complex, but probably harmo- nious mixture of affective ties, money-raising, business-sharing and cultural and art- istic engagement," Paola Pugliatti explains. Together, Henslowe and Alleyn represent a group of "arts- and entertainment-producers who were in the process of gaining a social status of their own, granted by the public success of their trade, but still dependent on patronage and protection."[33] Yet Alleyn managed to accrue both the wealth and status to move even beyond the limits of this "producer" status. In 1605, he purchased the manor of Dulwich—a large plot of land a few miles south of London. In essence, this made him "lord" of the manor, with attendant sei- gneurial rights, such as influence over the parish of Camberwell (which lay within his lands). He set about establishing a charitable enterprise, known as the "hospital" in Dulwich, with an educational institution attached intended to be called the

FIGURE 5.1 British School, *Joan Alleyn*, 1596, oil on panel, 79.1 × 63.2 cm, DPG444. Dulwich Picture Gallery, London.

"College of God's Gift" (now Dulwich College), both begun in 1613 and formally opened in 1619. Alleyn also built an alms-house for ten people elsewhere in north London. Such "acts of public charity could bolster a man's reputation (and credit perhaps) in his own eyes as well as those of his contemporaries."[34] Alleyn's actions demonstrate the links between charity and theatrical enterprise, both built at one man's behest. Indeed, the profits from the Fortune and other playing structures made such acts of piety and such community-orientated actions possible.

At the same time, Alleyn's rise in status can be seen as a part of the fabric of a playing industry that was, by the early seventeenth century, large and various. His diary suggests fundamental links between playhouse construction and status. This remarkable document records Alleyn's various movements around Dulwich and London, including meetings with everyone from local vicars to the King's treasurer, interspersed with the business of play—such as trips to the Hope and drinks with the playhouse's other partner, Jacob Meade.[35] The diary and associated leases and papers attest not only to Alleyn's abiding concern for charity—what W.K. Jordan somewhat *un*charitably described as being "almost fanatically interested in the plight of the poor"[36]—but also to a fanaticism about *building* itself. From the early 1600s, Alleyn was engaged in a constant negotiation with leases, builders, purchase of materials, legal arrangements, repairs, and rebuilding that lasted until his death. The diary demonstrates how the fine details of building and decorating formed part of his daily activities, from noting his expenses on wainscotting to payments to various joiners or carpenters. Moreover, in addition to the diary, Alleyn also kept a second memorandum book, which he tellingly termed his "building book."[37] Writing and building go hand in hand in the Alleyn archive. His experience building the Fortune playhouse with Henslowe in 1600 seemingly gave him the skills and confidence, over the course of several years, to become the initiator, financer, and overseer of numerous such projects. It does not seem a stretch to suggest that building became intrinsic to his identity. Physical construction, in turn, built status, community benefaction, and material wealth. Alleyn may never quite have achieved his desire for a coat of arms—the sign of confirmed gentlemanly status—but he had nonetheless advanced himself into a "new" gentry position, replete with personal portraits, books, and lordship of a whole manor, to boot.[38] Indeed, surviving portraits of Alleyn and his wife Joan (held at Dulwich Picture Gallery; see Fig. 5.1) testify to their cultivation of social distinction via cultural production; Robert Tittler recognises, for instance, the "affinity between portraits and arms," both of which were "tableaux of personal presentation" that conveyed both external and internal qualities[39] (as visible, for instance, in Joan's delicate ruff and red gloves, while holding what is likely a patterned or decorated prayer book in her right hand). Alleyn's career and the wider sample of playhouse building motivations in this brief overview should therefore help us follow Ingram in rejecting "facile generalizations about playhouse builders"[40] and recognising the plurality of hopes and desires that drove early modern individuals of all backgrounds to lay bricks, knock down walls, or hammer in posts in the name of play.

Building Playhouses

It was possible to build in sixteenth- and seventeenth-century England with only a modest amount of capital and credit, but the question of finance was unsurprisingly first and foremost when it came building a playhouse. One of the more famous models, today, is the system employed to finance the Globe, which offered shares to investor-owners. Cuthbert Burbage claimed during a later dispute, in 1635, that he and his brother built the Globe with "sums of money taken up at interest, which lay heavy on us for many years; and to ourselves we joined those deserving men, Shakespeare, Heminges, Condell, Phillips, and others, partners in the profits of that they call the House."[41] The exact split of the shares remains unclear, though Burbage explained that each lease was issued for 21 years. "The labour of building and financing the Globe was in its way and its time heroic," according to Andrew Gurr, "and aptly enough was adjudged a Herculean effort by its supporters." He sees the agreement as

> an exceptionally cooperative act. It arose from the professional players' custom as touring companies of 'sharing' the profit and loss of their enterprises. Sharing in a playhouse extended the tradition of sharing the company's main assets, their playbooks and costumes, into a more material form.[42]

Other playhouses worked similarly. When Alleyn began to rebuild the Fortune in brick, almost immediately after its timber predecessor burned down in 1621, he avoided footing all of the construction costs himself by setting up what Berry labels a "consortium" of 12 shareholders, each of which held leases to the ground on which the playhouse would stand. Only a minority of these were actors at the Fortune itself, indicating the reach and appeal of the playhouse business model beyond the playing company. In turn, "he, she or they received a twelfth of the profits of the playhouse, paid a twelfth of the expenses, and agreed not to convert the place into something other than a playhouse."[43] The Second Blackfriars playhouse, too, followed a similar model to the Globe.[44] The sharers' practice that typified many playing companies during this period was therefore sometimes transferred onto the financing of playhouse structures.

The model of sharing investment, either in a playhouse or a company, was not particularly exceptional in the period. Many businesses depended upon such arrangements. Henry S. Turner calls this the "corporate commonwealth"—the range of bodies and groups whose formal existence structured the country:

> by the sixteenth century, corporations aggregate had become even more various: they were educational, ecclesiastical, charitable, political, and commercial, and they ranged in size from the universal church, extending across territories and indeed across time, to the angels in heaven—who formed a spiritual corporation, according to Richard Hooker—to the kingdom, or the community of the realm; to Parliament; to English corporate towns; to the two universities of Oxford and Cambridge; to the new joint-stock companies devoted to trade and exploration; and down to individual parish churches, chantries, and hospitals.[45]

Turner identifies the playing industry as part of this corporate aggregate, especially in the later part of the sixteenth century. In these years, as we saw in earlier chapters, regulation of play increased on both a local and national scale. Such policing accordingly resulted in "great formalization in company structures."[46] Indeed, scholarship has drawn parallels between the playing company and the craft company—those ancient if shifting "guild" bodies responsible for membership and management of an occupation or occupations.[47] The comparison might be extended out from the company to the physical spaces they inhabited. The sports complex at Congleton or the playhouse at Wine Street discussed in Chapter 4 suggest models for the management of playing spaces by corporate or semi-corporate bodies with both commercial and civic imperatives in mind. The structural similarity between playing and corporation activities (from the civic to the occupational) indicates the growing commercialisation of early modern England noted above, and the increase in joint-stock financing and incorporated towns across the country had inevitable consequences for an expanding leisure industry.

The sharers' models of the Globe or Fortune survive in contemporary paper-work, leases, and lawsuits. Yet the founding arrangements of many playhouses are not so well-documented. Indeed, the putative originality of the Globe's model must remain speculative, given that we do not know the full financing situation of Walton's London stages or of sites like the Canterbury bullstake or the Shrewsbury amphitheatre. Many sought to build playhouses predominantly using capital or credit. James Burbage and John Brayne spent large sums of both to support the building of the Theatre, with some contemporary estimates putting it at around 1,000 marks—a figure to add grist to the mill of religious opponents, given it translates to roughly £666.[48] That amounts to roughly 36 years' worth of wages of a skilled tradesmen.[49] The two were forced to pawn the lease the year after it was completed and eventually mortgage the property, and both men continued to struggle with liquidity in the wake of the mammoth undertaking.[50] However, not all playhouse projects required substantial investment. Those who owned buildings that already catered for the service industry, such as inns, could adapt with relatively little expense (perhaps using capital or profits from the existing business). Henry Houghton, owner of the Bell, recorded a back room, casement, a number of other rooms, a cell, a hall, chambers, and a kitchen, with two garrets, in the 1570s, and it was this property that featured regularly as a sports and performance venue in the later sixteenth century.[51] In a similar manner, Richard Farrant's establishment of the first playhouse at the Blackfriars was achieved by collapsing a single wall, a simple architectural act discussed in Chapter 1 of this book. Renovating with a playhouse in mind may well have required small extensions. In the years leading up to the opening of Bristol's Wine Street playhouse, for example, proprietor Nicholas Woolfe was awarded permission to enlarge his tenement.[52] These models suggest the many ways one might set about financing and building a playhouse in the sixteenth or seventeenth centuries, on a sliding scale from the frighteningly expensive to the relatively straightforward.

Indeed, we have seen that building a playhouse did not necessarily mean building from scratch. Early modern England's built environment was characterised by use and re-use, meaning adaptation and conversion could also mean "building" a venue. Such categories, however, took on particular charge from the 1570s in London, where concerns about space initiated new legislation over real estate. The city's corporation were eager to curb the trend of exploiting tenements by turning them into unsafe multiple-occupancy housing. At the same time, they reiterated building regulations issued by the Queen in a proclamation of 7 July 1580, which prevented any "new building" with fresh foundations. London accordingly sought to "enquire […] of all offences against the said proclamation in places pretended exempt and within three miles compass without the walls of the said city."[53] These orders help make sense of the trend of conversion discussed in Chapter 1 and remind us of the multitude of approaches that could qualify as playhouse construction. Nor was this a London-only phenomenon. The same restrictions applied to built-up cities outside of London, offering context for Woolfe's expanded playhouse-tenement. In 1607, Bristol emphasised a similar restriction on new building, when they ordered

> That no Burgess or Inhabitant of the said City shall at any time hereafter erect any new building or cause any new building to be erected and sett up within the said City or liberties thereof before such time as the same building and place which it is to be set up be first viewed and allowed by the Surveyors of the Lands of the said City or by three of them at the least with the Chamberlain of the said City for the time being[.][54]

The precept extended to "every Carpenter Mason or Workman that shall be Employed in the erecting or setting up of any such building or wall," who must observe these strictures or be fined. Such close regulation of urban space proscribes unlimited building activity in the centre. The entry suggests a parallel with London's actions some 30 years earlier and may well repeat earlier restrictions on building in central Bristol—an area that was characterised in this period by expansion and adaptation of medieval structures.[55]

Finance, availability of land, and restrictions on new buildings shaped how one might go about building a playhouse, but the skills and approaches required to complete such a project nonetheless applied to all the possible architectural iterations. Chief among them were the talents of the carpenters, masons, and workmen noted in the Bristol precept. We have already met a number of such individuals, who were responsible for re-edifying Congleton's cockpit or setting up a specialised trade in stage building in 1520s London. Peter Streete stands tall among such individuals, guaranteed posterity thanks to his building of the Globe. He was born to a joiner father but became apprenticed to a carpenter and went on to make a substantial living practising the craft, taking on 20 apprentices from all over England and Wales during his lifetime.[56] Streete's apprentices remind us that even London builders came from all over the country, and some may well have returned to their provincial homes after their terms. They would have taken with them a raft of knowledge and perhaps even something of Streete's predilection for play construction. In 1599, Streete was employed by the Burbages to dismantle the Theatre and take some of its timbers to Bankside, where he was to set up a new playhouse in the form of the Globe. When caught in the act of disassembly in Shoreditch, Streete told an enquirer, "that they took it down but to set it up upon the premises in an other form."[57] The comment is not entirely untrue, given that they were to set it up (elsewhere) in another form, but it does remind us of how commonplace it was to recycle building materials. Streete was used to such practices—even to the audacity and borderline illegality with which Elizabethan builders seemingly sometimes conducted themselves. Nine years earlier, he was pulled before the Star Chamber for stealing building materials from a dismantled property. He allegedly brought bills, swords, daggers, pistols, and a whole crew of confederates to the site he was working on, in order to commandeer "the Timber and Lead of [the complainant's] old house." His employer had tasked him to "pull Down the said old Tenement and in the place and Room thereof to erect and set up and perfectly to finish one other new Tenement."[58] Both his skills in reuse and his adeptness at theatrical construction earned Streete rapid new commission after building the Globe: Henslowe and Alleyn recruited him to build the Fortune the following year. Streete therefore gives us both a career and some character to help personalise those involved in the playhouse building industry.[59]

Yet "building" was in many ways a management task, one that fell to the proprietors or prospectors involved. William C. Baer's work into house-building and renting in early modern England underlines the boom in the building trade that occurred from the mid-sixteenth century, expanding London's suburbs considerably. While there is limited data available about those who built and sold property, it is clear that (in particular) following the regulations of 1580 and the threat of fines, prohibitions, and competition, it took "especially determined persons to build houses speculatively and get them sold or leased despite this daunting environment."[60] Baer also notes that construction was not for many builders their main profession; rather, they had other trades, which sometimes fell within the building trade and therefore allowed them to capitalise on their own skills. Even so, builders came from a variety of backgrounds and, generally, did not require huge amounts of capital to undertake such a project. While Baer's studies focus on those building accommodation, these same factors apply to those constructing recreational spaces. His description of a builder fits many of the individuals across this study perfectly:

> They were the projectors, promoters and leaders who conceived and initiated the project, lined up land and financing and oversaw it to completion. Builders could hire the variety of special trade or craft functions and professional skills that they could not perform themselves.[61]

The relationship between project management and the many skills involved in construction provides a salient reminder that playhouse building was always a collaborative enterprise and that we often do not know the names, background, or even job roles of so many instrumental individuals—a point expanded upon below.

Builders of leisure facilities therefore took a range of approaches to construction. Sometimes they "new built," raising capital through sharers or leveraging what money they could through loans or re-mortgaging. Others adapted structures as they saw fit. In the case of Francis Wood of East Coker, Somerset, he and a group of "confederates" simply took advantage of a chapel that had been set aside to be used as a grammar school. In its compass, they set up a fencing school and a "Cockpit game," apparently drawing diverse disordered persons on a daily basis.[62] In some cases, the act of "building" could be very light touch—a case of dressing an existing room and taking one's game there. In that sense, the question of how to build a playhouse takes us full circle back to the archetypes discussed in Chapter 1 of this book: playhouses came in all shapes and sizes and, accordingly, necessitated different approaches to building and maintenance. Sometimes, intent and practice could transform a space just as much as physical construction. Indeed, the ongoing labour demanded by all playhouses—from lawsuits to structural repair—made the act of building (business and edifice alike) a perpetual process, as indicated in this chapter's final section.

Who Made Playhouses Possible?

This book has already implicitly indicated the range of people who built, converted, adapted, or ran playhouses, from town corporations to entrepreneurial joiners, grocers, or dyers. This section considers commercial operators beyond men like Burbage or Henslowe and the collaborative practices that made playhouses possible. As noted above, building projects lend themselves to those with some knowledge of the trade. It is therefore no surprise that the playhouse constructor James Burbage, builder of the Theatre, was a joiner, or that Henry Walton, involved in so much theatrical construction in the 1520s, was the keeper of the London Mercers' timber yard. Yet other business people and more-than-business-people paralleled these individuals' access and expertise, providing specialist skills of their own or, indeed, simply hard graft. I accordingly focus here on the procurers of the playing industry—those central to the booking and networks of commercial play—as well as the extensive female involvement in and management of early modern leisure venues. In reflection of these various and widespread narratives, this section is structured by the biographical frameworks of three early modern Marges: Margaret Woolfe (Bristol), Margaret Brayne (London), and Margery Swayne (Congleton).

Margaret Woolfe

Recent studies have demonstrated the extent to which women were active in the early modern theatre industry, particularly in their ownership or management of venues. David Kathman has importantly shown how three major playing inns in sixteenth century London were owned or managed by women during their period of operation as playhouses: Margaret Craythorne either owned or leased the Bel Savage for 23 years from 1568, Alice Layston owned the Cross Keys from 1571 to her death in 1590, and Joan Harrison ran the Bull after her husband Matthew died in 1584 until 1589.[63] Meanwhile, Anne Farrant had financial control of the First Blackfriars playhouse for a short but important duration (in a decade in which the playhouse's repertory as published by the female publisher, Joan Brome).[64] These questions about playhouse ownership, leasing, and daily management extend into the seventeenth century, which saw Jane Poley and Susan Woodliffe with instrumental roles in the Boar's Head, Sybil Evans at the Second Blackfriars, Winifred Burbage Robinson for both the Second Blackfriars and the Globe, and Margaret Grey with the Fortune, as well as to the other individuals discussed in this chapter.

Far from being improper or exceptional, female property ownership and management was relatively common in early modern England. Yet the law was not equal and, certainly, early modern England was deeply chauvinistic in its legal practices. The borough of Manchester in the 1580s, for instance, sought to punish by fine or imprisonment any single woman who "shall sell any ale or bread" or "keep any house or chamber" in the town.[65] However, looking beyond statute or prescription and towards actual lived experience indicates, as always, a much more nuanced picture:

> The reality of women's receiving large amounts of property and exerting power over it in a distinctive way does not change the fact of oppression, but it does highlight the disjuncture between theory and practice. It also exhibits the ingenuity of many ordinary women in working within a massively restrictive system.[66]

Indeed, growing public and legislative concern about exploitative rental markets and property development (connected to the building restrictions discussed above) often saw ordinances, complaints, or satire directed at landladies. Many owners of tenements or alleys listed in the records of the London Court of Common Council, as it sought to regulate the housing industry, were women. In what might appear in the context of this section as a running joke, one of them, bound upon several occasions to observe rental regulations in 1573, was even called Margaret:

> The Condition of this recognisance is such that where the said Margaret Hawkins has diverse times tenants dwelling in Alleys & other places within the ward of Farringdon-without, which some of them be very poor, of the said Margery do not at any times hereafter, after such tenants as now she hath be either dead or go Away, place an other tenant to dwell in any there tenements that shall be chargeable to the City or parish or go a-begging.[67]

The distance between these domestic lettings and recreational spaces was not so great as it might seem on the surface. Alleys, as Chapter 1 indicated, brought together domestic accommodation and sport, not least through the bowling alley, which itself overlapped with playhouse construction.[68]

Contemporary commentary blurred the lines between landlordism and recreational management. Henry Chettle's *Kind-Hart's Dream* (1593) sees the late clown Richard Tarlton reanimated as a ghost to deliver a posthumous complaint about the rental market. Chettle himself rounds out the disapproval by offering his own representative sketch of London housing:

> Some Landlords having turned an old Brew-house, Bake-house, or Dye-house into an Alley of tenements, will either themselves, or some at their appointment, keep tippling in the fore-house (as they call it) and their poor tenants must be enjoined to fetch bread, drink, wood, coal, and such other necessaries, in no other place: and there till the week's end they may have any thing of trust, provided they lay to pawn their holiday apparel: nay, my Land-lady will not only do them that good turn, but if they want money, she will on Monday lend them likewise upon a pawn eleven pence, and in mere pity ask at the week's end not a penny more than twelve pence.[69]

Here, the landlady is not only a domestic letter but manager of a tippling house, moneylender, and keeper of an enclosed market for goods. It is telling that Chettle's representative figure is female. His decision to make her a woman not only enables the tract's underlying misogyny, in its attack on female enterprise (albeit a seemingly exploitative one), but also indicates that such arrangements were not atypical. After all, the imagined Land-lady had a real-life equivalent in the serial offender Margaret Hawkins. It should be no surprise, therefore, that we find numerous recreational enterprises also managed by women, from Kathman's innholders to the Widow Dichfield, who had possession of the "Cockpit House" in Prescot for some period in the 1600s.[70]

Margaret Thomas, later Margaret Woolfe, of Wine Street in Bristol offers one such case study in female playhouse ownership that brings together many of these concerns with inheritance, management, and the early modern service industry. Her experience also points to the complex interaction between ownership and exclusion attendant on women of moderate or middling status (neither very rich nor very poor) in the early modern period and the inequities inherent in any collaborative venture. Accounts of the Wine Street Playhouse to date have largely framed it as a one-man operation, focused on Nicholas's business motivations and capabilities. But surrounding legal information pertaining to the Woolfes' activities on Wine Street indicates that it was a much more collaborative venture than such a model allows.[71]

Margaret's first husband, Thomas Thomas, left her various goods after his death, including "one messuage tenement or Inn within the City of Bristol called the sign of the White Harte & sundry other houses lands tenements," which she proceeded to manage herself, in her own words, "to her great profit and commodity."[72] By the time she married her new husband, Nicholas Woolfe, in February 1605, the couple owned an impressive suite of recreational property on Wine Street, with the White Hart complementing the Playhouse near Christ Church. Indeed, contemporary legal testimony identifies Margaret as the co-owner and co-operator of the Playhouse. One deponent in a lawsuit makes a point of noting that he handed money to Margaret, rather than Nicholas, when he entered the venue. The deponent also noted that *both* of "the defendants took money" from comedians who performed at the venue.[73]

Margaret therefore not only brought into her second marriage capital, property, and goods but was possessed of valuable skills. She had experience managing an inn for "profit" and in turn would have had facility with playhouse management—a role that she seems, from her front-of-house collection, to have taken up. The qualities of business enterprise typically associated with the "middling" sorts were quite clearly held by the likes of Margaret Woolfe.[74] Her management and sometime ownership of both the inn and the playhouse suggest that women's roles in this area of society extended beyond running a domestic household (a space that already merged work and leisure) to more substantial commercial operations. Indeed, Margaret adds to the list of women central to the expanding urban leisure industry of early modern England.

Yet business savvy was no shield against both structural oppression and gender inequality. Margaret's wider experience of marriage indicates the precarity of both social and economic status. Although her widowhood from Thomas Thomas granted her a degree of financial autonomy, Margaret's remarriage significantly affected her agency. Motivations for remarrying in early modern England were vast, complex, and ultimately difficult, if not impossible, to ascertain.[75] As a widow, Margaret claimed to have run the White Hart inn by herself to her "profit and commodity," placing her alongside other widows in Bristol who had established themselves up as confirmed craftspeople or traders.[76] Indeed, "most widows were active economic agents,"[77] who built on skills developed throughout their lives (including activities during marriage) and who sometimes pursued their late husband's businesses, from agricultural concerns to the developing craft of painting.[78] Yet Margaret's marriage to Nicholas affected her freedom, not least given that she seemed to have conveyed most of her property into the marriage. According to her account of their relationship, domestic life was not entirely happy. Woolfe provided nothing in his will for Margaret and indeed bequeathed the property she had brought into the marriage to his other family members. A subsequent court case on Margaret's behalf lamented that Nicholas had not left "Margaret one penny in goods or otherwise saving only houseroom during her life, in so much as she became very poor and miserable and was enforced to crave relief of others."[79] Margaret herself had testified in an earlier lawsuit (concerning the inheritance of Nicholas's son, a topic addressed in the Chapter 4) that her husband "carried himself so hard and greedy upon [Margaret's] meanes and estate," even though "he were wealthy and of good estate."[80] During their life together, Margaret witheringly remarks, Nicholas was so tight with his money that he had never made for her a single gown. When her brother "in his charity" had given Margaret one, Nicholas took shears to it and "cut out in pieces to make him the said nicholas woolfe doublet and hose."[81]

Margaret's depiction of their marriage in court emphasises her late husband's selfishness and parsimony and presents the Bristolian cutler as something of a miser. Nicholas, of course, was not alive to rebut these claims, and they may well reflect

Margaret's legal literacy and skilful self-presentation in court, where claims of poverty and ill-treatment were commonplace when widows were (often rightly) dissatisfied with the outcomes of probate. Yet her husband's will clearly robbed her of property once rightly hers, and whatever joint enterprise existed around the playhouse and the White Hart while the two were married counted for little upon Nicholas's death. Margaret, saddled with a stingy husband and with no legal claim to an inn she once owned and ran to her "commodity," was left only with houseroom. The apparent sadness and injustice of this narrative reminds us that business and property ownership was always contingent upon contemporary social and legal practice. Evidence of female playhouse management does not always indicate escape from a patriarchal world.

Margery Swayne

Venue ownership and management were not the only ways in which business people and more-than-business-people were instrumental to commercial playing enterprises. Indeed, ownership or proprietorship is in many senses a narrow model for understanding a playing industry that was expansive, imbricated with other crafts and occupations, and collaborative. Like the architectural structures surveyed in Chapter 1, which were often porous and adaptable, the business structures discussed here relied on a raft of surrounding skills and inputs. Natasha Korda has emphasised the significance of labour surrounding playing venues. Her exploration of the "lost history" of women who worked in and around playhouses considers commercial venues "within the broader economic landscape of early modern London." Her work emphasises how

> the professional stage relied on the labor, wares, ingenuity, and capital of women of all stripes, including ordinary crafts- and tradeswomen who supplied costumes, properties, and comestibles; wealthy heiresses and widows who provided much-needed capital and credit; wives, daughters, and widows of theatre people who worked actively alongside their male kin; and immigrant women who fueled the fashion-driven stage with a range of newfangled skills and commodities.[82]

The present discussion of Swayne and Brayne, and Woolfe above, is shaped by and follows in the footsteps of Korda's important recovery of surrounding labour, which includes consideration of account-keeping and the female creditors of early modern London, such as Elizabeth Burbage, Elizabeth Hutchinson, and Agnes Henslowe.[83] This section, like the section on Bristol above, seeks to find "lost labours" in locations outside of London, where such work is often doubly hidden as a result of inattention to the playing capacities of smaller regional towns and cities. In the next section, I then return to London to consider how Margaret Brayne shaped the playing industry not only through her labour but through forthright ownership and claims to business equity.

Margery Swayne was one individual whose labour supported and enabled play. On our visit to the Congleton cockpit and playing complex in Chapter 4, we met a number of people responsible for "dressing" or "making" the cockpit on a yearly basis. Margery was at the heart of this dressing and making, thanks to her work as a straw-drawer or thatch-drawer. Straw- and thatch-drawers prepared hay, rye, wheat, and other material for use, including for roofing, decorative plaiting, or, as here, lining or preparing a space for animal sports. In 1589, Swayne was paid 16 pence for three days' work drawing thatch. Ten years later, she appears again in the Town Council's Order Books for the sixpence paid to her for drawing 23 thraves of straw "bestowed upon the Cockpit" and again around Easter time for her work on wheat and rye straw for the site. The following year, as work was underway "in mending the Cockpit" ahead of the "great Cockfight Week," Swayne was paid another sixpence for "drawing carrying & watering four thraves of Rye straw."[84] These are but a handful of payments, but they indicate a span of at least 11 years of labour on the Congleton playing complex. Intriguingly, individuals sometimes go unnamed in relation to such work. The earliest records in the town accounts accord money for barley straw and rye straw "to the cockpit and schoolhouse" but do not name a recipient for the five shilling fee, suggesting there may be more instances of individuals like Margery Swayne—or Swayne herself—involved with cockpit preparation throughout the period.[85] Yet beyond these payments, it is hard to find details about her life. She seemingly left no will—itself not an unusual occurrence if one's possessions or worth was relatively insubstantial—and the paper trail surrounding Margaret or Margery Swayne or Sweyne (or potentially other variations in spelling) does not go far beyond these records.[86]

This documentary scarcity places Swayne alongside the six lives reconstructed by Elisabeth Salter, whose research recognises the challenges involved when it comes to using small details to generate even a slim biography. Salter explores, for instance, Elizabeth Philip, who worked for Henry VIII's royal household producing materials for the wardrobe: for such women, as for Swayne, there is a difficulty finding evidence "that directly reflects their own lives in any detail"—a common trial when it comes to recovering the lives of those from lower status or otherwise marginalised groups or demographics. For Salter, the appearance of her subject's name in the royal wardrobe accounts makes it possible "to investigate the ways that a woman such as Elizabeth Philip came into contact with the splendid richness of the culture of display at this royal household" and to consider the opportunities and experiences that contact provided.[87] Swayne may be distant from centres of royal activity and record-keeping, but the few accounting entries in the Congleton corporation records place her as a similar figure to Philip. The biographical survey here is brief and set alongside analogous activity of other women involved in play; it suggests the "richness" of opportunity provided by playing spaces in a medium-sized provincial community.

Indeed, Swayne's skill-set and her community labour allow for some biographical speculation. It is possible, for instance, she was employed as a servant. Jane Whittle's research has shown that female servants were employed for non-"domestic" tasks from cherry picking to hay-making.[88] The job need not have restricted and may even have facilitated participation in municipal life, as workers were not confined to the household or fields. Charmian Mansell has demonstrated, for instance, how female servants involved with such work were present and active in the wider early modern community. Mansell's study of the experiences of individuals in church court depositions establishes that "the female servant's sphere of interaction was not limited to her employers or their family. Both within and beyond the home, opportunities to exchange news, gossip, and establish friendships were abundant."[89] In the case of Swayne, these opportunities would have extended to paid community work, her labour supporting the corporation's leisure infrastructure. Swayne may alternatively have been what we would now think of as self-employed or freelance, taking on work that would add to a husband's profits or wages or that simply provided income for herself.[90] Rural households engaged in a diverse array of money-making labours. Studies of Kentish "husbandmen," for instance, reveal flexibility in craft and production with "distinct temporal rhythms across the year."[91] Like the widow Elizabeth Ringer in Tara Hamling and Catherine Richardson's study of domestic life and work, Swayne could have engaged in numerous forms of production.[92] The seasonal work of straw-drawing may have represented for her or her household one of the many "by-employments of those of lower social status."[93] The Congleton corporation's particular need for and use of straw folds such seasonal work into the playing industry. Swayne therefore represents one of the many roles held by men and women across the country adjacent but instrumental to playhouse development.

Other such individuals were responsible not for "making" or "dressing" spaces but for procuring the play that took place within them. Indeed, procurement was a central feature of commercial performance, sport, and game and is key to recovering the wide-reaching labour of leisure in more rural areas. *Play procurers* were individuals who sourced and solicited play on behalf of their community or their own establishment. The term itself would have been familiar to someone like Margery Swayne. It was used in Congleton to explain payment to "John Pursell for Riding to procure Bears in the night for the wakes," clearly on the Corporation's behalf.[94] On another occasion, William Stonyer was paid in 1601 "for bringing a letter to Shelmerdyne [the bearward]."[95] These payments suggest that physical journeys and a correspondence network (relying on deliverers or post people) provided the town with play at necessary or desired occasions.

As with all elements of the playing industry, procurement was not a male preserve. Women can be found hiring or supporting bearwards in Cheshire and beyond, such as in the legal records in the north, where procurers were frequently cited for breaking laws or "entertaining" bears and bearwards. "John Foster of Peever," near to Congleton, confessed that "his wife did hire a Bearward called by the name of Thomas Gorst to beat at his house this day and tomorrow."[96] Back in Congleton itself, Goodwife Brodhurst was paid the rather large sum of 22 shillings and 8 pence for providing a "bearward's diet," suggesting quite an appetite after days at the town's wakes in 1611.[97] As well as directly procuring the bears and bearwards, then, related forms of aid or support were crucial to the playing ecologies surrounding regional playing spaces. Proprietors of those spaces some-times took on several of these roles, from procurement to accommodation. When Eleanor Cox hosted bearwards at her alehouse in Wells, she had to endure slander in the streets a few days later from a drunken neighbour. The foul-mouthed Miles Brokenburrowgh announced loudly "Thou were drunk at Bristol, when thou went after the Bearwards which had been at thy house, for thy money."[98] Although part of a defamation case that put the facts and behaviour in question, this curious detail suggests that Cox acted as a regional landlady for the bearwards. Perhaps, like Goodwife Brodhurst, she provided lodging and diet; perhaps the bears were even baited at her inn or alehouse.

Such instances reflect a playing business that goes beyond management and ownership and that relied upon individuals like Swayne, Pursell, or Brodhurst to provide networks and infrastructure that made play possible. Given the peri-patetic nature of much of the bear-baiting and playing industries (characterised in the provinces by travelling bearwards and troupes), these procurers were of utmost importance. They were the factors who made entertainment happen. These procurers and hosts formed part of the playing industry's essential human resource network across the country—those individuals who sourced entertainers, managed logistics, or maintained venues. Margery Swayne is particularly illustrative of this wider playing infrastructure. We can place her with certainty in the playing venue of the Congleton cockpit-schoolhouse, thanks to payments from the corporation, but beyond these details we have little to go on. Her labours in service of the leisure industry are testament to the many individuals whose names or details we may no longer know and the extent of whose work and involvement may no longer be apparent. For us today, playhouses and surrounding complexes—as both businesses and community operations—in many ways, relied upon the activities of strangers.

Margaret Brayne

The activities represented by and surrounding Margaret Woolfe and Margery Swayne demonstrate how shared labour was intrinsic to early modern playing places. The sharers' or joint-stock models that financed playhouses like the Globe represent another collaborative model, one in which risk and reward were collect-ively distributed. However, there were other fundamental forms of collaboration across the early modern playing industry—both within one institution and between different venues. The final part of this chapter returns to a longstanding crux in early modern theatre history concerning the relationship between the Theatre and the Curtain in Shoreditch. I suggest that the enigmatic profit-sharing arrangement between these two playhouses might be more productively approached via Margaret Brayne, co-builder of the Theatre.

In January 1565, Margaret Stowers married John Brayne in St Dionis Backchurch, London.[99] The couple spent most of their marriage resident in Bucklersbury, in St Stephen's Walbrook parish. As a grocer, John Brayne would have been at home in the parish, given it was the heart of the city's grocery trade. John, as we saw in the opening chapter, built a playhouse at the Red Lion sometime around 1567. It is possible that Margaret had some involvement in or experience of playhouse construction as part of her husband's early venture. Certainly, that was true of his second theatrical building project, the collaboration with his brother-in-law James Burbage in building the Theatre. Indeed, in a later court case, Margaret explained that she and her husband "were driven to labour in the said works for saving of some of the charge in place of 2 labourers."[100] In a similar fashion to the work put in by Swayne in Congleton, Margaret Brayne's labour was integral to the playhouse—in this case, through her physical involvement in laying its foundations: she was a playhouse *builder* in a literal as well as a figurative sense.

Choice elements of Margaret's activity are recorded for posterity, thanks to the tortuous legal proceedings she initiated. The many complicated legal documents about the Theatre and its land are held at the UK National Archives, and Herbert Berry has set out a handlist that helpfully classifies each suit and their respective documents. Some concern land disputes between the landlord Giles Allen and the Peckhams (A), the Earls of Rutland (B), and the Burbages (D), but Berry's "Category C" documents relate to the quarrel between the Burbages and the widow Brayne.[101] Brayne contended that she was owed the sum of two bonds (a total of £600) from the Burbages, or, alternatively, that she should receive half the profits of the playhouse. Her claims arose from the substantial sums of money put in by her late husband, who had even bankrupted himself through the playhouse's financial demands. The Burbages disputed her right to a "moity"—or half of the profits—and this fundamental disagreement formed the crux of the lawsuits.[102]

Margaret was joined in her legal odyssey by one of her late husband's creditors, Robert Miles. The two had a rather dramatic relationship. Margaret initially blamed Miles for her husband's death, and Miles and John Brayne had been put further out of pocket, thanks to another unrewarding investment in an inn called the George (a property Miles allegedly insinuated himself into owning). Miles in return kicked her out of the inn, prompting Margaret to take him to court on a murder charge as well as suing him for a share in the George. Then, an almost implausible about-turn saw them become "close friends."[103] The nature of their relationship was publicly called into question during the lawsuits[104]—not least because Margaret had responsibility for a child, Katherine, born some months after her late husband's death, whose parentage was a matter of damaging speculation.[105] The circumstances of Katherine's birth had a bearing on the suit, because if John Brayne had died without legitimate children, the playhouse ownership would defer to Burbage's own heirs. Accordingly, Katherine's birth, if legitimate, gave Margaret a further basis for her claim. Given this fact, the Burbages fell to the convenient conclusion "that Miles was the father and that he and Margaret Brayne had conspired to murder John Brayne."[106]

The messy relations between Margaret Brayne and Miles on the one hand and the Burbages on the other prompted a knotty set of cases: first, Margaret ventured at common law to collect two bonds and secure half the title of the Theatre and its profits; in 1588, James Burbage "sued [Robert Miles and Margaret Brayne] in

Chancery to get the bonds cancelled and to stop them from making claims on the playhouse," before Margaret counter-sued Burbage. "The two lawsuits in chancery jogged on side by side for seven years. Then, with Margaret Brayne dead and Miles carrying on by himself, Chancery returned the case to the point at which it had begun."[107] Miles (and by extension Margaret) were ultimately unsuccessful in their quest. The documents produced by this seemingly unending (and technically unended) dispute provide not only historical vignettes stranger than fiction but happily furnish us with a great deal of (albeit often contested) knowledge about the theatrical affairs of early modern London.

Margaret's quest to secure a right to the Theatre led her not only to the court but into the playhouse itself. Just as Swayne's straw-dressing places her as an actor (if not a performer) in the Cheshire sports complex, so Margaret too engages in a form of public action at the doors to her putative business. Ralph Miles (son of her co-litigant Robert) gave eyewitness testimony of the lively drama occasioned by the quarrel. He stated before the court that he had been

> requested by […] Margaret Brayne and […] Robert Myles [his father] to go with them to the Theatre upon A play day to stand at the door that goeth up to the galleries of the said Theatre to take & receive for the use of the said Margaret half the money that should be given to come up unto their said Galleries at that door.

Miles showed James and Richard Burbage an order issued by Chancery, which allegedly proved that Margaret had the right to collect half the profits taken at the galleries. In response, "James Burbage & the wife & his son Rychard Burbage, did with violence thrust [Ralph] and the said Margaret and Robert Myles away from the said door going up to the said Galleries," issuing numerous threats to beat them. When Robert Miles repeated their right and intention of taking box office money, Richard and his mother Ellen Burbage "did set upon the said Robert Myles & beat him with A broom staff calling him murdering knave with other vile and unhonest words."[108] This extraordinary scene not only suggests the height of feelings surrounding the playhouse lawsuit but shows two women—Margaret Brayne and Ellen Burbage—making claims upon theatrical space and physically, as well as legally, asserting right and ownership within the playing industry.

Brayne's lawsuit extended beyond the law court and the playhouse doorstep to feature in national print circulation. Henry Chettle alluded to it in a disparaging quip in *Kind-Harts Dream* (1593). Not only does the pamphlet, as we saw above, satirise exploitative landladies, it takes aim, too, at ambitious claimants like Margaret Brayne. While celebrating the virtue of players in the city, the ghost of Tarlton takes pause to chide a widow who "complains against one or two of them, for denying a Legacy of forty shillings sum." Should she secure the portion, Chettle writes, "she intends to set up an Appleshop in one of the Inns."[109] Given Brayne's lawsuit was still at issue in the year of publication, this appears to be a thinly veiled reference to the Theatre and connected buildings, including the Curtain and her late husband's East London inn, the George. Chettle implies, in the phrase "appleshop," that Brayne might invest the money in a brothel,[110] but the term is vague enough to acknowledge both the commercial and theatrical impetus behind her suit.[111] The allusion suggests that Brayne's claims to playhouse ownership were not just known by the courts and a small circle of those directly implicated but were the subject of wider London knowledge and gossip.

The Theatre lawsuit is fundamentally concerned with collaboration. The exact financial relationship between John Brayne and James Burbage is at the heart of the finer details of the different cases and extends to hearsay and speculation from those involved in labour on and around the playhouse. On the one hand, therefore, it suggests the trickier side of the collaborative processes involved in building and business. Yet these documents also reveal other networks of collaboration— including between playhouses. The proprietor of the Curtain playhouse in 1585, Henry Lanman, explained in one of the Chancery cases that he had agreed with Burbage and Brayne that they would take "the Curtain as an Esore to their playhouse," so that "the profits of the said 2 Play houses might for 7 years space be in dividend between them."[112] Duncan Salkeld is frank about the difficulty this sentence has long posed for theatre historians: "This word 'Esore' has often been rendered as 'easer' and interpreted as referring to a financial 'easement', here established by way of a neighbourly agreement. In truth, we do not know what this word means."[113] Salkeld speculates that it may in fact refer to "Esau," the Biblical character, who (in parallel to the Curtain's relationship to the Theatre) was "rougher" than his younger brother: "The Curtain, then, may have been an Esau to the Theatre's Jacob, rough and plain since its inception, a slightly elder brother to the younger, more attractive sibling."[114] This ingenious suggestion troubles our sense of precedence (discussed in Chapter 1), though it perhaps does not enlighten us about the exact business arrangements, which remain obscured by the word (whatever its precise modern transliteration), if sketched out faintly in Lanman's predominantly financial language of profit and dividend.

Either way, the 50/50 profit-sharing set-up between the owners of the two playhouses factored into Margaret Brayne's understanding of the Shoreditch playing industry. Local resident Henry Bett told the court in 1591 that shortly after her husband's death, Margaret "did take up some money at the play house, called the Curtain," while John Allen (an actor and the brother of Edward Alleyn) noted that, given this profit-sharing arrangement, "he doth think the complainant is to have her dividend […] aswell as her moity of the Theatre," emphasising "And so ought she to have the whole moity of the Theatre […] & half of the other Moity of the profits of the Curtain."[115] The "dividend" suggests a joint-stock split not in the ownership of one single playhouse, as with the Globe, but a super-company that pooled profits between the two playhouses. It may well be that Lanman's arrangement reflected a nascent playhouse conglomeration (nearly 25 years before the King's Men occupied both the Globe and the Blackfriars and some fifteen years before Henslowe doubled his playhouse tally by building the Fortune). The arrangement meant that the owners could maximise their share of London's available recreational profits.

Seeing the "Esore" from Margaret Brayne's point of view suggests one model for understanding the playing industry of late sixteenth century London. Even in the midst of contention, Brayne championed collaboration—that, after all, was the grounds for all of her legal claims. Her husband had invested large sums in the building of the Theatre in partnership with his brother-in-law, and both, in turn, had agreed another collaborative venture with Lanman. Her approach to what is now a historical textual crux—the "Esore" arrangement—was to turn up at the Curtain and collect her dues. Hers is the only documented instance of a proprietor setting foot, in the name of business, in both the Theatre and the Curtain (though doubtless not the only such occurrence). Her movements in Shoreditch while chasing box office money thereby provide physical connections between two otherwise separate playhouses (even if the legal status of her activities remained muddy) and embody the precarious collaborative practice between them. Indeed, the surrounding history of the Shoreditch "Esore" radically rejects sole, male playhouse ownership. It is rather a picture of sharing and sharing gone wrong, in which—like the architecture of so many across the country—the boundaries of playhouses are shown to have been porous, overlapping with other nearby leisure institutions. It is also a picture of female playhouse ownership both assumed and contested, in the lawcourt, in the forecourt, and in bookstalls. Playhouse business was messy, but it was abundantly plural.

The more-than-business-people involved in the early modern playing industry were not just commercially-driven owners of playhouses. While profit-hunting, modelled dramatically in the stand-off between Brayne and Miles and the broom-wielding Burbages, was perhaps a prime motive for constructing recreational venues, it was not the only one. The Woolfe family of Wine Street had a complicated relationship with both inn and playhouse, with Nicholas invested equally in the cultural legacy of the theatre and the cultural literacy of his son. His wife, meanwhile, brought business acumen to theatrical management but suffered, as many women of the period did, from the threat of precarity and probate inequity. Margery Swayne only fleetingly appears in the documentary archive, paid for her work on the cockpit at Congleton, but her work is evidence of the skills and labour brought to the playing industry by numerous lower-status individuals.

Playhouse building required substantial, if not prohibitive, investment, as we have seen, and joint-stock models offered one way in which capital could be generated. Builders were in many ways project managers, overseeing a complex operation in which many different skills came together. Leisure venues therefore give us insight into the processes of the early modern building trade and the regulatory frameworks within which it operated. At the same time, but from a different angle, each of the three Margarets discussed in the final part of this chapter demonstrates specific ways to build—by converting an inn and merging businesses, by drawing straw and shaping an arena for animal sport, or by laying the bricks of a playhouse oneself and then seeking to reclaim a moiety of those foundations at court. Indeed, Margaret Brayne is an exemplary figure when it comes to thinking about the who's who of the early modern playing industry. As the widow of John Brayne (whose formal investment legally tied her to both the Theatre and the Curtain), she claimed a stake in both playhouses—a claim featured in popular print as well as in court. Her extensive legal battles to be recognised as a playhouse proprietor offers the chance for revisionist theatre history not to rewrite the past or impose modern narratives upon it, but rather to reflect claims of ownership and management asserted so determinedly at the time.

Notes

1 Carol Chillington Rutter, "Introduction," *Documents of the Rose Playhouse*, rev. ed. (Manchester: Manchester University Press, 1999): 1–35. p. 6.
2 Rutter, p. 5.
3 William Ingram, *The Business of Playing: The Beginnings of the Adult Professional Theater in Elizabethan London* (Ithaca: Cornell University Press, 1992), p. 16.
4 For a selection that touches on these narratives and wider questions of business, see: Douglas Bruster, *Drama and the Market in the Age of Shakespeare* (Cambridge: Cambridge University Press, 1992); Neil Carson, *A Companion to Henslowe's Diary*, 1988 (Cambridge: Cambridge University Press, 2005); Ingram, *Business*; William Ingram, *A London Life in the Brazen Age: Francis Langley, 1548–1602* (Cambridge: Harvard University Press, 1978); Theodore B. Leinwand, *Theatre, Finance, and Society in Early Modern England* (Cambridge: Cambridge University Press, 1999); and the many studies of Henslowe (and sometimes Burbage) within the economic contexts of the early modern theatre.
5 REPS 19 fo 18 (8 Dec. 1575), COL/CA/01/01/021, MS, London Metropolitan Archives, London.
6 C24/228/10, MS, The National Archives, Kew, London.
7 Irwin Smith, *Shakespeare's Blackfriars Playhouse: Its History and Its Design* (New York: New York University Press, 1964), p. 467.
8 LM 413, MS, Surrey History Centre, Woking, UK.
9 Ingram, *A London Life in the Brazen Age*, p. 111.
10 Harleian 286, fo. 102, MS, British Library, London.
11 Ingram, *Business*, p. 147.
12 Cotton CH 26 fo. 41, MS, British Library, London; REPS 18 fo. 168v (2 Mar. 1573), COL/CA/01/01/020, MS, London Metropolitan Archives, London.
13 John Stockwood, *A Sermon Preached at Paules Crosse on Barthelmew Day* (London, 1578), K1r.
14 Craig Muldrew, "The 'Middling Sort': An Emergent Cultural Identity," *A Social History of England, 1500–1750*, ed. Keith Wrightson (Cambridge: Cambridge University Press, 2017): 290–309.
15 John Northbrooke, *Treatise Wherein Dicing, Dancing, Plays and Interludes, with Other Idle Pastimes* (London, 1577), N3r.
16 Martha C. Skeeters, "John Northbrooke," *Oxford Dictionary of National Biography*. Online. Accessed 20 Oct. 2021.
17 Judith M. Bennett, "Conviviality and Charity in Medieval and Early Modern England," *Past and Present* 134 (1992): 19–41. p. 21.
18 Bennett, p. 21.
19 E36/227 fos 31v-32r, MS, The National Archives, Kew, London.

20 See Elizabeth Goldring, *Nicholas Hilliard: Life of an Artist* (New Haven: Yale University Press, 2019).

21 Robert Tittler acknowledges that only the most fashionable London-based painters "had begun to think of themselves as professionals and gentlemen, practitioners of a liberal art rather than mere craftsmen," *Portraits, Painters, and Publics in Provincial England, 1540–1640* (Oxford: Oxford University Press, 2012), p. 60. Hilliard's treatise, *The Arte of Limning*, frames his work as part of a venerable intellectual tradition as well as positioning himself strategically as a leading artistic figure: Goldring, pp. 243–7.

22 MS 01454/47 sheet 4*, MS, London Metropolitan Archives, London.

23 Ingram, *Business*, pp. 119–49.

24 C3/328/28, MS, The National Archives, Kew, London.

25 Christopher Marsh, *Music and Society in Early Modern England* (Cambridge: Cambridge University Press, 2010), p. 14.

26 Nicholas was practicing his trade of cutler and training apprentices up to his death (after which his nephew Isaac took over his final apprentice, John Sutchecombe), F/AU/1/ 18 p. 157, MS, Bristol Archives, Bristol.

27 Marsh, p. 168. Marsh observes, for instance, that Bristol had a particularly high ownership of virginals among non-gentry and tradespeople, p. 181.

28 Jennifer Bishop, "Utopia and Civic Politics in Mid-Sixteenth-Century London," *Historical Journal* 54.4 (2011): 933–53. p. 938; p. 940. David Kathman, "The Rise of Commercial Playing in 1540s London," *Early Theatre* 12.1 (2009): 15–38.

29 Jessica Winston, *Lawyers at Play: Literature, Law, and Politics at the Early Modern Inns of Court, 1558–1581* (Oxford: Oxford University Press, 2016).

30 For this and further biographical details, see S.P. Cerasano, "Alleyn, Edward (1566– 1626)," *Oxford Dictionary of National Biography*. Online. Accessed 21 Oct. 2021.

31 See Henslowe's letter to Alleyn, 28 September 1593, in which he asks to send word to his wife about how much Goodman Hudson pays in rent, so she can deal with the situation in London. *Documents of the Rose Playhouse*, ed. Carol Chillington Rutter, rev. ed., (Manchester: Manchester University Press, 1999), pp. 75–7.

32 See S.P. Cerasano, "Edward Alleyn, the New Model Actor, and the Rise of Celebrity in the 1590s," *Medieval and Renaissance Drama in England* 18 (2005): 47–58.

33 Paola Pugliatti, "'My Good Sweet Mouse': Letters in a Time of Plague," *Journal of Early Modern Studies* spec. issue (2020): 1–23. p. 9.

34 Anita Gilman Sherman, "The Status of Charity in Thomas Heywood's 'If You Know Not Me You Know Nobody,'" *Medieval and Renaissance Drama in England* 12 (1999): 99–120. p. 109.

35 MSS 009, MS, Dulwich College Archive, Dulwich, London. This document is freely available online at the *Henslowe-Alleyn Digitisation Project* (https://henslowe-alleyn.org. uk), where it has also been transcribed by Grace Ioppolo, who provides a helpful introduction and glossary of names.

36 Quoted in Sherman, p. 109.

37 Grace Ioppolo, "The Diary of Edward Alleyn (1617–1622)," *Henslowe-Alleyn Digitisation Project*. Online. Accessed 21 Oct. 2021. p. 13. See Dulwich College, MSS 001, Article 101, 1r.

38 For more on Alleyn and the idea of the "New Gentry," see the *Middling Culture* website (www.middlingculture.com).

39 Tittler, *Portraits*, p. 115.

40 Ingram, *Business*, p. 181.

41 *English Professional Theatre*, eds Glynne Wickham, Herbert Berry, and William Ingram (Cambridge: Cambridge University Press, 2000), p. 226.

42 Andrew Gurr, "Why the Globe is Famous," *The Oxford Handbook of Early Modern Theatre*, ed. Richard Dutton (Oxford: Oxford University Press, 2009): 186–208. pp. 189–90.

43 *English Professional Theatre, 1530–1640*, p. 638.

44 For detail on the ownership structure of the Blackfriars, see Lucy Munro, "Who Owned the Blackfriars Playhouse?", *Shakespeare Quarterly* 70.4 (2019): 247–69. See also "Introduction," *Moving Shakespeare Indoors: Performance and Repertoire in the Jacobean Playhouse*, eds Andrew Gurr and Farah Karim-Cooper (Cambridge: Cambridge University Press, 2014): 1–12.

45 Henry S. Turner, *The Corporate Commonwealth: Pluralism and Political Fictions in England, 1516–1651* (Chicago: Chicago University Press, 2016), p. 14.

46 Turner, pp. 121–2.

47 See David Kathman, "Players, Livery Companies, and Apprentices," *The Oxford Handbook of Early Modern Theatre*, ed. Richard Dutton (Oxford: Oxford University Press, 2009): 412–28; Roslyn Knutson, *Playing Companies and Commerce in Shakespeare's Time* (Cambridge: Cambridge University Press, 2001).

48 STAC5/A12/35, MS, The National Archives, Kew, London.

49 According to The National Archives' free and entertaining Currency Converter, 2017. "Currency convertor: 1270–2017," *The National Archives*. Online. Accessed 21 Oct. 2021.

50 See Ingram's account in *The Business of Playing*, pp. 192–216.

51 C2/Eliz/B24/63, MS, The National Archives, Kew, London.

52 Roger Leech, *The Topography of Medieval and Early Modern Bristol: Part I* (Bristol: Bristol Record Society, 1997), pp. 172–3.

53 REPS 20 fo. 136v, COL/CA/01/01/022, MS, London Metropolitan Archives, London.

54 04273/1 p. 136 (1607), MS Bristol Archives, Bristol, UK.

55 Roger Leech, *The Town House in Medieval and Early Modern Bristol* (Swindon: English Heritage, 2014).

56 Mary Edmond, "Street, Peter," *Oxford Dictionary of National Biography*. Online. Accessed 21 Oct. 2021.

57 REQ 2/184/45, MS, The National Archives, Kew, London.

58 STAC 5/G17/29, MS, The National Archives, Kew, London.

59 For more on the processes involved, see John Orrell, "Building the Fortune," *Shakespeare Quarterly* 44.2 (1993): 127–44.

60 William C. Baer, "The House-Building Sector of London's Economy, 1550–1650," *Urban History* 39.3 (2012): 409–30.

61 Baer, p. 410.

62 STAC 8/49/8 item 10, MS, The National Archives, Kew, London.

63 David Kathman, "Alice Layston at the Cross Keys," *Medieval and Renaissance Drama in England* 22 (2009): 144–78. p. 144.

64 Callan Davies, Andy Kesson, and Lucy Munro. "London Theatrical Culture, 1560–1590." *Oxford Research Encyclopedia of Literature*. 28 Jun. 2021. Online. Accessed 9 Jul. 2021.

65 John Harland, *A Volume of Court Leet Records of the Manor of Manchester in the Sixteenth Century*, ed. John Harland (Manchester: Chetham Society, 1864), pp. 157–8.

66 Amy Louise Erickson, *Women and Property in Early Modern England* (London: Routledge, 1993), p. 19. For wider discussion of this quotation and subject, see Christine Churches' reappraisal of the topic, "Women and Property in Early Modern England; A Case-Study," *Social History* 23.2 (1998): 165–80.

67 REPS 17 fo. 427v (20 Jan. 1573), COL/CA/01/01/019, MS, London Metropolitan Archives, London.

68 For more, see Callan Davies, "Bowling Alleys and Playhouses, 1560–1590," *Early Theatre* 22.4 (2019): 39–66.

69 Henry Chettle, *Kind-Hart's Dream* (London, 1593), F1v-2r.

70 *Records of Early English Drama: Lancashire*, ed. David George (Toronto: University of Toronto Press, 1991), pp. 77–84.

71 *Records of Early English Drama: Bristol*, ed. Mark C. Pilkington (Toronto: University of Toronto Press, 1997); Siobhan Keenan, *Travelling Players in Shakespeare's England* (Basingstoke: Palgrave, 2002).

72 P/StP&J/R/1/1, n.p, MS, Bristol Archives, Bristol; C3/328/28, MS, The National Archives, Kew, London.

73 REQ 2/296/80, MS, The National Archives, Kew, London.

74 Callan Davies, "The Woolfes of Wine Street: Middling Culture and Community in Bristol, 1600–1620," *English Historical Review*, 137.585 (2022).

75 For cultural overview of female remarriage, see Jennifer Panek, *Widows and Suitors in Early Modern English Comedy* (Cambridge: Cambridge University Press, 2004).

76 See, for instance, Mrs Slye, *The Company of Soapmakers, 1562–1642*, ed. Harold Evan Matthews (Bristol: Bristol Record Society, 1940), p. 104.

77 Jane Whittle, "Enterprising Widows and Active Wives: Women's Unpaid Work in the Household Economy of Early Modern England," *The History of the Family* 19.3 (2014): 283–300. p. 297.

78 Tittler, *Portraits*, p. 81.

79 C2/JasI/W4/59, MS, The National Archives, Kew, London.

80 C3/328/28.

81 C3/328/28.

82 Natasha Korda, *Labors Lost: Women's Work and the Early Modern English Stage* (Philadelphia: University of Pennsylvania Press, 2011), p. 1.

83 See Korda, pp. 27, 60.

84 *Records of Early English Drama: Cheshire (including Chester)*, Vol. 2, eds Elizabeth Baldwin, Laurence M. Clopper, and David Mills (Toronto: University of Toronto Press, 2007), p. 617; p. 622; pp. 626–7.

85 *REED Cheshire*, Vol. 2, p. 616.

86 There was a John and a Peter Swayne resident near Congleton in the late sixteenth and seventeenth centuries, both fathers to a number of children in parish registers in the location, but there is unfortunately no clear relation to Margaret. The name is not especially uncommon throughout England.

87 Elisabeth Salter, *Six Renaissance Men and Women: Innovation, Biography, and Cultural Creativity in Tudor England, c. 1450–1560* (Aldershot: Ashgate, 2007), pp. 2–3.

88 Jane Whittle, "Housewives and Servants in Rural England, 1440–1650: Evidence of Women's Work from Probate Documents," *Transactions of the Royal Historical Society* 15 (2005): 51–74.

89 Charmian Mansell, "Beyond the Home: Space and Agency in the Experiences of Female Service in Early Modern England," *Gender and* History 33.1 (2021): 24–49. p. 45.

90 For a survey of women's involvement in the labour market in agriculture and beyond, see Jane Whittle and Mark Hailwood, "The Gender Division of Labour in Early Modern England," *Economic History Review* 73.1 (2020): 3–32.

91 Tara Hamling and Catherine Richardson, *A Day at Home in Early Modern England* (New Haven: Yale University Press, 2017), pp. 150–1; Darron Dean, "Wrotham Pottery: An Analysis of Vernacular Ceramics in South-East England, 1600–1740," unpublished MA thesis, V&A and Royal College of Art.

92 For this and a wider discussion of income from female trades for and in the household, see Hamling and Richardson, pp. 150–1.

93 Hamling and Richardson, p. 151.

94 *REED Cheshire*, Vol. 2, p. 639.

95 *REED Cheshire*, Vol. 2, p. 626.

96 *REED Cheshire*, Vol. 2, p. 744.

97 *REED Cheshire*, Vol. 2, p. 637.

98 *REED Bristol*, pp. 164–5.

99 Herbert Berry, "Brayne, John," *Oxford Dictionary of National Biography*. Online. Accessed 22 Oct. 2021.

100 C24/226/11, MS, The National Archives, Kew, London.

101 Herbert Berry, "A Handlist of Documents about the Theatre in Shoreditch," *The First Public Playhouse: The Theatre in Shoreditch, 1576–1598*, ed. Herbert Berry (Montreal: McGill-Queen's University Press, 1979): 97–133.

102 For a full account and attempted reconstruction of the payments and financial difficulties surrounding the building of the Theatre, see Ingram, *Business*, pp. 182–218.

103 Herbert Berry, "Brayne, John," and "Shylock, Robert Miles, and Events at the Theatre," *Shakespeare Quarterly* 44.2 (1993): 183–201.

104 C24/228/11 and C24/228/10, MSS, The National Archives, Kew, London.

105 William Ingram and Herbert Berry differ in their conjecture about the child, Katherine. Ingram suggests it could have been John Brayne's child from an illicit liaison, which he had acknowledged and made provision for in his will by asking Margaret to provide for her (*Business*, p. 216), whereas Berry suggests Katherine was Margaret's own child (perhaps by Brayne in his final months).

106 Berry, "Shylock, Robert Miles, and Events at the Theatre," p. 193.

107 Berry, p. 117.

108 C24/228/10.

109 G4v-H1r.

110 "Applesquire" was a familiar slang term for a male bawd, according to John Florio in *World of Words* (London, 1578), O1v.

111 See Callan Davies, "Playing Apples and the Playhouse Archive," *Practices of Ephemera in Early Modern England*, eds Callan Davies, Hannah Lilley, and Catherine Richardson (London: Routledge, forthcoming).

112 C24/226/11.

113 Duncan Salkeld, *Shakespeare and London* (Oxford: Oxford University Press, 2018), p. 38.

114 Salkeld, p. 39.

115 C24/226/11, C24/228/10.

CODA

Archives and Afterlives

A visitor did not have to travel far in early modern England to find a commercial playing place. Upon entry, they might have encountered a variety of different play forms. Together, the structures and the activities they were designed to host point us towards a sense of playhouse-ness. We might accordingly regard the early modern playhouse less as a type or category than a family, one whose iterations varied across time and place but shared some key characteristics. This book has explored both common and idiosyncratic features, ranging from architectural structure to the playhouse's impact on surrounding communities, roads, and economic activities. Indeed, the playhouse was both a commercial enterprise and a community hub, both a business and a space where creativity, social status, and aesthetic and technological development melded together.

But how do we visit the playhouse once its bricks and mortar—or scaffolds, timber, straw, thatch, paving, or quarry walls—have crumbled? I have largely depended in this book on documentary archives, using materials, for example, from UK's The National Archives, British Library, and London Metropolitan Archives; from regional record centres like Bristol and Lancashire Archives; and building on the extraordinary range of archival extracts published by the *Records of Early English Drama* project. These documents give clues to the size and location of playhouses, the fights that took place within and outside them, the business quarrels that raged around them, the finances that underwrote them, or the individuals who built and used them. Yet reading documentary archives in this way inevitably imposes some form of order and narrative on what are often scrappy details.[1] "As early modernists with an interest in the literary culture of Shakespeare's time," write Roslyn Knutson, David McInnis, and Matthew Steggle—pioneers in the consideration of early modern theatrical "loss"—"we work in a field that contains many significant losses: of texts, of contextual information, and of other forms of cultural activity," and it is "important to recognize that loss is not restricted to playtexts

DOI: 10.4324/9781003231127-7

alone."[2] Indeed, playhouses themselves sit alongside playtexts as "lost" artefacts. Many of them are difficult and perhaps impossible to recover at this distance, as indicated by the chance discovery of documents describing a stage built at the Red Lion in Mile End (discussed in the introduction). Knutson, McInnis, and Steggle's collection demonstrates how "lostness is a continuum, not an absolute state, and that valuable things can be said" about things that do not survive whole. Indeed, "more remains to be discovered—in relatively inaccessible archives; in easily accessible ones; in printed sources; and in electronic databases."[3] The scholarship around lost plays models one important and effective way in which scrappiness, obscurity, or outright disappearance might be approached.[4]

Other discoveries can be found in the architectural materials themselves. We saw in Chapter 1 how assumptions have long been made about playhouses whose information survives partially and potentially misleadingly in archival records. In 2016, MOLA (Museum of London Archaeology) discovered the Curtain playhouse just off a busy road in Shoreditch, back from a carwash company and line of bars and pubs. The playhouse was not, as scholars had long thought, round—a derivative mirror image of its neighbouring Theatre—but was a large, rectangular building. The discovery of the Curtain's material remnants offers fresh physical evidence to sit alongside and shape our gleanings from historical documents. It apprises us of dimensions, access routes to and from the stage and the "tiring house" at the back, or the possible audience capacities of a site. Since then, the Boar's Head in Whitechapel and the Red Lion complex at Mile End have also undergone revealing archaeological digs, the latter indicating a vaster leisure complex than suggested by the structures mentioned in documents.[5] Excavations also furnish us with insights into the material culture of the playhouse—from small glass beads worn on costumes dotted around the building's floors to shards of pottery from drinking vessels and legions of long-discarded oyster shells.

Like archival research, however, archaeology does not offer a set of concrete answers to the question posed in the title of this book. Mike Pearson and Michael Shanks stress the "need to work upon understanding archaeological things and the creative event that is the construction of archaeological knowledge." Shanks champions "interpretive archaeology"—a term used to designate

> a set of approaches to the ruined material past which foreground interpret-ation, the ongoing process of making sense of what never was firm or certain. This archaeology entertains no final and definitive account of the past as it was, but fosters multivocal and multiple accounts: a creative but none the less critical attention and response to the interests, needs and desires of different constituencies (those people, groups or communities who have or express interest in the material past).[6]

Shanks's *ongoing process* and Knutson, McInnis, and Steggle's *continuum* necessitate attention both to the historical uses of playhouses and to contemporary historical recoveries. They also ask us to reflect on how we treat "discovered" playhouses today: sites like the Rose or the Curtain survive as markers on a London map, as visitor centres or performance venues, and in the popular imagination as "playhouses." Yet in early modern England they were transformed from tenements or houses into playhouses and eventually back into tenements.

Early modern playhouse-builders and -goers may therefore have found our fossilisation of these spaces—fixing them as historic playhouses—as rather curious. As we saw in Chapter 5, the period's building industry regarded buildings as perpetually mutable. The built environment was defined by the "common practice of moving buildings around, of taking down a sizeable structure and reconstructing it elsewhere, a practice that was not only cost-effective but efficient and, in many cases, something that could be performed fairly quickly."[7] Indeed, playhouses were often subject to demands to change their use if not their structure; the Shoreditch landlord Giles Allen said he would only reissue a lease if the owners of the Theatre "would Convert the same to some other better use."[8] These features emblematise what S.P. Cerasano deems the "transitory playhouse," a fundamentally evanescent structure.[9] They also point to the gap between our attitude to materiality today and the different mindsets of sixteenth- and seventeenth-century individuals. "Fictions of preservation have long underwritten our ideas of loss," Sarah Wasserman points out.[10] Yet stasis and endurance were not inherent features of early modern commercial playing structures.[11]

The matter turned up by archaeological investigation therefore reminds us that playhouses sat and continue to sit within an *ongoing process*. Playhouses were constructed from more than timber and sometimes depended on nutshells for flooring or discarded food remains that merged into the physical structures of the buildings.[12] Their organic matter included everything from discarded shellfish to bear bones and dog remains,[13] all of which form a capacious archive of construction, modification, and leisure activity. The playhouse archive, then, is not just textual but physical and environmental. These elements alert us to the importance of change and transmutation in histories of early modern structures. The materials that made and make up early modern playhouses are perpetual "substances-in-becoming": "Whatever the objective forms in which they are currently cast, materials are always and already on their ways to becoming something else."[14]

The playhouse archive might therefore be framed not only around loss but around generative forms of disintegration. "Degraded artifacts," Catherine DeSilvey explains, "can contribute to alternative interpretive possibilities even as they remain caught up in dynamic processes of decay and disarticulation."[15] For DeSilvey, these processes not only help reframe questions about historical sites and their heritage value today but offer benefits for the environment around them: "processes of decay and disintegration can be culturally (as well as ecologically) productive."[16] DeSilvey's study thinks about the benefits for physical decay for everything from insects or rodents (who appear as new occupants of these once human spaces) to new ways of framing historical narratives: "cultural remembering proceeds not through reflection on a static memorial remnant but through a process that slowly pulls the remnant into other ecologies and expressions of value, accommodating simultaneous resonances of death and rebirth, loss and renewal."[17] Such a framework resonates with the playhouse archive. Although it is formed of both artefacts ("a relic of human manipulation of the material world") and ecofacts ("a relic of other-than-human engagements with matter, climate, weather, and biology"),[18] distinctions between such categories rarely hold up. Even the documentary archive—made up of "old and stretched animals' skins, pulped and reshaped woods or rags, and chemical compounds"—is an ecology "where the materials of remembrance are living, dying, and being devoured."[19] Playhouses were built from and persevere in the space between nature and culture.

The playhouse archive therefore spans far beyond the materials considered in this book. There are crucial stories lying beneath the ground and across physical, cultural, and legal borders. These chapters have moved beyond scholarly focus on London by considering playhouses across England, but that national framework can also misleadingly contain the energies of early modern play. There are manifold overlaps, connections, and exchanges between different modes of performance across Europe, from touring players or the travelling tumblers we met in Chapter 2 to the movement of theatrical materials of all kinds.[20] The suggestive relationship between Shoreditch's Curtain playhouse and continental spaces, gestured at in Chapter 1, indicates the many social and cultural contexts not only beyond playhouse walls but beyond the country's shoreline.

Vital scholarship also urges us to recognise how archival violence and elision can pre-determine scholarly questions.[21] Ayanna Thompson's edited collection, *The Cambridge Companion to Shakespeare and Race* (2021), reflecting decades of scholarship, emphasises that the early modern theatrical world was and is determined by "the specifics of racialized discourses, rhetoric, and performances." Essays throughout the collection acknowledge "the historical and cultural milieu of the fifteenth, sixteenth, and seventeenth centuries […] and the archives that hold the historical documents from these time periods," but emphasise the need to think about histories of imperialism and "alternative archives that reveal more about the various lives of people of colour in the early modern world."[22] Those alternative archives perhaps require more personal forms of engagement or expression. Indeed, Kim F. Hall's powerful reflection on working at the Schomburg Center for Research in Black Culture (as part of a project on Othello, Shakespeare, and race) the day after Trump was elected to the White House is an extraordinary testament to the fact that many historical "citings"—and individual experiences working in an archive—do not fold into "traditional scholarly narrative."[23] Hall's essay, though, is also more than that and poignantly and forcefully articulates what it means to work through a racist archive and an archive of racism as a scholar of colour.

"Alternative archives" can encourage us to think more broadly about the history of the playhouse during a period in which it became, in some instances, an institution of local government, community, parish, or neighbourhood—and therefore part of the power structures and regulatory systems that shaped early modern society.[24] How might the playhouse as an institution, for instance, reflect race-making processes and actions? The "documentary evidence of race," Ambereen

Dadabhoy points out in Thompson's collection, has often been narrowed by a refusal "to see the operations of race and racism" in texts thought of as separate from or irrelevant to these questions.[25] The observation might extend to physical structures and spaces, too. The social and cultural place of the playhouse is not limited to individuals directly named in connection with those spaces in contemporary documents. The Wine Street playhouse in Bristol came into operation at a moment of expanding colonial trade, "accomplished primarily by numerous small exporters, most of them Bristolians, who still sent every variety of manufactured item along with servant labor to the planters in return for their produce, primarily sugar and tobacco."[26] The playhouse's place within Bristol's leisure economy, in which sugar and tobacco (like virginals and other luxury goods and materials discussed in this volume) were sold and consumed,[27] align the playhouse with larger global concerns and inequities. The middling individuals who founded it and those who frequented the venue and related sites of commerce and recreation therefore capitalised on a rich material culture made possible by colonialism and exploitation.

"Alternative archives" also encourage us to think about the experience of playhouses for more-than-human actors. In sites on the Bankside, animals—from dogs and bears to horses—far outnumbered humans in the operational elements of the playhouse or baiting arena. They also featured in inn- or alehouse playhouse venues, too. Richard Tarlton entertained audiences at the Cross Keys in London with an impromptu skit with "a horse of strange qualities," in which the horse in question responded to its master Bankes' request to "go fetch me the veriest fool in the company" by marching up to Tarlton, as explored in Chapter 2.[28] Bankes' horse may have carried its rider some distance across the country on their journey to the playhouse. Turning our attention to animals' interaction with the institution of the playhouse can further expand our sense of the traffic and journeys discussed in Chapter 3 or the types of non-human "community" that found themselves together (perhaps in a stable or yard, or perhaps directly interacting with performers and audiences) during a playhouse performance. Holly Dugan and Karen Raber's introduction to the *Routledge Handbook of Shakespeare and Animals* reminds us that archival evidence or zooarchaeological detail cannot always bring us to see "individual animals" and points to the limitations of historical knowledge about the past.[29] At the same time, chapters such as Dan Brayton's on "Shakespeare's Fishponds" note how surrounding ecological features can inform our understanding of playhouse activity and push us beyond the built world itself when generating narratives about theatre.[30] Dugan and Raber recognise that all such questions alert us to "our current ecological crises."[31]

These ecological crises were current for early modern individuals, too, whose own environmental consciousness expanded during the years covered by this book.[32] Thomas Day set out a climate warning in 1583: "The Lord hath forewarned us a great while [...] by his creatures, and miraculous tokens, strange monsters, blazing comets, unwanted enumbrations of waters, strange fishes, perilous wars, earthquakings, and last of all, fiery constellations."[33] This vision of environmental destruction was sometimes a reality within early modern playhouses. In 1594, severe floods forced the Admiral's Men to depart to the Playhouse at Newington Butts, Laurie Johnson explains, while repairs were made to the Rose on Bankside.[34] These were transitory spaces not only in their design—built of re-useable materials and open to changes of function—but in their susceptibility to the forces of the natural world. After all, playhouses began to emerge during a mini-Ice Age characterised by grain shortages, failed harvests, and "environmental degradation" that ranged from deforestation to increased reliance on coal for fuel.[35]

The natural world also emerges in the playhouse archive in tangible and unsettling ways. Animal remains within manuscripts carry a macabre reflection of animals' presence in the playhouse itself. Erica Fudge, faced with the challenge of speaking with animals who "had no voices and left no textual traces," was confronted with a different documentary presence while researching and writing a book that helped establish early modern animal studies: the

> absent-presence of animals was firmly, and ironically, underlined for me on the label recording the British Library's 'Record of Treatment, Extraction, Repair, etc.' stuck into the back cover of Thomas Taylor's *A Vindication of the Rights of Brutes* (1792). In the column next to the word 'Adhesives' is written by hand 'ANIMAL GLUE'.[36]

Animals not only lie—many no doubt undiscovered—among the physical remnants of playhouse buildings but bind together the archival documents in which textual traces of those buildings are conveyed. Fudge's archive therefore reaches beyond the binary of human and animal to find stories about humans in animals and vice versa: "the animal can never be studied in isolation."[37] These approaches suggest an enabling model of interconnectedness, in which both past and present ecologies shape our sense of playhouse-ness.

Feminist studies have helpfully modelled ways to approach the playhouse's contemporary contexts by thinking about performance more widely—both within and beyond the theatrical institution itself—using both social and cultural history as well as the study of imaginative texts. Natasha Korda, for instance, offers an "in depth study of several categories of female labor and commerce in and around the theaters as they were depicted in dramatic texts, on the stage, and in the culture at large."[38] Attending to the labours that made and shaped playhouses recognises participation in play beyond a narrow social stratum (as modelled by early modern book history): "Focusing on women's work enables the recognition of the various forms of labour—textual and social as well as material and commercial—in which women of different social classes participated."[39] Indeed, meaningful engagement with women's play activity prompts us to talk less about "theatre" and instead to embrace the more capacious term, "performance."[40] Emily Mayne's special issue on the subject suggests how the playhouse archive might be shaped by such vocabulary: "in early modern usage the word 'performance' (noun and verb) most often relates to *doing*: to the carrying out of an action." In turn, the word is broad enough to evoke a range of early modern cultural and social practices that include specific scripted performances on stage without being confined to them, while nonetheless retaining a persistent association with scripted, staged drama. The term 'performance' thus has the potential to draw early modern performances of both stage- and non-stage-based varieties into dialogue.[41]

Accordingly, Mayne's special issue explores perambulatory performance (Matthew Woodcock), libel and status (Clare Egan), accountancy (Mark Chambers), and coronation pageants (Mayne). Playhouse-ness was not simply a question of dramatic companies or playtexts but was fundamentally entwined with the wider social practices and performances of early modern England. In turn, they direct us to a raft of different archives from the material and architectural to the textual and even to performance-as-research or practice-research. Contemporary performance methods raise questions about how to enliven and embody the past and in turn open the creative possibilities of multipurpose performance spaces.

Such rich and urgent veins of scholarship will hopefully encourage readers to explore these avenues further and to build on the work presented in this book. I have aimed to show across the preceding pages, through a diverse array of microhistorical studies, how playhouses were heterogeneous spaces. Not only were play venues enjoyed by individuals from all walks of society, they were built, rebuilt, and run by everyone from town corporations to Cheshire straw-drawers. Accordingly, they often looked radically different from each other: some like the round amphitheatre we might encounter today as a reconstruction under the name of the "Globe," others somewhat architecturally distinct: an adapted quarry, a current or former schoolhouse, a multi-room inn building. The various communities that surrounded these different structures and that I have explored in this book urge us to think beyond London as the epicentre of "Renaissance drama" and to recognise the rich cultural lives of those in towns and cities across the country. They also remind us that "drama" was by no means the only play on offer at playhouses (in and out of the capital); one might enter to see anything from fencing and animal sports to improvised performance, acrobatic feats, or Olympian contests. I have also dwelt here with these communities outside the playhouse walls, with chapters charting journeys to playing venues or exploring the labour, skills, and the political structures that surrounded and supported them. I see playhouses, in other words, as part of the changing institutional landscape of early modern England, and accordingly they have a reach far beyond the immediate audience on, say, a cold Tuesday night in Shrewsbury. Play itself, an umbrella term for an array of commercial recreational activities, therefore offered political and economic influence (as well as controversy). Taken together, these elements should make us more relaxed about applying the term "playhouse" beyond a narrowly defined or situated structure, with the advantage that it opens up a great many more narratives about the cultural world of sixteenth- and seventeenth-century

England. With a larger complement of playhouses and greater appreciation of their socio-cultural impacts, we can appreciate the many "actors"—not just in the theatrical sense—who formed England's leisure industry and who shaped the country's social environments. Although it is often adopted as a convenient shorthand for the period, these were never "Shakespeare's playhouses," or at least no more than they were Henry Walton's, Sackerson the bear's, Congleton corporation's, or Margaret Woolfe's, Margaret Swayne's, or Margaret Brayne's.

There are many more such actors to be found and narratives to be told. The approaches raised briefly in this coda are but a fraction of research in early modern studies—from queer and trans studies to histories of the book—that can and will directly shape our answers to the question posed by this book's title. Playhouses touched everybody's lives in early modern England: human performers and exploited animals; neighbouring residents or business owners; the pragmatic regulator and the irascible antitheatricalist. The development of commercial institutions for play over the course of the sixteenth and early seventeenth centuries generated a language for the industry that endures even now. At the same time, the vocabularies that were so fluid at the time remain alive and contestable today.

Notes

1 For more discussion of the imposition of narrative in theatre history writing, see William Ingram, "Introduction: Early Modern Theater History: Where We Are Now, How We Got Here, Where We Go Next," *The Oxford Handbook of Early Modern Theatre*, ed. Richard Dutton, 2009, (Oxford: Oxford University Press, 2011): 1–18.

2 Roslyn L. Knutson, David McInnis, and Matthew Steggle, "Introduction: Coping with Loss," *Loss and the Literary Culture of Shakespeare's Time*, eds Roslyn L. Knutson, David McInnis, and Matthew Steggle (London: Palgrave MacMillan, 2020): 1–18. pp. 1–2.

3 Knutson, McInnis, and Steggle, p. 11.

4 In addition to this collection, see *Lost Plays in Shakespeare's England*, eds David McInnis and Matthew Steggle (London: Palgrave MacMillan, 2014); David McInnis, *Shakespeare and Lost Plays* (Cambridge: Cambridge University Press, 2021), and the *Lost Plays Database* (lostplays.folger.edu).

5 Archaeology South-East, "Archaeological Excavations at Whitechapel Central, 85 Stepney Way: A Post-Excavation Assessment and Updated Project Design Report" (London: Archaeology South-East, 2020).

6 Michael Shanks, *Theatre/Archaeology*, 2001, (London: Routledge, 2005), p. xvii.

7 S.P. Cerasano, "The Transitory Playhouse: Theatre, Rose, and Globe," *The Text, the Play, and the Globe: Essays on Literary Influence in Shakespeare's World and His Work in Honor of Charles R. Forker*, ed. Joseph Candido (Madison: Fairleigh Dickinson University Press, 2016): 95–120. p. 105.

8 REQ 2/184/45, MS, The National Archives, Kew, London.

9 Cerasano, "The Transitory Playhouse."

10 Sarah Wasserman, *The Death of Things: Ephemera and the American Novel* (Minneapolis: University of Minnesota Press, 2020), p. 236.

11 For more on early modern ideas of fleetingness, see essays in *Practices of Ephemera in Early Modern England*, eds Callan Davies, Hannah Lilley, and Catherine Richardson (London: Routledge, forthcoming).

12 For more discussion of the relationship between fruit remains and playhouses, see Callan Davies, "Playing Apples and the Playhouse Archive," *Practices of Ephemera in Early Modern England*, eds Callan Davies, Hannah Lilley, and Catherine Richardson (London: Routledge, forthcoming).

13 "Empire Warehouse, Bear Gardens," Archaeological Evaluation Report (London: London Borough of Southwark, 2008). Anthony Mackinder, with Lyn Blackmore, Julian Bowsher, Christopher Phillpotts. *The Hope Playhouse, Animal Baiting and Later Industrial Activity at Bear Gardens on Bankside, Excavations at Riverside House and New Globe Walk, Southwark, 1999–2000.* Archaeology Studies Series 25 (London: Museum of London Archaeology, 2013).

14 Tim Ingold, *Making: Anthropology, Archaeology, Art, and Architecture* (Abingdon: Routledge, 2013), p. 31.

15 Catherine DeSilvey, *Curated Decay: Heritage Beyond Saving.* (London: University of Minnesota Press, 2017), p. 37.

16 DeSilvey, p. 5.

17 DeSilvey, p. 35.

18 DeSilvey, p. 28.

19 Miles Ogborn, "Archives," *Patterned Ground: Entanglements of Nature and Culture*, eds Stephan Harrison, Steve Pile, and Nigel Thrift (London: Reaktion, 2004): 240–2. p. 240.

20 David Amelang, "A Day in the Life: The Performance of Playgoing in Early Modern Madrid and London," *Bulletin of the Comediantes* 70.2 (2018): 111–27; Barbara Fuchs, *The Poetics of Piracy: Emulating Spain in English Literature* (Philadelphia: University of Pennsylvania Press, 2013); Robert Henke, ed., *A Cultural History of Theatre in the Early Modern Age* (London: Bloomsbury, 2017); Jerzy Limon, *Gentlemen of a Company: English Players in Central and Eastern Europe, 1590–1660* (Cambridge: Cambridge University Press, 1985); Jerzy Limon, "The City and the 'Problem' of Theatre Reconstructions: 'Shakespearean' Theatres in London and Gdańsk," *Actes des congrès de la Société française Shakespeare* 28 (2011): 159–83; Eric Nicholson and Robert Henke, eds, *Transnational Exchange in Early Modern Theater* (Aldershot: Ashgate, 2008).

21 In different ways, Duncan Salkeld and Saidiya Hartman suggest how elision or gaps might form part of historical narratives in the face of violence or absence: Hartman, "Venus in two Acts," *Small Axe* Number 26 12.2 (2008): 1–14. Salkeld, "Shakespeare Studies, Presentism, and Micro-History," *Cahiers Élisabéthains* 76.1 (2009): 35–43.

22 Ayanna Thompson, "Did the Concept of Race Exist for Shakespeare and His Contemporaries? An Introduction," *Cambridge Companion to Shakespeare and Race*, ed. Ayanna Thompson (Cambridge: Cambridge University Press, 2021): 1–16. p. 4.

23 Kim F. Hall, "I Can't Love This the Way You Want Me to: Archival Blackness," *Postmedieval* 11 (2020): 171–9.

24 The institutionalisation of play sits alongside other institutional changes that served to sharpen the divide between narrow ruling elites or middling power-brokers and a popular "culture of poverty," Keith Wrightson and David Levine, *Poverty and Piety in an English Village* (New York: Academic Press, 1979), p. 183.

25 Ambereen Dadabhoy, "Barbarian Moors," *The Cambridge Companion to Shakespeare and Race*, ed. Ayanna Thompson (Cambridge: Cambridge University Press, 2021): 30–46, p. 43.

26 David Harris Sacks, *The Widening Gate: Bristol and the Atlantic Economy, 1450–1700* (Oxford: University of California Press, 1991), p. 279.

27 There were numerous comments about tobacco smoke, for instance, in early modern English playing venues. See, for instance, Horace Walpole, *Paul Hentzner's Travels in England* (London, 1797).

28 Richard Tarlton, *Tarltons Iestes* (London, 1613), C2r-v.

29 "Introduction," *The Routledge Handbook of Shakespeare and Animals*, eds Karen Raber and Holly Dugan (London: Routledge, 2020): 1–10. p. 5.

30 "Shakespeare's Fishponds: Matter, Metaphor, and Market," *The Routledge Handbook of Shakespeare and Animals*, eds Karen Raber and Holly Dugan (London: Routledge, 2020): 21–33.

31 Dugan and Raber, p. 6.

32 Bruce Boehrer, *Environmental Degradation in Jacobean Drama* (Cambridge: Cambridge University Press, 2013).

33 Thomas Day, *Wonderful Strange Sights* (London, 1583), A3v.

34 Laurie Johnson, *Shakespeare's Lost Playhouse: Eleven Days at Newington Butts* (Abingdon: Routledge, 2018).

35 Boehrer, p. 21.

36 Erica Fudge, *Perceiving Animals: Humans and Beasts in Early Modern English Culture* (Basingstoke: MacMillan, 2000), p. 2.

37 Fudge, p. 2.

38 Natasha Korda, *Labors Lost: Women's Work and the Early modern English Stage* (Philadelphia: University of Pennsylvania Press, 2011), p. 217.

39 Valerie Wayne, *Women's Labour and the History of the Book in Early Modern England*, ed. Valerie Wayne (London: Bloomsbury, 2020), p. 2.

40 Clare McManus, "Women and English Renaissance Drama: Making and Unmaking 'The All-Male Stage,'" *Literature Compass* 4/3 (2007): 784–96. p. 793.

41 "Introduction: Rethinking Early Modern Performance," "Rethinking Performance in Early Modern England: Sources, Contexts, and Forms," spec. issue *Early Theatre* 23.2 (2020): 113–22. pp. 115–6.

INDEX